DAVID GARRICK

DAVID GARRICK
from a painting by Gainsborough in the
possession of Mrs Kay

DAVID GARRICK

BY

JOSEPH KNIGHT, F.S.A.

WITH ETCHED PORTRAIT

BY

W. BOUCHER

From a Painting by Gainsborough in the possession of Mrs. Kay

BENJAMIN BLOM  New York

First Published 1894
Reissued 1969 by
Benjamin Blom, Inc., Bronx, New York 10452

Library of Congress Catalog Card Number 74-91904

Printed in United States of America
at Westbrook Lithographers, Inc.
Westbury, New York

PREFACE.

MATERIALS for a biography of Garrick overflow.
Apart from the mass of letters edited in 1832 by
Boaden, in two volumes, under the title of "The
Private Correspondence of David Garrick," an immense amount of matter, much of it unedited and
unused, is in the Forster Collection at South Kensington. These sources have been laid under contribution. Lives of Garrick have been written by
Thomas Davies, the bookseller and actor (London,
2 vols., 1780, reprinted 1780, 1781, 1784, and
with notes by Stephen Jones, 1808); by Arthur
Murphy, the dramatist (London, 2 vols., 8vo, 1801);
by Boaden, prefixed to the correspondence mentioned
above; and by Mr. Percy Fitzgerald (London, 2 vols.
8vo, 1868). The last-named life, long out of print,
is inaccurate in some details, but is a work of much
research and value, to which justice has not been
done. What is almost a life is included in Forster's
"Life and Times of Oliver Goldsmith" (London,
2 vols., 8vo, 1877, sixth edition). Shorter lives are
in existence in the "Dictionary of National Biography" and elsewhere. The literature and the
memoirs of the second half of the last century are full
of anecdote concerning Garrick or references to him.

The chief difficulty of the biographer has been accordingly that of selection. Indebtedness in the compilation of the following monograph to the sources named, and especially to Mr. Percy Fitzgerald, is fully acknowledged. Among those to whom a special debt is due, are Mr. Walter Herries Pollock, who has placed at the compiler's service material accumulated with a view to a work on Garrick which, unfortunately for the lovers of literature and the stage, has not been written; and Mr. Sketchley, the erudite and obliging Librarian of the Dyce and Forster Collection at South Kensington. Originally intended to form one of a series of lives of actors, the biography aims only at supplying the leading facts of Garrick's career, and makes no pretension to furnish full information concerning the scenes and characters amidst which he dwelt or to chronicle the stories that have been invented concerning him.

27, Camden Square,
        September, 1893.

ERRATA.

p. 56, l. 6, *after* exist *insert* a full stop.

p. 108, l. 26, *for* Howard *read* Havard.

p. 140, l. 6, *for* Fitzgerald *read* Fitzpatrick.

p. 200, l. 7, *for* Fitzgerald *read* Fitzpatrick.

p. 203, l. 4, *for* couroune *read* couronne.

DAVID GARRICK.

CHAPTER I.

AMONG those whom the repeal of the Edict of
Nantes drove to seek shelter in England was a
Huguenot gentleman of the name of David Garric, a
member, it is said, of a noble family, De la Garrique,
established near Saintonge, and connected by birth or
marriage with the most illustrious families of L'An-
goumois and Périgord. At the period of his flight
David Garric was living in Bordeaux. So hard
pressed was he in his efforts to escape that he left
behind him his wife and child. By way of St. Malo
he reached Guernsey, and on the 5th October, 1685,
arrived in London. Here, two months later, he was
joined by his wife, who, after escaping by sea from
Bordeaux, had undergone imminent risk of ship-
wreck and capture. Not until the 22nd May, 1687,
were they gladdened by the arrival of their son Peter,
an infant of two years, who came over in the charge
of Mary or Marie Mongorier, a nurse. Other
children were born to David Garric after his arrival
in England, where he was joined by a brother and
sister, fugitives like himself, who came to him from
Rotterdam. Of the children born to David most

died in infancy, his wife, whom he had married in 1682, dying in 1694. Three, however, survived— Peter, who was put into the English army ; David, who took to the wine trade and settled in Portugal ; and Jane, who married an exile of the name of La Condé.

Concerning the early career of Peter Garric history is all but silent, and the name of the regiment which he joined is unknown. All that is known is that the young officer, whose first commission is dated 12th May, 1706, was quartered in Lichfield, where he married, on the 13th November, 1707, a Miss Arabella Clough, a lady of Irish descent, the daughter of a vicar-choral of the cathedral in that city. Promotion followed, and before the birth of his first son, Peter, 24th September, 1710, Peter Garric was a lieutenant. A daughter, Magdalene, arrived 29th April, 1715 ; and on 19th February, $17\frac{16}{17}$, a second son, David. Captain Garrick was then quartered in Hereford on recruiting service, and it was in the Angel Inn, in that city, that David Garrick, the future actor, first saw the light. Nine days later he was christened at All Saints' Church, in the same city, the register giving the name Garrick, as it is now spelt.

Other children followed : Jane, born 1st April, 1718 ; William, 8th March, 1720 ; George, 22nd August, 1723 ; and Merriall, 19th December, 1724 ; besides Daniel, Arabella, and Anna Maria, all of whom died in infancy.

At ten years of age David was put into the

Grammar School at Lichfield. The head-master of this establishment at that time was Hunter, a man the severity of whose discipline has been commemorated by Samuel Johnson, the immediate predecessor of Garrick. Johnson charges Hunter with brutality, and with failure to distinguish between want of knowledge and neglect of knowledge. Men of this stamp were common at this time, and for a century later. His capacity to teach was owned by Johnson, who more than once spoke of him as a good master. The under-masters were, moreover, men of ability, and the school, on the whole, contrasted favourably with most schools of its epoch. Young David was not, however, destined to enjoy an unbroken course of tuition. He had, as may be supposed, from the first, much vivacity and a certain amount of mimetic power. A bent to the stage was acquired while he was still in his first years at school. A visit was paid to Lichfield by a company of strolling players, whose performances were witnessed by the boy. A result of their visit was an amateur performance, of which he was the director, of "The Recruiting Officer" of Farquhar. That this piece should have commended itself to a youth whose earliest recollections of his father were as a recruiting officer is natural. In the representation Garrick played Sergeant Kite. Who were Captain Plume and Captain Brazen, Worthy, Melinda, and Sylvia history does not record. Lucy, the chambermaid, was assigned to one of Garrick's sisters. As the performance is reported to have come off about 1727,

when the Sergeant Kite was ten years old, it may
well have been his earliest appearance upon any
stage.   Not long afterwards an invitation for David
Garrick was received from his uncle David, now
established as a prosperous wine merchant in Lisbon,
to join him for the purpose of learning the business.
An offer such as this was too good not to meet with
immediate acceptance from Captain Garrick, who
had now exchanged into a marching regiment, the
same, it is said, once commanded by the infamous
Colonel Kirke, and who subsequently found himself
compelled to go on half-pay.

In Lisbon the success of young David appears to
have been social rather than commercial.   We hear
of his declaiming to the English community speeches
from plays, and delighting them with exhibitions of
mimicry and sprightly sallies of various kinds.   Some
aristocratic acquaintances were contracted, and the
youth records his intimacy with the Duke d'Aveiro,
who subsequently, on the 13th January, 1759, was
broken on the wheel and then burnt alive for con-
spiracy.   Neither now, however, nor when he subsequently adopted it, had the profession of wine
merchant much attraction for the mercurial youth,
who was found too volatile for trade, and was sent
back to resume his studies under Hunter.

An opportunity of exchanging his half pay for full
pay and foreign service now presented itself to the
captain, who, in 1731, proceeded to Gibraltar, the
garrison of which had been largely augmented.   Upon
his progress to London he was accompanied by Mrs.

Garrick, whose health at this period was infirm, and who was for some time unable to return to Lichfield. David now presents himself in an engaging light. He corresponded constantly with his father, supplying him with the domestic particulars which are of keenest interest to an exile, and displaying a gaiety of spirits and a keenness of perception not wholly removed from humour. This correspondence has fortunately been preserved, and is now accessible in the Forster Collection in the South Kensington Museum. Extracts from the letters have been published in the "Life of Goldsmith," by Forster, and in that of Garrick by Mr. Percy Fitzgerald. One or two of them may, however, with advantage be quoted *in extenso*. The first of the series, given with its eccentricities of spelling, etc., and dated Lichfield, Jan^{ry} ye 21, 1732-3, is as follows :—

> " Hon^{d.} Sir,
>
> " It is not to be exprest ye Joy that the family was in at ye Receipt of Dear Pappa's Letter which we Receiv'd the 7th of this Month. My poor Mamma was in very good Spirits two or three Days after she receiv'd your Letter but now begins to grow moloncolly again, and has little ugly fainting fits, she is in great hopes of ye Transports going for you every Day, for we Please ourselves with ye hopes of your spending this Summer with y^r Family. My Mamma rec'd ye thirty Pounds you was so good to send her, she has Paid ten Pounds to Mr. Rider for one Year's Rent, and ten Pound's to the Baker, and if you can spare a little more as you tell her you will, she is in hopes of paying all ye Debts that you may have nothing to fret you when you come home. My Mamma staid six Weeks in London after you left her at Mr. Bronker's for she was

very much out of order when she was there, and they would
not part with Her before & was very good to her.   Mr.
Adair came twice to see my Mamma at Mr. Bronker's &
was prodigiously civil and obliging and beg'd her to send
him some Ale which she designs to do very soon.   My
Mamma paid for your Stockings & Holland as soon as you
left her, and as soon as she came down to us, not to her
great Joy, she found us very shabby in Cloaths, & in all
our accoutrements that we was rather like so many beggars
than Gentlemen Soldiers, but with much ado at last she
equipt us out a little better, and now with a great deal of
Mending and Patching we are in Statu quo.   We receiv'd
a Letter from Brother Peter which was directed to you,
and we thought it would be too troublesome to send it
inclos'd so have sent you a Coppy of it on yᵉ other side.
at Present we have but little News.   Doctor Hector
is married to Miss Jop [or Top] Smith, & Mr. Lawrence
who is at London is married to yᵉ Lady who you saw at
Capᵗⁿ Goddard's a very pretty woman only she squints a
little, (as Capᵗⁿ Brazen says in yᵉ Recruiting officer) Capᵗⁿ
Weldon has parted wᵗʰ his Commission, and has half Pay
as Lieutenant of a Man of War, every Body loves and
likes Mrs. Weldon, but he has quarell'd with most of yᵉ
People in this Place, which gives yᵉ poor woman a great
deal of uneasyness, but they are both highly Civil to our
family.   Mr. & Mrs. Harvey came to see my Mamma as
soon as she came to Town, she is a very fine Lady & has
return'd but few of her visits.   I am a great favourite of
both of them and am with them every Day. Mr. Walmesley
has had a very great quarrel with Capᵗⁿ —— [name
marked through and not decipherable in MS.] & I
think (Considering he being always so civil to yᵉ Officers)
us'd him very ill, but at Present all is over but they dont
visit one another.   I have been to Mr. Ofleys who sent a
Man & horse for me with Mr. & Mrs. Harvey & Mr.
Walmesley were I got acquainted with his two Sons, who
are fine young Gentlemen.   Mr. Walmesley gave me slyly

half a crown for y{{e}} Butler & another for y{{e}} Groom, for my
self which made me look very grand. All y{{r}} friends are
very well, we had a letter from my Uncle Day [qy.
contraction for Uncle David] who says that Mr. Lowe
preacht a Sermon which was thought by every body one of
y{{e}} Best they had heard for a long Time. Mrs. Lownds
sends love & service, but has not yet conquer'd her fever.
My Grand mother [Clough] is very poorly & sends her
blessing & would fain live to see you once more, my
Brothers & Sisters their Duty and am in a particular
manner.

> " Dear S{{r}}
>> " Y{{r}} ever Dutifull Son
>>> " DAVID GARRICK.

"P.S.—D{{r}} Sir if you could possibly send Mr. Walmesley
a little Wine, I am sure he would take it as a Particular
Favour." [A few words are here obliterated.]

This letter of a boy not yet sixteen has much interest and significance. How close on the family was
the grip of poverty is everywhere apparent. During
his early life Garrick was to know the sufferings that
accrue when narrowness of means accompanies the
necessity of maintaining a respectable appearance.
Speaking of the youth of Garrick, Johnson says, in
well-known lines, " He began the world with a great
hunger for money ; the son of a half-pay officer, bred
in a family whose study was to make fourpence do as
much as others made fourpence-halfpenny do." (Life,
by Boswell, iii. 387, ed. Hill.) In view of the
charges of parsimony and avarice subsequently brought
against Garrick, these early experiences of poverty
assume importance. The reference to "The Re-

cruiting Officer " shows how, at this early age,
his thoughts and reading were directed to the
stage.

The second letter is dated the 3rd December, 1733,
and is principally occupied with politics, the probability of war, the wedding of the Prince of Orange,
and the misdeeds of a Mr. Woodhouse.   Before the
third, dated the 18th March, 1734, was written, David
has incurred some rebuke for slackness in writing,
and has found his pleasure at hearing from his father
greatly damped thereby.   His apologies are warm,
vehement even, and it must be held of him as of the
player Queen in " Hamlet," that he doth " protest
too much."   It would, he holds, were he guilty, be
the worst of ingratitude, and he ought to be esteemed
the worst of wretches did he neglect what he thought
would give the least pleasure and satisfaction to
one of the best of fathers.   He then proceeds to
moralize :—

> " If those Persons who have not in any measure receiv'd
> what tenderness and affection, I have, from their Parents,
> are accounted Reprobates, if they omitt to pay all ye Regard
> and obedience to them they possible can, what on ye con-
> trary can be said for him who in every instance of Life has
> had ye greatest indulgence from a most kind father, whose
> study has always been to promote the welfare of his Chil-
> dren, such a one I think that does non [t ?] return Parental
> affection is ye most odious Monster, and rather fit for y^e
> Society of Brutes than that of Men.   In my poor opinion
> Nature seems to have done her endeavour to have planted
> in him all ye contraries, to obedience, virtue, morality,
> gratitude and what is most commendable in any Young

Person, tho He had but y° least share of what Fatherly love and goodness I enjoy,"

and so forth.

In further letters David tells how sisters Lenny and Jenny [Magdalene and Jane] need money to buy lace for their head-dresses, otherwise how are they to be distinguished from vulgar madams? His dear " Pappa " is also informed that David himself is turned quite philosopher. To show, however, that he is not unduly vain of his new profession, he owns that he would gladly " get shut " of the philosopher's characteristic, " to wit, a ragged pair of breeches (especially as he has had lately a pair of silver breeches-buckles presented to him) ; wherefore, if the gallant captain would cure his son of philosophic contempla-tion, the only way will be to send some handsome thing for a waistcoat and breeches as aforesaid." Then follows a hint that he is told " velvet is very cheap at Gibraltar." Trivialities are these matters. Not often, however, is a glimpse of the kind obtained into the boyish life and ambitions of one destined to equal eminence. A letter from Mrs. Garrick to the absentee husband may serve to depict the domestic surroundings amidst which Garrick grew. Of this, which is undated, a copy only is preserved in the Forster Collection :—

" I must tell my Dear Life & Soul that I am not able to live easy longer with out him for I grow very jealous —but in the midst of all this I do not blame my dear. I have very sad dreams for you . . . but I have the pleasure when I am up, to think were I with you how tender [torn

here] my Dear Soul would be to me, nay was when I was
with you last.   O that I had you in my armes I would tell
my Dear Life how much I am his.

"A. G."

Few opportunities of realizing this natural wish
were in the event afforded. Once more Garrick
writes and states that there is a piece of Le Grout's
(a miniature artist of the day) which he values
above all the pieces of Zeuxis or Apelles, and
it gives him more pleasure to have one glance of
that than to look a whole day at the finest picture
in the world; nay, it has this effect upon him : that
whenever he looks upon it he fancies himself at Gibraltar, sees the Spaniards, and sometimes mounts
garrison. The picture, which is in his hand, he
cannot adequately describe :—" It is the figure of a
gentleman, and I suppose military by his dress; I
think Le Grout told me his name was one Captain
Peter Garrick ; perhaps as you are in the army you
may know him, he is pretty jolly, and I believe not
very tall."   Concerning this pleasant and affectionate
banter, Forster writes with pleasant but exaggerated
enthusiasm, " Is not the letter a bit of comedy in
itself, a piece of character and feeling such as Farquhar might have written ? "   (Goldsmith, i. 227.)

Views had been entertained as to the expediency
of sending David to a University ; but the idea had
been postponed on account of narrowness of means.
A tentative scheme of Gilbert Walmesley's was then
suggested, to send the youth to Edial, near Lichfield,
in Staffordshire, where, according to an advertisement

in the *Gentleman's Magazine* for June and July,
1736, "young gentlemen are boarded and taught
the Latin and Greek languages by Samuel Johnson."
Thither, accordingly, David went. His stay was
confined to a few months, when Johnson's experiment broke down, and teacher and pupil are next
heard of travelling together to London in search of
the fame which awaited both.

Previous to this time Garrick, who had been made
much of by the officers in Lichfield, had more than
once gone near embracing his father's profession.
He had sent to his father some satirical verses of no
particular merit upon an officer in whom he had
scented a rival, had made one or more excursions to
London, and had, while at school with his brother
George at Edial, excited the laughter of his companions by some not too delicate mimicry of
Johnson.

When all notion of the University had been abandoned, and the choice of some profession for David,
then nineteen years of age, was imperative, Gilbert Walmesley, the Registrar of the Ecclesiastical
Court in Lichfield, and the constant friend and
patron of Garrick, was naturally consulted. The
bar was the profession selected, and as some
preliminary study was necessary, David, on his
journey to London, was provided with a letter from
Walmesley to his friend the Rev. John Colson, a
Lichfield man, master of the new mathematical school
founded in Rochester by Sir Joseph Williamson. In
this letter, which stands first in the interminable

series of the Garrick Correspondence collected by
Boaden, and is dated from Lichfield, 5th Feb., 1736,
are some passages of great interest. The occasion
of writing Walmesley declares to be as follows :—

> " My neighbour, Captain Garrick, (who is an honourable,
> valuable man,) has a son, who is a very sensible young
> fellow, and a good scholar, and whom the Captain hopes,
> in some two or three years, he shall be able to send to the
> Temple, and breed to the Bar. But at present his
> pocket will not hold out for sending him to the University.
> I have proposed your taking him, if you think well of it,
> and your boarding him, and instructing him in mathema-
> tics, and philosophy, and humane learning. He is now
> nineteen, of sober and good dispositions, and is as in-
> genuous and promising a young man as ever I knew in
> my life. Few instructions on your side will do, and in
> the intervals of study, he will be an agreeable companion
> for you. His father will be glad to pay you whatever you
> shall require, that is within his reach ; and I shall think
> myself very much obliged to you into the bargain. This
> young gentleman, you must know, has been much with me,
> ever since he was a child, almost every day ; and I have
> taken a pleasure often in instructing him, and have a
> great affection and esteem for him ; and I doubt not but
> you will soon have the like, if it suit with your convenience
> to take him into your family."

Acknowledging the favourable reception given his
first letter, Walmesley then introduces (2nd March,
17$\frac{36}{37}$) another neighbour of his, one Mr. Johnson, who goes to try his fate with a tragedy. Of
Johnson he speaks as a very good scholar and poet,
who, he hopes, will turn out a fine tragedy writer.
The letter is otherwise interesting, and states that on

the day on which it is dated "Davy" Garrick and Johnson set out for London together.

Concerning this journey to London, which proffers all the opportunities of romance, little serious information is obtainable. Garrick subsequently stated that they rode and tied, which Boswell characterizes as an effort at embellishment. On another occasion, Johnson, in a large company, in a spirit of rather malicious banter of Garrick's assumptions, referred to some event as having taken place in the year in which he came to London with twopence-halfpenny in his pocket. This drew from Garrick the inquiry: "Eh? what do you say? with twopence-halfpenny in your pocket?" "Why, yes," responded Johnson; "when I came with twopence-halfpenny in my pocket, and thou, Davy, with three halfpence in thine."

Such means as the pair possessed were at any rate speedily consumed during a short residence in London, and they then made, at Garrick's suggestion, application to Wilcox the bookseller for a loan. With more insight and good nature than are customary, Wilcox, according to Hawkins ("Life of Johnson," p. 43), was so moved by their artless tale, that he advanced them five pounds, which is all that their modesty permitted them to ask. It is satisfactory to be able to chronicle that the loan was repaid.

Garrick meanwhile had entered himself duly at Lincoln's Inn, on the 9th of March, 1737, paying for his entry the sum of three pounds, three shillings and fourpence, thus showing that Johnson's statement as to the amount of funds he carried with him to

London was ironical. The death of Garrick's father trod close upon the heels of the admission into Lincoln's Inn. That David figured for the sum of one shilling in his father's will, proved the 7th April, 1737, which left the other children from three to five hundred pounds each, is assumably due to the fact that David Garrick, the Lisbon wine merchant, had left his namesake a thousand pounds, as against five hundred to his other nephews and nieces. Not long had David to wait for his legacy; his uncle's death and that of his mother also being assigned to the year 1737. Some attempt to carry out the educational scheme with Colson seems to have been made, but Garrick's residence in Rochester cannot have extended much beyond a year, since in 1738 he was once more in Lichfield. Peter, his elder brother by seven years, had given up the navy, and was also in his native city. As the result of a family council, it was determined that the forensic scheme should be abandoned, and that the slight training David had obtained in the wine trade, during his residence in Lisbon, should be turned to account. Joining their modest capital together, the two brothers started business as wine merchants in Durham Yard, a small street leading riverwards from the Strand. The site of their business premises was swept away when the brothers Adam made their famous architectural changes. By the arrangement, Peter the elder was to remain in Lichfield and look after the sale of wines among his father's friends. To David was assigned the place of London

manager, assumably involving the functions of purchasing and superintending storage. To this occupation, Foote, in the days of Garrick's prosperity,
was accustomed to refer, saying that he remembered
Garrick in Durham Yard, with three quarts of
vinegar in the cellar, calling himself a wine merchant.

At this time, Garrick had acquired a reputation
as a talker and a mimic, shortly to be supplemented
by that of a poet and a wit. A position more
dangerous than that he occupied cannot easily be
conceived. In the mere search after business it
was natural that he should, in spite of an inherent
sobriety, attributable partly perhaps to his French
descent and partly to his habits of economy,
haunt taverns and coffee-houses, where readiness to
join in conviviality was indispensable to success.
His place of business was in immediate proximity to
Covent Garden, then, as since, the haunt of those
most nearly connected with the stage. From the
crapula of such surroundings he kept himself free,
but the seductive influence he was unable to resist.
He became a veritable denizen of Bohemia, an
associate of actors, a frequenter of the green-room,
and the avowed lover of a reigning actress. That
his business suffered from such habits and pursuits
may be surmised, though there is no evidence of the
fact. A friendship which he formed with Macklin
did much to foster his longing for the stage, and
his admiration for Margaret Woffington acted as an
irresistible provocative. When he first made the
acquaintance of Peg Woffington is uncertain. It

was probably during her one year's engagement 1740-41 at Covent Garden. To neither of these acquaintances, but to Giffard, did he owe his appearance on the stage.

Before the final plunge, Garrick, it is said, made one tentative experiment, taking characters, the names of which are unknown, in performances of Fielding's "Mock Doctor" and a burlesque of "Julius Cæsar," given at St. John's Gate, Clerkenwell, where Cave was then conducting the *Gentleman's Magazine.* Permission for this had possibly been obtained by Johnson from Cave, who, besides admitting into the *Gentleman's Magazine* for September, 1740, a new epilogue to the "Mock Doctor," signed G, and ascribed to Garrick, accepted also some of the love verses which Garrick had begun to write. Closer still was drawn the connection with the stage when, on the 15th April, 1740, for the benefit of his friend, and subsequent manager, Henry Giffard, Garrick's "Lethe" was performed at Drury Lane. This piece, to be heard of again, was a mere sketch of manners, and had scarcely the pretence of a plot. Permission is accorded to mortals to cross and recross the Styx and taste of the waters of oblivion. Æsop receives the visitors and inquires into their motives in taking the journey. These prove in every case to be base or contemptible, and the whole is a mere satire, into which, previous to its revival, Garrick introduced new characters. Though acted anonymously, as appears, it was treated with consideration; Taswell being

Æsop; Beard, Mercury; Macklin, the Drunken Man; Woodward, the Beau; Rafter, Mr. Thomas; and Mrs. Clive, Miss Lucy. A prologue and epilogue were spoken. The latter is by Garrick, and was delivered by Thomas and Miss Lucy.

CHAPTER II.

Such indulgences and experiences as have been mentioned could have in Garrick's case but one result. For the stage he was qualified by gifts altogether exceptional, and to it he had for many years been drifting. "Nature," says Cumberland, "had done so much for Garrick, that he could not help being an actor—she gave him a frame of so manageable a proportion, and from its flexibility so perfectly under command, that by its aptitude and elasticity he could suit it to any sort of character—his eye was so penetrating, so speaking, his brow so moveable, and all his features so plastic and accommodating, that wherever his mind impelled them they would go, and before his tongue could give the text his countenance would express the spirit and passion of the part he was charged with." With a modesty rare in his profession he elected to make his first appearance, or what was practically such, under an assumed name and with a darkened countenance in the country. Mr. Percy Fitzgerald has shown that his actual first appearance was at Goodman's Fields, where, Yates being indisposed, he went on in his place as harlequin. Curious as was the experiment, it may scarcely count as a *début*. The chief interest is in showing that the courage of the young wine merchant was on a par with his ambition.

In the summer of 1741, Garrick accompanied Giffard, the manager of Goodman's Fields theatre, and Dunstall to Ipswich, where, under the name of Lyddal, which was the maiden name of Giffard's wife, he made his first appearance as Aboan, the black officer in " Oroonoko," the drama founded by Southerne upon a pathetic and an interesting narrative of Mrs. Behn. Success with a country audience means comparatively little. Such, however, was achieved. Other parts followed, including Chamont in "The Orphan," Sir Harry Wildair in Farquhar's comedy of that name, and Captain Brazen in "The Recruiting Officer." From the outset accordingly Garrick's empire was divided between tragedy and comedy.

Emboldened by his success, Garrick, on his return, applied for engagements at both Covent Garden and Drury Lane. The stage doors of the patent houses did not then or subsequently open very readily to the histrionic aspirant, and the advances of Garrick were repelled. Destiny had decided that under Giffard Garrick's first ventures were to be made, and Goodman's Fields was selected for his London *début*. The portal was not only small, but in a sense surreptitious.

On October 31st, 1729, Odell opened, in Ayliffe Street, Goodman's Fields, a theatre, the management of which he soon resigned to Giffard, who, in 1732,

substituted for it a handsome and more commodious
house, built from designs by Shepherd, the architect
of Covent Garden. Giffard and his wife were main-
stays of a theatre which during some years prevailed
against the class of opposition to which from the first
such institutions appear to have been subjected on
the part of the authorities. In answer to remonstrances, and in consequence of the freedom of satire
permitted himself by Fielding, the famous Licensing
Act was passed on the 21st June, 1737. The
bill, brought in on Friday, the 20th May, was called
a bill "to explain and amend so much of an Act
made in the twelfth year of the reign of Queen Anne,
entitled, *An Act for reducing the laws relating to
Rogues, Vagabonds, sturdy Beggars and Vagrants,
into one Act of Parliament ; and for the more
effectual punishing such Rogues, Vagabonds, sturdy
Beggars, and Vagrants, and sending them whither
they ought to be sent*, as relates to Common Players
of Interludes." The real significance of the Act, not
easily to be extracted from the words quoted, was to
restrain the number of play-houses, and regulate
that no dramatic composition, even to a prologue or
epilogue, should be exhibited or delivered without
the approbation of a licencer. In spite of much opposition, and in face of the brilliantly ironical speech of
the Earl of Chesterfield—one of the wittiest addresses
to which the House of Lords ever listened—the
bill was hurried by Sir Robert Walpole through
all its stages, and received the Royal assent. A
motion for leave to bring in a bill for restraining

the number of play-houses and for regulating common players had been conceded two years previously to Sir John Barnard, a respectable and influential magistrate, but had led to no action. Sir John's measure had been directed specially against Goodman's Fields, and he himself asserted that he had been on the look-out for such information as would bring the actors at that house within the vagrant laws. In 1737 Giffard was on the side of the Government, to which he carried the famous though to this day invisible "Golden Rump," which had been offered him for acceptance. According to what is known of this play, its production would have involved a scandal such as neither "Pasquin" nor "The Historical Register" had produced, and Giffard took it to the Government, little dreaming, it has been suggested, that he was an unconscious tool in its hands. He was duly paid for it a gratuity equal to what he might reasonably have expected from the representation. Walpole kept the MS., and the Licensing Bill was passed, William Chetwynd being the first licencer, and Odell, Giffard's predecessor in management, his deputy. Whatever the sum which Giffard received from Government, it can scarcely have compensated him for the disturbance in his business which followed the passage of the bill. After 1737 nothing is heard of Goodman's Fields until the 15th October, 1740, when the following announcement, curious in more respects than one, was put forth :—" At the *late* Theatre in Ayliffe Street a Concert of vocal and instrumental Musick, in two parts

—between the parts of the Concert will be presented *gratis* a Comedy, called ' The Stratagem '—by persons for their diversion." The word *late* denoted apparently not that the theatre had been destroyed, but that it no longer claimed to rank as a theatre. The insertion between the parts of a concert of a play given gratis was one of the devices by which, until well into the present century, the privileges of the patent houses were evaded. During the remainder of that season Giffard appears to have surmounted his difficulties, since many pieces, including several by Shakespeare, were performed. At the beginning of the next season the old precaution was observed. In the second volume of his Memoirs (pp. 111—114) Charles Lee Lewes reproduces a bill which for interest has, perhaps, not its equal in connection with the English stage. It is as follows :—

October 19th, 1741.

Goodman's Fields.

At the late Theatre, in Goodman's fields, this day, will be performed a Concert of Vocal and Instrumental Music, divided into Two Parts.

Tickets at three, two and one shilling.

Places for the Boxes to be taken at the Fleece Tavern, next the Theatre.

N.B. Between the two parts of the Concert, will be presented, an Historical Play, called,

The Life and Death of

King Richard the Third.

Containing the distress of K. Henry VI.

The artful acquisition of the Crown

by King Richard.

The murder of young King Edward V.
and his brother in the Tower.
The landing of the Earl of Richmond; and the death of King
Richard in the memorable battle of Bosworth-field, being the
last that was fought between the houses of York and Lancaster.
With many other true Historical passages.
The part of King Richard by a Gentleman (who never
appeared on any Stage),
King Henry by Mr. Giffard; Richmond, Mr. Marshall; Prince
Edward by Miss Hippisley; Duke of York, Miss Naylor;
Duke of Buckingham, Mr. Patterson; Duke of Norfolk, Mr.
Blakes; Lord Stanley, Mr. Pagett; Oxford, Mr. Vaughan;
Tressel, Mr. W. Giffard; Catesby, Mr. Marr; Ratcliff, Mr.
Crofts; Blunt, Mr. Naylor; Tyrrel, Mr. Puttenham; Lord
Mayor, Mr. Dunstall; The Queen, Mrs. Steel; Duchess of
York, Mrs. Yates;
And the part of Lady Anne
By Mrs. Giffard.
With Entertainments of Dancing,
By Mons. Froment, Madam Duvall,
and the two Masters and
Miss Granier.
To which will be added
A Ballad Opera of One Act, called,
The Virgin Unmask'd,
The part of Lucy by Miss Hippisley.
Both of which will be performed gratis, by persons
for their diversion.
The Concert will begin exactly at six o'clock.

The announcement that this was Garrick's first
appearance on any stage was one of those trade lies
to which, in all ages, the stage conscience has apparently reconciled itself. Garrick's success in Richard
was uncontested and epoch-marking. A career so
prosperous as his, from the outset to the close, has

rarely, if ever, been chronicled. No experience of country struggle, no breathless fight with poverty, no moment of serious gloom and discouragement, ever attended this favourite of Fortune. Some few obstacles had to be surmounted before he could make his mark ; some few clouds had to be dispersed before he showed himself at his meridian altitude. These were no more, however, than add zest to enjoyment. A contest is necessary to the pleasure of victory, a spice of opposition is indispensable to the rapture of conquest. In the words of Middleton (" Women beware Women ") :—

> " When we invite our best friends to a feast
>   'Tis not all sweetmeats that we set before 'em ;
>   There's something sharp and salt both to whet appetite
>   And make 'em taste their wine well, so methinks
>   After a friendly sharp and savoury quarrel
>   A kiss tastes wondrous well and full o' the grape."

Only calculated to give the kisses of Fortune the required taste of the grape were the rebuffs Garrick experienced. If in later life he was to find that enjoyment palled, that those who most admired him fell for no reason away from him, and that he could not through a long life ride always on the crest of the wave, he had an experience which none that ever drew breath has escaped, and to which actors perhaps more than all others are exposed.

Reflections such as these belong, however, to a later day in Garrick's career. At present he is steeped in the glow of a transcendent triumph, and his difficulty is to know how to wear publicly as well as becomingly his laurels, to break with his past, and to convey to the quiet home at Lichfield the intelligence that he is now a man of importance and a statutory "rogue and vagabond."

The appearance of Garrick in Richard was in many respects a revelation. Exaggerated importance was attached to it in its day, and his earliest biographers and critics were disposed to credit him with the invention of an art—that of natural delivery. This was at best but a recovery. That a very sorry method of delivery had crept into use we have on incontestable authority. At what date it was introduced is unknown. Of Mrs. Barry, in his "Brief Supplement" to Colley Cibber, Tony Aston says: "Neither she nor any of the actors of those times had any *tone* in their speaking, too much lately in use;" and he quotes from "The Orphan" a speech which she delivered in a natural manner and with much charm. This very scarce work is undated, but from an allusion it contains, must have been written after 1747. Aaron Hill, also, in his dedication of the "Fatal Vision" to Dennis and Gildon, complains of the "affected, vicious, and unnatural tone of voice" common on the stage, and exempts Booth alone among tragedians from "a horrible theatric way of speaking," which is destructive of the effect of dramatic poetry. This is a different matter from the question of chant, and is a reproach that has been levelled against English actors in all generations.

The first delivery of tragedy was in a species of chant, not unlike that, it may be supposed, still heard in Jewish worship, rising, perhaps, in lyrical portions, to a faint kind of melody. Tragedy was, as all know, in itself a form of worship, and the tendency to intone such has continued to our day. In countries where, as in France, the drama is directly transmitted from classic sources, a similar method has been retained on the stage. That the tragedies of Shakespeare could have been delivered in any such fashion is inconceivable. We are without any absolute light on the subject, but are justified in believing that the system of intonation was transmitted to us from France. From that country, after the Restoration, we took almost everything connected with the stage, and it is natural that those who imported plays, costumes, scenery, actors, should import also methods of delivery. It is obvious from the words of Aston that Betterton and the great actors of his period were free from this vice, and we know that soon after the appearance of Garrick it died. The rhymed and lackadaisical tragedies of the intervening period seem intended for some species of sing-song, to which they lend themselves as easily as the rhymed Alexandrines of the French classical drama, with its strongly accentuated cæsura, a measure which it has been the fashion in England to undervalue. The utmost service, then, with which Garrick's Richard can be credited is the restoration of a natural delivery, which had fallen into disuse. It is illustrative of the hold which the abuse of delivery had taken that Quin, after seeing Garrick act, declared peremptorily that if the young fellow was right he [Quin] and the rest of the players had been wrong.

Concerning the audience which witnessed the opening performance of Garrick we know nothing. That the personal popularity of the actor would have enabled him thus early in his career to crowd the house is improbable. A sprinkling of friends is all of which we hear. As he hid his name on his opening venture, it is possible that the knowledge of his experiment was confined to a few warm friends and supporters. No full and trustworthy record concerning the first presentation survives. It would be pleasant to accept as authentic the vivacious picture given by Murphy, who, however, at that time was a boy. Davies might have been present, but obviously was not, and the description given by both is drawn in part from hearsay and in part from subsequent observation. Such, Murphy declares, was the power of Garrick's imagination, that he transformed himself from the first into the very man. In sight of the audience the passions chased themselves quickly over his face, and the expression of each was conveyed before a word had been spoken. An astounding effect was produced by the rage and rapidity with which he spoke—

"The North !—what do they in the North
When they should serve their Sovereign in the West?"

(The version, it will be perceived, is Cibber's.) In what is known as the tent scene the descriptions were

realized to a great extent by the actor, who on starting from the dream presented " a spectacle of horror ;"
called out in " a manly voice," " Give me another
horse ; " with a " countenance of dismay," cried, in
a tone of distress, " Bind up my wounds ; " and then
falling on his knees, said in the most piteous accents,
" Have mercy, Heaven." This description, so far
as it goes, is no doubt accurate, since it is difficult
to see in what other way the whole could be given.
Davies is even more vague, speaking of Garrick's
style as " easy and familiar yet forcible," and praising
the " just modulation of the words and concurring
expression of the features from the genuine workings
of nature ; " things to which he says the audience
had long been strangers. The delivery of the long-
famous words :—

> " Off with his head,—So much for Buckingham,"

roused the audience to loud congratulations, as did
the death of Richard.

Doubt as to the success of the performance is impossible. The *Daily Post* of the following day, after
noting that the tragedy of " King Richard the Third "
was performed *gratis* at the late theatre in Goodman's
Fields, and that the character of Richard was taken by
a gentleman who never appeared before, speaks of the
reception as " the most extraordinary and great that
was ever known on such an occasion." A slightly
later comment, reprinted by Mr. Percy Fitzgerald
from a cutting from the *Champion*, now in a private
collection, gives a curiously naïve but intelligible

criticism, praising Garrick's voice, and saying it is " neither whining, bellowing, nor grumbling, but perfectly easy in its transitions, natural in its cadence, and beautiful in its elocution. He [Garrick] is not less happy in his mien and gait, in which he is neither strutting nor mincing, neither stiff nor slouching. When three or four are on the stage with him, he is attentive to whatever is spoke, and never drops his characters when he has finished a speech by either looking contemptuously on an inferior performer, unnecessary spitting, or suffering his eyes to wander through the whole circle of spectators. His action is never superfluous, awkward, or too frequently repeated, but graceful, decent, and becoming."

With its testimony so often and so curiously negative to Garrick's qualities, this quaint criticism recalls the expression used a century previously by Margaret Cavendish, Duchess of Newcastle, a member of the family of Lucas, Earl of Colchester, called on a monument in Westminster Abbey " a noble family, for all the brothers were valiant, and all the sisters virtuous." Of those brothers and sisters her Grace says, in words by which the critic of the *Champion* might have been inspired, they were " every ways proportionable, likewise well-featured, clear complexions, brown hair, but some lighter than others, sound teeth, sweet breaths, plain speeches, *tunable voices, I mean not so much to sing or in speaking, as not stuttering*, nor wharling in the throat, or speaking through the nose, or hoarsely, unless they had a cold, or squeakingly, which impediments many have."

Now that his profession has been deliberately adopted, and that his capacity for it is avouched, there comes upon Garrick the necessity, long shirked, of communicating to his brother and partner the change in his prospects and plans. Instances have been not infrequent in which the two occupations of actor and vintner have been reconciled. Such, indeed, are still known. Not easily reconcilable are, however, a life on the stage and a family business as a wine merchant in a Cathedral city. Garrick approached his brother very carefully and gingerly. Fortunately for him an elderly, staid, and reputable gentleman of Lichfield, a Mr. Swynfen, was among the favoured spectators of the first performance. It is a justifiable surmise that Garrick saw in this trustworthy personage an unimpeachable witness, and solicited his assistance. What is known is, that on the following day, the 20th, Swynfen sent a letter which presented matters in the precise light in which Garrick would have had them put, and bears, indeed, a suspicious resemblance to Garrick's own style. " Many people there are," says Mr. Swynfen, " who, because their fathers were called gentlemen, or themselves the first so called, will think it a disgrace and a scandal that the child of an old friend should endeavour to get an honest livelihood, and is not content to live in a scanty manner all his life because his father was a gentleman." Not of these, the writer holds, is Mr. [Peter] Garrick, who he is convinced " has not the same sentiments ; and he knows better of his friend's judgment than to suppose him partaking of the prejudices of other country friends of theirs, who have been most used to theatrical performances in town halls, etc., by strollers, and will be apt to imagine the highest pitch a man can arrive at on the stage is about that exalted degree of heroism which they two, in old days at Lichfield, used to laugh and cry at, in the Herberts and the Hallams ; but, as he does not doubt but that Mr. Peter will soon hear ' my good friend David Garrick performed last night at Goodman's Fields Theatre,' for fear he should hear any false or malicious account that may perhaps be disagreeable to him, he [Mr. Swynfen] will give him the truth, by which he had been most pleased." He then continues, " *I was there*, and was witness to a most general applause He gain'd in the character of Richard the Third ; for I believe there was not one in the House that was not in Raptures, and I heard several Men of Judgment declare it their Opinion that nobody ever excelled Him in that Part ; and that they were surprised, with so peculiar a Genius, how it was possible for Him to keep off the Stage so long."

This curious and interesting document owes its preservation to John Forster, in whose collection it is included and by whom, with other letters with which we have now to deal, it is given in his admirable life of Goldsmith. By the same post went David's own letter, the pith of which is the same. David, however, coquets with one or two matters before he comes to the all-important subject. He begins with things domestic, owning the receipt of a shirt ; then refers to what he supposes Peter may already have heard.   Before being more precise, he will premise some things in order that he may appear less culpable in his brother's sight than he might otherwise do.   He has looked carefully into business matters, taking stock of wine and money out at interest, and finds that since the beginning of the partnership, he has "run out near four hundred pounds."   Trade is still in a bad way, and he is very sensible that something must be done to recover the lost ground.   Now comes the confession: "My mind (as you must know) has been always inclined to ye Stage, nay so strongly so that all my Illness and lowness of Spirits was owing to my want of resolution to tell you my thoughts when here." Poor David! what throes he must have undergone when meeting his brother, and what a picture of irresolution has he drawn for us!   "Finding," he continues, "at last both my Inclination and Interest requir'd some new way of Life, I have chose ye most agreeable to myself, and though I know you will be much displeas'd at me, yet I hope when you find that I may have ye genius of an Actor without ye vices you will think less severe of me, and not be asham'd to own me for a Brother."

Relapsing into business, he professes his willingness to put himself into his brother's hands, will take a thorough survey of the vaults and will send Peter his share or do whatever is judged expedient.   Then changing once more his topic he blurts out the fact, "Last night, I played Richard ye Third to ye Surprise of Everybody, and as I shall make very near £300 per annum by it, and as it is really what I doat upon, *I am resolv'd to pursue it.*" After the expression of what was doubtless a sincere and unchangeable resolution, he returns to business, and the means of paying for his part of the wine at Lichfield. He prays for an immediate answer, and concludes, " I am Dʳ Brother yʳ sincerely D. Garrick." Some supplemental information follows : " I have a farce (yᵉ Lying Valet) coming out at Drury Lane." Peter's reply to this epistle and his answers generally are unfortunately not included in Forster's collections. The correspondence is thus one-sided. No difficulty is experienced in gathering the general tenour, nor is much imagination requisite to picture the state of the Lichfield dove-cotes which had been thus fluttered. Garrick's next letter, dated the 27th October, assures his brother that the uneasiness he has experienced at the receipt of his letter is inexpressible. The shock had, however, been anticipated, and he had, so far as was possible, guarded himself against it. His strong resolution even now might be sacrificed to the love he bears his brother and to the arguments to which he had listened, but necessity convinced him that he was less to blame than Peter seemed to believe. That his uncle should upbraid his brother with their joint reticence concerning their affairs, surprises him. What he had himself " run out " was doubtless more " owing to his own wilfulness than any miscarriage in trade ; but run out he had, and let him live never so warily, must run out more."

Now comes a touch showing how much influenced in his views of life he had been by his association with men of fashion. He holds that Peter, on reflection, will see that no trade they have would have enabled him (David) "*to maintain himself and a servant handsomely*." The stage in general deserves Peter's censure, but some, as Booth, Mills, Wilks, Cibber, &c., have lived reputable and been admitted into the best company. He then continues: "As my Genius that way (by ye best Judges) is thought Wonderful, how can you be averse to my proceedings when not only my Inclinations, but my Friends who at first were surprised at my Intent, by seeing me on ye stage are now well convinc'd 'twas impossible for me to keep off." The best company in town is desirous of his. Mr. Glover—Richard Glover, the author of "Leonidas," then a man of influence and distinction—has been every night to see him, and proclaims, as does every one he meets, that he has not seen such acting for ten years before. Brother as Peter is, to tell him all that is now said would be too vain. His name has not yet been put in the bills, and he has only played the part of Richard the Third, which brings crowded houses every night. Not less flourishing are his finances than is his fame, and he has not upon him a debt of twenty shillings.

Very far from being convinced is Peter Garrick, and a fresh appeal is necessary. This is dated the 10th November. Sorry as he is that Peter remains averse to what he is so inclined to and to what the best judges think he has the greatest genius for, David affirms that the great, nay, incredible success and approbation he has met with from the greatest persons in England, have almost made him resolve, even, he is sorry to say, against dear Peter's entreaties, to pursue the profession by which, if health continue, he shall certainly make a fortune. He receives at present six guineas a week, though this is a secret, and has been offered £120 for his benefit. If his brother will come to see him it shall cost him nothing. David then says : " Mr. Littleton, Mr. Pit, and several other members of Parliament were to see me play Chamont in ye Orphan, and Mr. Pit, who is reckon'd ye greatest Orator in ye House of Commons, said I was ye best Actor ye English Stage had produc'd, and he sent a Gentleman to me to let me know he and ye other Gentlemen would be glad to see Me. The Prince has heard so great a Character of me that we are in daily expectations of his coming to see me."

Peter remains inexorable. No amount of reputation that David can earn in London, not even the anticipated smiles of royalty, can compensate for the irreparable injury inflicted upon the family position in Lichfield. He is, however, slightly mollified, and on the 24th November, David rewards the small change by a half offer to let his brother have his whole capital, and declares, " I know I shall soon be more able by playing and writing to do you service than any other way."

Further triumphs have to be recorded. He is

told by the best judges, who to a man are with him, that he will turn out, nay, already is " not only the best tragedian but comedian in England." Fortified by such opinions, he may venture to tell his brother that he is " very near *quite* resolved to be a player." On his own merits he would not expatiate to anybody but his brother, " but as this may somewhat palliate my folly, you must excuse me. Mr. Littleton was wth Me last Night, and took me by ye hand and said, he never saw such playing upon ye English Stage before." They have had finer business than at either Drury Lane or Covent Garden, from the managers of which he has had great offers. Mr. Giffard, the manager, has given him yesterday twenty guineas, and he (David) purposes next week purchasing £200 of stock out of his profits of playing. He even takes courage to send his brother a copy of his farce, " The Lying Valet," the performance of which goes with a general roar from beginning to end, and in the character of Sharp, though far different from any other he has played, he has got, he believes, no less reputation.

Though somewhat anticipating matters, this profoundly interesting correspondence may as well be closed and dismissed. On the 22nd December, things being now for good or ill definitely settled, he says, addressing the same Peter, " You, perhaps, would be glad to know what parts I have play'd: 'King Rich^d,' Jack Smatter in ' Pamela,' Clody (*sic*) ' Fop's Fortune,' Lothario ' Fair Penitent,' Chamont

'Orphan,' Ghost 'Hamlet,' and shall soon be ready in Bays in y⁰ 'Rehearsal,' and in yᵉ part of Othello, Both of which I believe will do Me and Giffard great service. I have had great success in all, and 'tis not yet determin'd whether I play Tragedy or Comedy best. Old Cibber has spoke with yᵉ Greatest Commendation of my Acting."

Once more, at a somewhat later date, 19th April, 1742, we are favoured with a self-painted picture of his success. "The favor I meet with from yᵉ Greatest men has made me far from repenting of my choice. I am very intimate with Mr. Glover, who will bring out a Tragedy next winter upon my accᵗ. Twice I have sup't wᵗʰ yᵉ Great Mr. Murray, Counsellʳ, and shall wᵗʰ Mr. Pope, by his introduction. I sup't with Mr. Littleton, ye Prince's Favourite, last Thursday night, and that with y⁰ highest Civility and complaisance. He told me he never knew what Acting was till I appear'd, and said I was only born to act wᵗ Shakespear writ. These things daily occurring give me Great Pleasure. I din'd with Lᵈ Halifax and Lᵈ Sandwich, two very ingenious Noblemen, yesterday, and am to dine at Lᵈ Halifax's next Sunday with Lᵈ Chesterfield. I have the Pleasure of being very intimate, too, with Mr. Hawkins Browne, of Burton. In short, I believe nobody (as an Actor) was ever more caress'd, and my Character as a private Man makes 'em more desirous of my Company. (All this *entre nous*, as one Brothʳ to another.) I am not fix'd for next year, but shall certainly be at yᵉ Other End of

ye Town.   I am offered 500 guineas and a Clear
Benefit, or part of ye management."

In no case of a man of approximately equal importance have we so trustworthy an insight into the
obstacles—they can scarcely be called difficulties—
that beset an opening career as these letters afford.
There is much naïveté and sincerity, and as much
frankness as was to be expected under the circumstances, in these letters, written for a purely domestic
purpose, and appearing little likely, it must be owned,
ever to again see the light.   In one's own despite the
temptation comes over one to wish to know more of the
little domestic comedy thus opened out.   When did
Peter relent ?   The sisters, we may be sure, were soon
reconciled.   Their personal dignity would be less
compromised, and the opportunity of gossip over
David's success and his fashionable acquaintances
would be compensation for a little social embarrassment.   Visitors from Lichfield must from time to
time have visited London, and would naturally flock
to Goodman's Fields to see their play - acting
townsman.   The reports they brought back could
not be other than favourable, seeing that Garrick's
early career knew no disgrace, scarcely even a check.
A glow of satisfaction must then in time have
mounted as they heard of triumph unprecedented
even in a career such as that of an actor.   Some
wonder is, however, inspired when the fish-blooded
Peter first saw his brother act, and whether he yielded
to the emotions which David's acting was accustomed
to produce.   Did his sisters, after a time, come to

town at David's expense to see the new marvel? Peter was, before long, to draw on him for a sum of money, to be repaid at his convenience. George was to be sent up to be established, by David's influence, in a solicitor's office, and to be during the remainder of his life Garrick's dependent. Some glimpses into this not unfavourable metamorphosis which converts the disgrace of a family into its honour and its prop are afforded. One would be thankful for more.

CHAPTER III.

DURING Garrick's earlier performances the pretence of anonymity was maintained. Each succeeding character was presented by a gentleman who made his third, or tenth, or twentieth appearance upon any stage. So soon as all was known in Lichfield the reasons for an affectation of mystery were over. Garrick was naturally anxious to wear publicly his laurels. Before, however, the curtain was raised, and the *secret de Polichinelle* stood revealed, he had played, as has been seen, many characters, including some original creations, and his name was as familiar in the purlieus of Covent Garden as that of Macklin or Quin. On the 28th October, 1741, he essayed his second part, that of Clodio, in "Love Makes a Man; or, The Fop's Fortune," a play extracted by Colley Cibber from "The Custom of the Country" and "The Elder Brother" of Beaumont and Fletcher. Clodio, a coxcomb, had been "created" by Cibber himself, but had passed from him to Garrick through Bullock, jun., Theophilus Cibber, and Chapman. Not otherwise interesting is it than as the first experiment of Garrick in London in comedy, and it was shortly afterwards dropped, not to be resumed. Chamont, in "The Orphan" of Otway, followed on the 6th November, and was another success. Three days later, on the 9th, Garrick was the original Jack Smatter in "Pamela," an adaptation from Richardson by James Dance, who produced it and other works under the pseudonym of "Love." Thanks in part to Garrick's performance of a vivacious and taking part, it ran for twelve successive nights, eclipsing thus, so far as the actor was concerned, the success of Richard. On the 30th November Garrick, now obviously master of the situation and the mainstay of the house, produced his own two-act comedy, "The Lying Valet," a clever adaptation of "All without Money," the second of the five pieces which form Motteux's "Novelty: Every Act a Play." In this Garrick played Sharp, the lying valet, who, to serve his impecunious master, lies like "a scientific expert." The subject is as old as the beginning of comedy, and Sharp is the same character that has appeared under a hundred aliases—Xanthias, Davus, Sganarelle, Figaro. Sharp is witty and resourceful rather than brilliant, his inventions having no great originality, and still less promise of success. Garrick also recited as Sharp an epilogue of his own composition, which is a vindication of his assumed character. After the fashion of the author of "The Lie," Raleigh or another, he taxes the heads of the various professions with falsehood. It begins—

> "That I'm a lying rogue, you all agree,
>   And yet look round the world, and you will see
>   How many more, my betters, lye as fast as me."

Lothario, in "The Fair Penitent," played by Garrick for the first time 2nd December, 1741, became one of his favourite parts and remained long in his repertory. On the 9th December he played the Ghost in "Hamlet" to the Hamlet of Giffard, his manager, and the Ophelia of Miss Hippisley. His "Lethe" was revived at this house on the 2nd January, 1742, though there is no reason to suppose that he acted in it. On the 5th he played Fondlewife in "The Old Bachelor" of Congreve, and on the 14th Costar Pearmain, in "The Recruiting Officer" of Farquhar. Aboan, in "Oroonoko," was added to his repertory on the 23rd January; Witwoud, in Congreve's "Way of the World," on the 27th; and Bayes, in "The Rehearsal," perhaps the most conspicuous triumph of his first season, on the 3rd February.

Not half the marvels of this wonderful season, the most remarkable ever known in the case of a tyro on the stage, are told, but a pause in the enumeration of new characters undertaken is expedient. Garrick's first appearance under his own name had taken place on the 2nd December, when he acted for his benefit Lothario. By that time all difficulties had been surmounted, and London was ringing with the fame of the young actor. The patent houses might with advantage have closed their doors, since all the town was flocking to worship at the new shrine. One or two men of influence held aloof. Gray, writing to Chute, says: "Did I tell you about Mr. Garrick, that the town are horn-mad after him? There are a dozen

dukes of a night at Goodman's Fields sometimes"
("Works," ii. 185); but adds, "And yet I am stiff
in the opposition." Horace Walpole, too, remained
captious, and, though owning Garrick to be a good
mimic, confessed that he saw nothing wonderful in
his acting. "It is heresy," he adds, "to say, as the
Duke of Argyll says, he is superior to Betterton"
("Coll. Lett." i. 189).

Compensation for these adverse verdicts, if ever,
which is doubtful, they reached his ears, came to
Garrick in abundance. The hostility of a few old
stagers, even when they were men of so much eminence as Cibber, was in itself a compliment. Cibber,
moreover, knew too much of his art to remain implacable, and his aside to Mrs. Bracegirdle, "I' faith,
Bracey, the lad is clever," though a trifle grudging,
must be taken as a recantation, and as near an approach to an amends as Cibber was likely to give.
Pope, however—then, though near the close of his
life and failing in health, the most prominent literary
figure of the epoch—was a convert. His interest in
the stage had died. At the instance of Lord Orrery
he revisited the theatre, saw Garrick, and said, "That
young man never had his equal, and never will."
Meanwhile, as has been seen, the gates of Literature
and Society were held wide open to receive the young
actor. Among his friends and supporters was the Rev.
Thomas Newton, subsequently editor of Milton and
Bishop of Bristol. A native of Lichfield, where his
father had been a brandy and cider merchant, he had
doubtless, though much the senior of Garrick, known

the actor in early days. Newton, now Reader and
Afternoon Preacher at Grosvenor Chapel, South
Audley Street, and a tutor in the family of Lord
Carpenter, encouraged Garrick in his choice of a profession, declared a belief—always entertained—that
Garrick was a born actor, and told him that his
adoption of the stage would make his fortune without
hurting his character. The correspondence was maintained throughout Garrick's season at Goodman's
Fields. In his first letter Newton ventures on some
criticisms of Garrick's methods, speaking of certain
shortcomings as oversights rather than faults, and
declaring that his beauties and excellences are innumerable. With judgment uncommon in those days,
he declares that the alterations made in Shakespeare's
plays have rarely been judicious, and adds, "Even
the character of Richard the Third, as now drawn, is
not quite judicious." He takes to Goodman's Fields
Mrs. Porter, a famous actress then retired, who says
over the table at Lord Carpenter's, "Good God!
what will he be in time?" and declares that he must
excel in everything. Not less enchanted are the
ladies of Lord Carpenter's family, who constantly
revisit the theatre, and attach much importance to
obtaining seats whence they can see his play of feature. Pulteney, ever absorbed as he is in politics,
wishes to see Garrick. Newton's criticisms are always
judicious. In more than one of his letters he chides
Garrick for his choice of parts. "I was almost angry
with you to see your name last week in the bills for
Costar Pearmain. I am not fond of your acting such

parts as Fondlewife, or even Clodio, nor should be of 'The Lying Valet,' if it was not of your own writing." Less wise is his counsel to Garrick to play only high-class parts. He finds Garrick in Bayes superior to old Cibber in many things, holds young Cibber by comparison insufferable, and declares Garrick, in the opinion of good judges, superior in some characters to Booth, and even equal to Betterton.

Bayes had been a prodigious, but not altogether worthy, success. Cock-a-hoop at his triumph, Garrick undertook in his performance of this part to turn to account his powers of mimicry, and make sport of the actors of the day. Already at rehearsal he had wounded some susceptibilities by the manner in which he had instructed older actors and told them how to deliver the speeches allotted to them. He now determined to imitate the chief supporters of Drury Lane and Covent Garden. With a view to reconciling the rest, he obtained from Giffard, his associate in management, permission to deal with him first. If a cock-and-bull story, told without authority in Cooke's "Life of Macklin," is to be trusted, this led to a hostile encounter between the two. Giffard had supposed that Garrick would treat him lightly, merely glancing at his peculiarities, or, as he would prefer to say, his excellences. So ridiculous, on the contrary, did Garrick make him, that he retired in a rage, and sent the ebullient actor a challenge, which Garrick accepted. A meeting took place, in which Garrick was wounded in the sword arm, necessitating thus a postponement of the play for a fortnight, until a principal performer had recovered from an indisposition. Demonstrably false in the last part is this statement, since Garrick played Bayes every night for a week subsequently. Doubt is thus cast upon the whole story.

Delane, who, as the chief performer at Drury Lane, was held to be at the head of the profession, was the next selected. According to Murphy, Garrick "retired to the upper part of the stage, and drawing his left arm across his breast, rested his right elbow upon it, raising a finger to his nose; he then came forward in a stately gait, nodding his head as he advanced, and in the exact tones of Delane, spoke the famous simile of the boar and sow." Endowed with a tall and handsome figure, and a voice of much range and melody, Hale, of Covent Garden, had obtained a reputation in lovers. Garrick chose a speech suited to the occasion, and in a soft, plaintive accent, without any real feeling, *vox et præterea nihil*, gave an exact resemblance of Hale in one of his favourite characters. After that came the turn of Ryan, whose voice, owing to an accidental injury to his jaw, had a drawling, croaking accent. Him Garrick imitated by speaking in a tremulous, raven tone of voice,—

"Your bed of love from dangers will I free."

These, with Giffard and Bridgewater, are the only actors with whom Garrick is known to have dealt.

For Quin, in certain characters, he had a sincere admiration. Quin, moreover, was not a man with whom it was expedient to take many liberties. Delane is said to have been hurt in reputation by the mimicry. So much ill-feeling was caused by these proceedings that Garrick was ultimately persuaded to abandon them.

The next novelty was " The Schoolboy ; or, The Comical Rival," in which, on the 22nd February, 1742, Garrick played Master Johnny. This is a farce reduced by Cibber from his own " Woman's Wit ; or, The Lady of Fashion." Master Johnny is a lout of fifteen years of age, a budding Tony Lumpkin. This was succeeded, on the 11th March, by " King Lear," another of Garrick's most conspicuous triumphs. On this character, in which no subsequent English actor, with the possible exception of Macready and Mr. Irving, has won general acceptance, Garrick stamped his mark from the first. Consideration of its merits belongs to the famous revival, when Garrick was pitted against Spranger Barry. Boheme, Quin, and Booth, however, among the successors of Betterton, were the rivals with whom Garrick contested supremacy. His first appearance as Lear satisfied neither himself nor the friends to whose opinion he trusted. It was accordingly reconsidered ; the weakness of age was more clearly indicated, and the fire of the two burning eyes was dimmed. Newton was now satisfied with it. It was of this performance, indeed, that two of Newton's friends, " one of the

masters of Westminster School and one of the chief
clerks in the Treasury," declared that in it he far exceeded Booth and equalled Betterton.   Newton continues : "The thing that strikes me above all others
is that variety in your acting and your being so
totally a different man in Lear from what you are
in Richard.   There is a sameness in every other
actor.   Cibber is something of a coxcomb in everything ; and Wolsey, and Syphax, and Iago all smell
strong of the essence of Lord Foppington.   Booth
was a philosopher in Cato, and was a philosopher in
everything else.   His passion in Hotspur and Lear
was much of the same nature, whereas yours was an
old man's passion, and an old man's voice and action ;
and in the four parts wherein I have seen you,
Richard, Chamont, Bayes, and Lear, I never saw
four actors more different from one another than you
are from yourself."   This criticism conveys an idea
of sincerity and competency, which is a marvellous
tribute to one who was still a youth and a
débutant.

A second benefit was accorded Garrick on the 18th
February, when, in order to show how wide were his
limits, he repeated Lear and the Schoolboy.   On this
occasion the announcement was made that " the
stage will be formed into an amphitheatre, where
servants will be allowed to keep places."   Two days
earlier Garrick had played Lord Foppington.   This
was once more challenging Cibber on his own ground ;
Lord Foppington was pre-eminently Cibber's part.
As Sir Novelty Fashion, in his own " Love's

Last Shift," Cibber made, in 1696, his first great success as actor and dramatist. In his "Relapse" Vanbrugh copied the character and raised it to the peerage. Cibber was again the exponent. The justness and finesse of the picture of the heartless, conceited, and impertinent fop were vindicated when Sheridan transported it into "A Trip to Scarborough." Once more Cibber used it in "The Careless Husband," in which piece Garrick was now seen. In this he did not score. His friendly monitor is at the trouble to tell him that he had pointed out Sir Charles Easy in the "Relapse" as "the properest part" for him to essay.

After these impersonations, it was a coming down to play Duretête, a good-natured, sheepish fellow in Farquhar's "Inconstant," and Captain Brazen, a lying soldier, in "The Recruiting Officer" of the same dramatist. For Miss Hippisley's benefit, on the 1st April, he made another experiment, playing Pierre in Otway's "Venice Preserved." In this heroic character he was commended mightily, though Newton could have wished that he had chosen rather the character of Jaffier, that being a part of greater compass and variety.

No other new part was essayed during the season, which lasted until the 24th April, when Garrick played Lothario and the Lying Valet. One more performance, in which Garrick did not participate, was given, and the theatre then closed to open no more. Owing to the oppressive powers possessed by the patent houses, the smaller theatres were always driven to desperate shifts. A success so brilliant as that of Goodman's Fields during the past season, and the deficiency of their own receipts, drove the managers of Drury Lane and Covent Garden to strong measures. The aid of Sir John Barnard, sometime Lord Mayor of London, the original mover of the Licensing Act, was invoked, and Giffard was frightened into closing the house, while Garrick was engaged for the following season at Drury Lane for six hundred guineas—a sum larger than had ever previously been paid. Before going to Dublin for a summer season Garrick " hanselled " his engagement by appearing for three nights at Drury Lane. These three nights were the 26th May, when he played Bayes; the 28th May, when he was King Lear to the Cordelia of Peg Woffington; and the 31st May, when he was Richard the Third, being the last time of his performing this season.

In his first season, then, Garrick appears to have acted about one hundred and forty times, playing eighteen different characters. It was no uncommon thing in those days, and for a century later, for an actor in the country to play, in a fashion, a repertory much larger than this. Even now, in some few country theatres at which a stock company is maintained, the interval between one night's performance and the next is all that is sometimes allowed to study and rehearse a new part. It is possible that Garrick's feat may, in a way, have been rivalled by Kean and some of the Kembles. Country audiences are, however, friendly as a rule, and not too critical. Regarded carefully, the feat accomplished by Garrick during the opening season is "phenomenal." Before the most cultivated and exigent audiences that London could supply, a young wine merchant, twenty-four years of age, with no more stage information than he could pick up, established a reputation that placed him foremost among the actors of his day. The width of range he exhibited is absolutely unparalleled. Challenging comparisons one day with memories of Betterton and the next with those of Cibber, the most illustrious of his predecessors, he put the actors of his own day out of court and commanded, as has been seen, terms such as had never previously been paid to one of his profession. In the most important characters he had assumed moreover, his acting had been regarded as a revelation, and a regeneration of the stage was confidently anticipated from his advent. It is a somewhat curious coincidence that the two most memorable performances at the theatre that have been known—memorable that is as regards the revelation they afforded, and the future they heralded— both consisted of Richard the Third. The first is, of course, the representation gratis between the two parts of a concert on the 19th October, 1741, of Richard by "a gentleman who never appeared on any stage;" the next the only less memorable first appearance, before a thin, cold, inexpectant audience, on the 26th January, 1814, of that embodiment of genius and passion, Edmund Kean. In favour of the earlier actor, however, it may be said that he was

in fact a novice. Kean, on the other hand, had had
a long, though heartbreaking experience.

In June, 1742, accompanied by Mrs. Woffington
and Giffard, Garrick arrived in Dublin. Mrs.
Woffington was the first to appear, opening at
Smock-Alley theatre the 15th June, in her
favourite " breeches part " of Sir Harry Wildair.
Garrick followed on Friday as Richard the
Third. His reputation had preceded him, and
the house was crowded to the roof with a public
agog with attention. The London verdict was
ratified, and the young actor sprang at once to
the height of popularity. Few particulars as to this
trip have survived. His second experiment was
Chamont in " The Orphan" to the Monimia of
Mrs. Furnival ; his third in " Lear," in which Mrs.
Woffington was Cordelia, and Giffard, Edgar. On
this occasion he played also Sharp, in his " Lying
Valet." Conditions were favourable to the experiment, for Garrick and Mrs. Woffington were closely
attached to each other, and derived the inspiration
which, in those acting together, such sentiments are
calculated to beget. Though boasting in Mrs.
Cibber a star of no small magnitude, the rival house
in Aungier Street found itself deserted, and Mrs.
Cibber, after a final appearance in Andromache,
quitted the inhospitable city, never to return, and
went to London, where she was destined, on many
important occasions, and not always with such un-
satisfactory results, to try conclusions with Garrick.

Through a season lasting until the 19th August,

Garrick was the idol of the impulsive Dublin public. Mrs. Woffington shared in the craze and aided him greatly, but was distinctly a "meaner light."

To Garrick's Clodio in "The Fop's Fortune," she was the Angelina, the Lady Anne to his Richard, and the Ophelia to his Hamlet, which he essayed for the first time in Dublin. Their latest assumptions were Captain Plume and Silvia in the "Recruiting Officer," the former a light comedy part, scarcely worthy of Garrick's ability; the latter, a delightfully vivacious character, in which Peg Woffington, who had played it in London, could once more masquerade as a boy. Across a century and a half one can hear in fancy the arch, mutinous delivery of the dialogue so suited to her as she entered, in her male attire, to the two recruiting officers, Captains Brazen and Plume :—

Silvia. Save ye, save ye, gentlemen !

Brazen. My dear, I'm yours.

Plume. Do you know the gentleman?

Brazen. No, but I will presently. [*To Silvia.*] Your name, my dear ?

Silvia. Wilful, Jack Wilful, at your service.

Brazen. What ! the Kentish Wilfuls or those of Staffordshire ?

Silvia. Both, sir, both ; I'm related to all the Wilfuls in Europe, and I'm head of the family at present.

After this performance Garrick and his companions returned to appear at Drury Lane. Two or three things in addition to fame and money came of this visit. It was Dublin, if authorities are to be trusted, that dubbed Garrick Roscius, a name which he kept. An epidemic attributed to excessive heat broke out in Dublin, and carried off large numbers of people. This in commemoration of the visit was christened the Garrick fever, a name destined subsequently to change its meaning and to be applied to the excessive homage accorded to the actor.

One more result of the jaunt was the establishment of close relations, to be yet further strengthened, between Garrick and Mrs. Woffington. Garrick was now twenty-five years of age, and Mrs. Woffington a year younger. Affection had sprung up while they were in London, probably before Garrick had gone on the stage. This, in the opportunities of intimacy forced upon both by circumstances, ripened into passion. The poetic stage had passed. The authorship of the song of Pretty Peggy has been denied Garrick, in favour of Sir Charles Hanbury Williams. Garrick's claim to it is not, however, disproved. The song is to Peggy, by D. G. It is higher than Garrick's ordinary experiments in metre, but the same may be said with equal truth of Hanbury Williams. Love has of old wrought equal miracles, and the title of Garrick to one of the prettiest songs of the epoch is not to be lightly abandoned. There is, of course, abundant affectation, the vice of the age, but the language is agreeable, and the whole has spirit and vivacity :

> Once more I'll tune my vocal shell,
> To hills and dales my Passion tell,
> A Flame which time can never quell
>   That burns for lovely Peggy.

Yet greater Bards the Lyre should hit;
For pray, what Subject is more fit,
Than to record the radiant wit
  And bloom of lovely Peggy?

The Sun, first rising in the morn,
That paints the dew-bespangled Thorn,
Doth not so much the day adorn
  As does my lovely Peggy.

And when in Thetis' lap to rest
He streaks with gold the ruddy west,
He's not so beauteous, as undrest
  Appears my lovely Peggy.

Were she Arrayed in rustic weed,
With her the Bleating flocks I'd feed,
And pipe upon my Oaten reed
  To Please my lovely Peggy.

With her a Cottage would delight,
All pleases when she's in my sight!
But when she's gone 'Tis endless Night—
  All's dark without my Peggy.

When Zephyr on the violet Blows,
Or Breathes upon the damask rose,
He does not half the Sweets disclose
  That does my lovely Peggy.

I stole a kiss the other day,
And trust me, Naught but Truth I say,
The fragrant breath of blooming May
  Was not so sweet as Peggy.

While bees from Flowers to Flowers rove,
And Linnets warble through the Grove,
Or Stately swans the waters love,
  So long shall I love Peggy.

And when Death, with his Pointed Dart,
Shall strike the blow that rends my heart,
My words shall be when I depart,
            Adieu, my lovely Peggy.

Versions of this song, differing slightly from each other, exist in much the same vein and with abundance of similar metaphors, is a second song to Silvia, also signed D. G., the authorship of which is not contested. Tributes of this kind both in verse and prose were familiar enough to the petted actress. In Ireland the unconventional relations between the pair of lovers were closely guarded, and little suspicion was aroused. An incident which is related shows that some risk was occasionally run. A young nobleman posing as a patron of the stage, or in other words, seeking to debauch its professors, called upon Mrs. Woffington. Anxious to escape observation, Garrick, who was with her, slipped into another room. The weather was, as has been said, oppressive, and Garrick, who had been sitting bareheaded, forgot his wig. This unfamiliar appurtenance of a lady's boudoir at once arrested the attention of the visitor, who recognized its ownership, and elected to be angry. Peg Woffington was equal to the occasion. Bursting into a fit of laughter at the display of jealousy, she owned that the wig was Garrick's. A simple explanation was ready. Peggy had to play a new " breeches part," and Garrick had lent her the wig to aid her in her study of the character. This she protested was the whole truth, and she forbade any further manifestation of discontent. So obvious an explanation was, of course, accepted by her dupe, who was not likely to stand against such artillery of intellect as Peggy was able to bring to bear.

When Garrick returned to London he seems to have been unaccompanied by his fair partner, who had, it is supposed, too many *adieux* to make to get immediately away. He arrived with Mrs. Cibber, on her way to Covent Garden, Dr. Arne, her brother, and Delane. Mrs. Woffington arrived shortly afterwards, and an experiment in joint housekeeping began. This strange arrangement was at first tripartite, Macklin joining the two in a house, No. 6, Bow Street, now vanished. No element of possible permanency existed in this. Garrick and his female companion soon retired to Southampton Street, Strand. The arrangement was that Garrick, whose salary had mounted to a thousand a year, should pay the bills for one month and Mrs. Woffington the next. From the beginning of this scheme the charge against Garrick of miserliness, for which Macklin was largely responsible, and from which Garrick could never free himself, began to be heard. That visitors to the house during the months when Peg Woffington was caterer were more fortunate than those who came under the Garrick *régime* may be granted. It is too early as yet to deal with the question of Garrick's curiously composite character, and with the strange mixture of economy and generosity which he displayed. Boswell, however, has crystallized, in the life of Johnson, one utterance in which Johnson bears witness to the anxiety with which Garrick regarded the lavish hospitality of his associate. "I remember," says Johnson, "drinking tea with him long ago when Peg Woffington made it, and he grumbled at her for making it too strong. He had then begun to feel money in his purse, and did not know when he had enough of it." Tea was then a costly luxury, and was ordinarily drunk weak. On repeating to Sir Joshua Reynolds this anecdote Johnson added a further remonstrance of the actor, who in answer, it must be supposed, to some denial on the part of his helpmate, added, "Why, it is as red as blood."

CHAPTER IV.

GARRICK's appearance at Drury Lane under Fleet-wood marks what may be considered the beginning of his established career. Fashionable as had been his performances at Goodman's Fields, they were in a sense surreptitious, and his assumptions in Dublin may be regarded as a country preparation for a London career. When on the 5th October, 1742, as Chamont in the "Orphan" to the Monimia of Mrs. Pritchard, and the Castalio of Havard, he appeared as a salaried actor at Drury Lane, he had broken entirely with his past and taken, with a celerity unprecedented and unequalled, his position as the foremost English actor. The time, as has been abundantly pointed out, was propitious. No man of towering ability was on the stage, and although there were actors of merit and of mark there was none from whom Garrick had to fear serious rivalry. Memories of Betterton lingered, and Cibber was alive to comment if not to contest. Barton Booth and Wilks had both been ten years dead, and the former had been fifteen years absent from the stage. So far as can be judged these actors founded no school, and left behind them in their most eminent

gifts no successors.   Ben Jonson, an inferior but a
good actor, had died during the previous season.

Two men of eminence were on the stage.   One,
Macklin, was as yet Garrick's friend, though shortly
to become his enemy, and was with him at Drury
Lane.   Quin, the second, was the chief light of Covent
Garden.   At him Garrick looked askance.   Too
many guns were carried, however, by the old actor,
and Garrick, though noways disposed to be lenient in
his dealings with his competitors, shrank from a trial
of strength, and directed his broadsides against the
smaller fry by which he was surrounded.   Such parts
as Garrick did not take at Drury Lane Macklin
monopolized.   With Macklin as Shylock the season
opened on the 11th September, 1742.   Before Garrick's appearance Macklin had played Touchstone,
Tom in "The Conscious Lovers," Ben in "Love for
Love," Numps in "The Tender Husband," Lovegold
in "The Miser," Sir Novelty Fashion in "Love's
Last Shift," and Peachum in "The Beggar's Opera."
Subsequently in the season he was to take Beau
Clincher in "The Constant Couple," Lord Foppington in "The Relapse," Marplot in "The Busy
Body," Teague in "The Twin Rivals," Clodio,
Fondlewife, and other parts of primary importance, of some of which Garrick, realizing the
significance of the present experiment, gradually
divested himself, leaving them in the hands of
Macklin.   None of the other male members of the
company came into the first rank.   Of these Delane,
whom Garrick had already caricatured, stood fore-

most. He was then at the height of his reputation, was accepted by the town in the less debauched heroes of comedy, had easy, well-bred manners, and was regarded as the only Alexander the Great. With him at Drury Lane were Milward—whom Davies declares to have been celebrated in Hamlet, Castalio, Jaffier, and Oroonoko, and excellent in characters where " distress is dignified by superiority of rank," or " rendered venerable by age,"—and Havard, " a second-rate actor, always decent, sensible, and perfect, with a comely person and the manners of a gentleman." To William Mills were assigned parts such as Orlando in " As You Like It," Scandal in " Love for Love," Bellmour in " The Old Bachelor," and Sir George Airy in " The Busy Body." Not at all to be confounded with his father John Mills, who had died six years earlier, is this tall, ungainly disciple of Thespis, whose maintenance of a place on the stage furnishes a proof to how low an ebb its fortunes had declined. No irony of Fielding that is preserved is more amusing than his recommendation of the benefit of " Billy Mills." Here is an extract:—" He was at all times a very safe actor; and as he never shocked you with any absurdity, so he never raised horror, terror, admiration, or any of those turbulent sensations, to that dangerous height to which Mr. Garrick (however good a man he may otherwise be) hath been guilty of carrying them. From the pinnacle of theatrical greatness, where he once was seated, he hath by degrees fallen; not through his own demerit, for he is now as good as ever he was, but the greatest

misfortune in the world, namely, successful rivals."
Taswell, a man of education, but a circumscribed
actor, confined to elderly parts, Polonius and Sir
Tunbelly Clumsy, and Hallam, who joined during
the course of the season, were mediocrities; and
Yates, who, like Garrick, came from Goodman's
Fields, though destined to ripen into a fine comedian,
was at this time but a youth.

Compensation for the weakness of the company as
regards male performers was made by its strength in
female.   Within the first month after Drury Lane
opened Kitty Clive was seen as Portia and Miss Prue,
Peg Woffington as Rosalind, Mrs. Pritchard as
Monimia, Mrs. Mills as Angelica in " Love for
Love," and Mrs. Macklin as Diana Trapes in " The
Beggar's Opera."

Of Covent Garden Quin was the mainstay.   A
commonplace and conventional, but trustworthy
actor, he had wit enough to realize the dangers of
the siege which Garrick had laid to tradition.   The
famous utterance concerning Garrick, " If this young
fellow is right we have all been wrong," indicates
how lively was his apprehension.   In comedy he was
acceptable, and his Falstaff stands foremost through
subsequent years.   Walpole, an acute if a spiteful
judge, said that it was as excellent as the Lear of
Garrick.   In tragedy he was seen to little advantage.
Booth is reported to have declined to challenge comparisons with Quin.   One picture of him that seems
lifelike is supplied by Cumberland, who says :—
" With very little variation of cadence, and in a deep,

full tone, accompanied by a sawing kind of action, which had more of the senate than of the stage in it, he rolled out his heroics with an air of dignified indifference that seemed to disdain the plaudits that were bestowed upon him. Unable to express emotions, whether violent or tender, he was forced or languid in action, and ponderous and sluggish in movement. In the great characters of tragedy he was lost, and the most trustworthy of contemporary critics declares that people will remember with pleasure his Brutus and his Cato, and wish to forget his Richard and his Lear."

From Quin to Ryan, another object of Garrick's satire, was a long drop. Ryan's features, naturally good, had been damaged by accident. He played the lovers in tragedy, and fine gentlemen in comedy at Covent Garden, and previously at Lincoln's Inn Fields, and was selected by Addison when young to be the original Marcus in " Cato." His voice was loud but harsh and dissonant. As Orestes, Macduff, Ford in the " Merry Wives of Windsor," and Lord Townly, he displayed sound sense, feeling and judgment. In Richard III. he moved the astonishment of Garrick, who went prepared to laugh at the slovenly, ungraceful, and ill-dressed figure, and found much to learn and to introduce into his own performance. Ryan continued to play youthful parts long after he was disqualified by age for their due presentation. To Bridgewater and Hale tragic and heroic parts were not seldom entrusted at Covent Garden. Both are chiefly remembered by the fact that Garrick once thought them worthy of mimicry. Hale had a tall and well-proportioned person and manly deportment, a harmonious voice and a not unpleasing action. He was monotonous in style however, and lacking in judgment, and ended his life in Bristol, where he was a favourite. Davies tells concerning him a story with a " plentiful lack of " point, that Hale was watching Garrick in Bayes, and laughing merrily at his imitations of Delane, Ryan, Bridgewater and Giffard, when on a sudden, Garrick spoke three or four lines, beginning

" Oh ! what a stranger am I grown of late ! "

in a style caricaturing so admirably the voice and manner of Hale that the house echoed with laughter and applause. Shocked and outraged, Hale felt, according to the lame termination of the story supplied by Davies, " the folly and injustice of approving that ridicule of others which he could not bear himself." For the rest, Hale, who was tolerable when he could be induced to employ any self-restraint, was so attached to the wearing of full-bottomed wigs, that he insisted on wearing one when playing Charles the First. Hotspur was his best part. Bridgewater, who reconciled for a time the occupations of actor and dealer in coals, and ultimately and wisely decided in favour of the latter, left it doubtful whether he pleased or displeased the more. In the Ventidius of Dryden (" All for Love ") he furnished an excellent picture of a rough, brave old soldier ; in Tamerlane he was pronounced " solemnly drowsy in speaking, and struttingly insignificant in action." In the " Suspicious Husband " he was as effective as he was disagreeable in Frederick (his original part) in Fielding's " Miser," and as good as Hubert in " King John " as he was offensive as King Henry in " King Richard the Third."

In comedy Covent Garden was better stocked, being able to boast Woodward, who though unable to play tragedy, as he wished, was an ideal Bobadil and an admirable performer in Mercutio, Parolles, Osric, and similar parts, and was accepted as a successor to Cibber in Lord Foppington ; Hippisley, who, thanks in part to a burn in his face, was held the drollest of actors, the Liston of his day, unparalleled too in the display of avarice or amorous dotage ; and Chapman, who, though his name scarcely survives, won highest opinions as Touchstone. Of the female characters of importance Mrs. Cibber, an admirably competent actress, had a monopoly, though Miss Hippisley was there to play Miss Hoyden and the like, and Mrs. Horton, Mrs. Bellamy, Mrs. Woodward, and Mrs. Hale were also available. Mrs. Porter, an actress of position, who had seen and approved Garrick, had quitted the stage, and took a special benefit under royal patronage on the 14th February, 1743. Yates and Mrs. Yates, and Cibber's daughter, the notorious Mrs. Charke, were at the new theatre in James Street, Haymarket.

Giffard (Garrick's former manager), a capable actor, and his wife, with Theophilus Cibber, were making a vain struggle at Lincoln's Inn Fields.

> " These were the prime in order and in might,
>   The rest were long to tell."

Serious opposition to Garrick was not to be feared from such. A " Triton of the minnows," he found when thoroughly launched few other than favourable gales, and had not even the contest with difficulties that stimulates to exertion.

Chamont in " The Orphan ",was, as has been said, Garrick's opening part. Bayes in " The Rehearsal " followed on the 7th and 8th October, and " Richard III.," with Mrs. Mills as Lady Anne, on the 13th. On this last date rivalry was attempted at Covent Garden, and Quin essayed Richard with Mrs. Cibber as his Lady Anne. As to the result of the competition nothing is known. It requires no wizard, however, to declare that the struggle of Covent Garden must have been hopeless.

> " Never yet
>   Was any nation read of so besotted
>   In reason as to adore the setting sun."

After playing Clodio in " Love makes a Man," Garrick assumed on the 19th October, for the first time in London, the part of Captain Plume in the " Recruiting Officer "; on the 26th October he reappeared as King Lear, and on the 1st November he was Fondlewife in " The Old Bachelor." His first appearance in England as Hamlet took place on the 19th. This was, of course, in Shakespeare's " Hamlet " or what passed for such. He was not yet so firm on his feet as to attempt alterations of his own in the text or business of Shakespeare A quarter of a century had to elapse before he took upon himself to acquit Laertes of all share in the projected death of Hamlet, to save the life of Ophelia, banish the grave diggers from the play, lead the Queen off the stage in a state of insanity, and bring about the death of the King in a combat with his nephew and stepson. No special features in his Hamlet are remembered, and the criticisms that survive concerning other impersonations belong to a later date. Archer in " The Beaux' Stratagem " of Farquhar was the first novelty he essayed. This part of a gentleman personating temporarily a valet seems to have suggested something to Marivaux in "Le Jeu de l'Amour et du Hasard," though the lovemaking in Farquhar is free as can well be conceived from any such delicacy of language or proceeding as justifies the application to it of the term Marivaudage. It is indeed frankly brutal.

In Fielding's " Wedding Day," produced the 17th February, 1743, Garrick was the original Millamour. Not too agreeable a play is this, the last of Fielding's dramatic works, in which a father is presented as married to his own daughter. It was an early work, written for Wilks and Mrs. Oldfield, and hastily furbished up for Garrick and Mrs. Woffington. In addition to these actors, Mrs. Pritchard and Mr. and Mrs. Macklin took part in the performance. Danger signals were visible from the first. A report of extreme indecency was circulated, the licencer insisted on excisions, and

Kitty Clive refused the part assigned her as objectionable. Garrick added solicitations to warnings, and begged that certain coarse and detrimental passages put into the mouth of Millamour might be excised. With the sovereign contempt he entertained for the general public, Fielding remained immovable. Saying to Garrick concerning the audience, " No, d—n them ; if the scene is not a good one, let them find that out," he retired into the green-room, where, according to Murphy, he solaced himself with champagne and tobacco. The sound of hisses reached him in his retreat. Turning to Garrick, he said, " What's the matter, Garrick ? What are they hissing now ? " " Why, the scene that I begged you to retrench," answered the actor. " I knew it would not do, and they have so frightened me, that I shall not be able to collect myself again the whole night." " Oh, d—n them," said Fielding. " They *have* found it out, have they ? " The result was naturally a failure. Thanks to the friendly disposition of Garrick and of Fleetwood the manager towards the author, the piece kept its place for six nights, but on the last night there were only five ladies in the boxes. For the author's share Fielding, then in straits for money, received only 50*l.* Garrick, according to Macklin, was unable to get by heart the comic prologue, which was consequently spoken by Macklin, who also claims to have supplied a curiously unconventional and skittish rhymed apology.

On March 3rd, for one of his numerous benefits, Garrick appeared as Hastings in " Jane Shore " to

the Jane Shore of Mrs. Pritchard, and played Sharp
in "The Lying Valet" to the Kitty Pry of Mrs.
Clive. His popularity was at its height, and the
stage was formed into side boxes, and seven rows of
the pit railed into boxes. To "The Lying Valet"
he contributed a new epilogue, which he spoke.
On the 17th, for the benefit of Mrs. Woffington,
he made his first appearance in her great part of Sir
Harry Wildair in the "Constant Couple." Concerning his performance in this character, his biographers have not a word to say. Tate Wilkinson
declares it to have been a failure. Probabilities and
circumstances alike favour the view that in this part
Garrick experienced his first rebuff. So firm a hold
had Woffington taken of Sir Harry, that the public
might well prove intolerant of a masculine substitute.
It was in this *rôle* that she became the heroine of a
story famous in stage annals. Coming into the
green-room flustered from an enthusiastic reception,
she said, "In my conscience I believe half the men
in the house take me for one of their own sex," and
received from a rival the reply, "It may be so, but
in my conscience the other half can convince them to
the contrary." Another writer attributes the reply
in a slightly altered form to Quin. Two nights
later, with the substitution of Kitty Clive for Peg
Woffington as Lady Lurewell, the piece was repeated,
after which the character was dropped by Garrick.

Supposing a snub to have been administered, it was
met by Garrick in the best way in which an adverse
opinion could be combated, by a supreme triumph

as Abel Drugger, which he essayed for the first time
the 21st March.   From the hands of Pinkethman, the
part of Abel Drugger in Jonson's " Alchemist " had
passed into those of Theophilus Cibber, who dis-
figured it with " grimace and vile squinting." These
things Garrick at once swept away, substituting for
them a natural and an easy manner.   His success
was won in part, at least, by disloyal means.
Davies taxes him with having robbed the part of
Kastril the Angry Boy, excellently played by Yates,
in order to enrich his own.   Kastril's great opportunity is that in which in the fourth act he confronts
and challenges Surly, and causes him to quit the stage.
These things Garrick, after the manner of the leading
actor, arrogated to himself.   " Before seeing him in
this character and in Hamlet," Hannah More said at a
much subsequent date, " I should have thought it as
possible for Milton to have written ' Hudibras,' and
Butler ' Paradise Lost,' as for one man to have played
Hamlet and Drugger with such excellence." Weston,
who took the part a score years later than Garrick,
all but shook the supremacy of Roscius.   His simplicity was irresistible, and his manner of breaking the
phial has been mentioned as an unsurpassable piece of
by-play.   A picture of Garrick in this character in
Act 2, scene vi. of the " Alchemist," was painted
by Zoffany, and engraved and published in 1771.
His companions are Burton as Subtle and Palmer as
Face.   This was Garrick's last new part in his first
season at Drury Lane.   From an early time a col-
lapse of the management had been seen to be im-

minent, and before the close of the season in May, it had arrived. Its consequences were destined to be unpleasant in many ways to Garrick.

Charles Fleetwood, the manager, was a man of fortune and fashion, whom the manifold seductions of a managerial career had tempted. He entered upon the theatre at a period of great depression, during the season of 1733-34. Deserted by his actors, who had started an opposition at what was then known as the little theatre in the Haymarket, now the Haymarket Theatre, Highmore, the previous manager, had sold his share, at a heavy sacrifice, to Fleetwood, who within a year or so obtained the remaining portions of the patent, and found himself absolute master. Being backed up by considerable capital and by many persons of distinction, Fleetwood won the seceders back to their allegiance, and made a prosperous and even brilliant start. By the close of the season of 1734-35, John Mills, Johnson, Theophilus Cibber, and other actors claimed to hold a lease of the house for fifteen years. Of this nothing further is heard. The misfortunes of Fleetwood were in no sense due to the ill-success of the theatre, but to his own recklessness and ill-conduct. He had taken to a life of gambling and dissipation, until, to use the phrase of Victor, his " body was as much impaired by an excessive gout as his fortune by his misconduct." He was, however, a man of great plausibility and charm of manner, and, like a later and more celebrated manager, Sheridan, was wont to beguile into further loans those who had come with the sternest resolution of recovering their debts. Macklin, who was his manager and his associate in his gambling excesses, had been a frequent victim, and only escaped by a very bold stratagem from being further plundered.

The time had now arrived when the results of Fleetwood's extravagance could no longer be disguised. The theatre was heavily mortgaged, and the duplicity of Fleetwood rendered his creditors little disposed to forbearance. Salaries were unpaid, and the bailiffs were in the house. Fleetwood himself received the complaints and remonstrances of the actors with courtesy and the promise of redress. Pierson, the treasurer, however, who farmed the receipts, and to whom all had to look, refused payment, and met complaint with insult.

A meeting of actors was accordingly held towards the end of the summer of 1743 for the purpose of concerted action. As a result of this, the players entered into a formal agreement not to accept any terms that did not obtain the acquiescence of all the signatories. Utterly powerless to concede their demands, Fleetwood got together a scratch company, and gave such exhibitions as were within reach of his recruits. Towards the close of his career he had inundated Drury Lane with tumblers, rope-dancers, and the like from Sadler's Wells, and with exhibitions of monsters.

Of the faction that was started, Macklin was the nominal head, but Garrick was the soul. Strong in the conviction that his aristocratic patronage would enable him to tide over every difficulty, the latter applied to the Lord Chamberlain for a licence for the little theatre in the Haymarket. The Duke of Grafton was, however, not to be moved. He asked the applicant the amount of his salary, and received for answer, five hundred pounds. Garrick's nominal salary was at that time six hundred and thirty pounds. "And this you think too little," the duke is reported to have said, "whilst I have a son, who is heir to my title and estates, venturing his life daily for his king and country at much less than half the sum." Inconclusive logic is perhaps this, but it is as convincing as any authority is in the habit of dispensing to applicants. Discontent now arose in the ranks of the mutineers, and an application to the manager became imperative. Fleetwood, whose little remaining property was melting away, was placable except upon one point. He would receive back at reduced salaries the whole of the malcontents, with the exception of Macklin, whom he regarded as the prime mover in the struggle, and with whom, as his former manager and counsellor, he was exceptionally angry. The actors had agreed to stand or fall together, and loyalty forbade their acceptance of the proffered terms. Loyalty among actors, and perhaps among members of other professions, is not always to be trusted when it conflicts with interest. That some of the rebels would make terms with Fleetwood was scarcely doubtful. Garrick found himself accordingly on the horns of a dilemma. Towards Macklin, one of his earliest friends and his constant adviser, he had the most amicable sentiments.

His espousal of Macklin's cause, however, meant something like ruin to those of the actors who stood by him in respecting the agreement. This method of regarding the situation, charitable rather than heroic, commended itself to Garrick, and Macklin was finally shelved.

Garrick, it is not to be doubted, did his best to smooth matters over, and made offers which, if sin· cere, must be regarded as handsome. That the pressure put upon him by his former friend was felt cannot be doubted. To Fleetwood he professed his willingness to play for one hundred guineas less, if he would engage Macklin, and to Macklin he proffered six pounds a week until Fleetwood should recall him. He obtained also a promise of an engagement of seven pounds a week for Mrs. Macklin at Covent Garden. He had to deal with two characters of kindred obduracy, and found himself practically "between the devil and the deep sea." The pressure meanwhile put upon him by the remainder of the associated actors was strong. A letter to Macklin dated the 7th November, 1743, and signed by W. Mills, E. Mills, F. Leigh, W. Havard, W. Pritchard, H. Pritchard, E. Berry, and E. Woodburn, affirms that Garrick's return to Ireland—a scheme he had contemplated—or his refusal to play with Fleetwood, would be destructive to their interests, and would not contribute one jot to Macklin's advantage or to his return to the theatre. Macklin is accordingly requested to sacrifice for awhile his own convenience to the interests of so many people. A letter to Garrick followed, entreating him to postpone until

the receipt of an answer from Macklin his visit
to Ireland, and impressing upon him that if any
tie or obligation was still subsisting, they had an
equal claim with Macklin. Not much better is
this logic than that of the Duke of Grafton. The
world is, however, not much influenced by logic, and
neither reason nor eloquence would have been of the
slightest use in changing the determination of Macklin.
Garrick's magnanimous offers were powerless to
palliate his conduct, and Macklin, with the blind and
unreasoning prejudice of a certain class of mind, chose
for the object of his antipathy, not the manager who
refused him an engagement, but the friend who had
fought his battle with earnestness and with a nearer
approach to chivalry than was to be expected.

On the 5th December Garrick was announced to
make his first appearance this season as Bayes in the
"Rehearsal." On the same day appeared a pamphlet
entitled "Case of Charles Macklin, Comedian," containing a statement of the quarrel from his point of
view. Garrick had at least been indiscreet, though
scarcely disingenuous. His visit to Fleetwood had
been made without Macklin's knowledge, and so was
a technical breach of the original agreement. It was
known, however, to the other actors, and was in no
sense furtive. The charge that Garrick secured an
increase of his own salary while allowing that of
others to be reduced is improbable, and is supported
by no evidence. A clique, headed by Dr. Barrowby,
a keen disputant and a man described, with
some justice, in the Rawlinson MSS. in the British

Museum, as "a monster of lewdness and prophane-
ness," espoused the side of Macklin. All that
Garrick could do was to issue a hand-bill, which was
distributed in the theatre. A small party can dis-
turb a performance, and Macklin's party was large.
Garrick upon his appearance was greeted with cries
of " Off ! " " Off ! " from all parts of the house. Peas
were thrown on the floor of the stage for the purpose
of rendering the foothold insecure, and rotten eggs
and apples were showered on the discomfited comedian. Garrick's bows and apologetic gestures were
vain, and he finally withdrew, and left the audience
to its triumph. He forthwith published a vindication, which was written by William Guthrie,
subsequently author of a "General History of Scotland." To this, on the 12th, Macklin retorted with
a frothy reply. Like most other literary and artistic
quarrels the polemic is wholly unedifying and inconclusive.

Weak as a manager, Fleetwood was the man to
meet a crisis such as had arisen. With the assistance of a Mr. Wyndham, of Norfolk, a great patron
of what was then called " The Fancy," he smuggled
into the pit on the occasion of Garrick's next appearance a party of thirty prizefighters, consisting, according to Kirkman, the biographer of Macklin, and a
strong partisan, of Fleetwood's "friends and associates from Hockley in the Hole and the Bear
Garden." When the music ceased one of these
worthies stood up and said in a loud voice :—
" Gentlemen, I am told that some persons here are

come with an intention not to hear the play ; I came
to hear it ; I paid my money "—a not wholly convincing statement this—" for it, and I desire that they
who came to interrupt may all withdraw and not stay
to hinder my diversion." An uproar followed. The
protectors of order had been well selected, however ;
and, falling upon the Macklinites, they drove them
wounded and in disorder out of the pit. In the
language of Milton, not, it is hoped, too irreverently
used, the defenders of order might say,

> " The terms we sent were terms of weight,
>   Of hard contents and full of force, urged home,
>   Such as we might perceive amused them all
>   And stumbled many."

The victory was complete and final. Garrick was
allowed to proceed in peace with Bayes, and no
further attempt at disturbance was made. Its result
was, however, to breed long-enduring animosity between the two former friends, and it was the first in a
deplorable series of quarrels in which Garrick was
engaged.

On the 10th December Garrick played Chamont
in " The Orphan." Other characters in which he was
familiar followed, and on the 7th January, 1744, he
made a long-promised appearance in " Macbeth."
Preliminary announcements that he intended to revive
the " Macbeth " of Shakespeare had fluttered actors so
accustomed to the " Macbeth " of D'Avenant that they
did not know of any other. Quin even was startled,
and asked what the youngster meant, inquiring

anxiously, " Don't I play Macbeth as Shakespeare wrote it ? " The name of Shakespeare was potent even in those irreverent days, and was not seldom used in the case of works that had very few traces of his handiwork remaining. Garrick's promise must not be understood to have been *quite* carried out. The presumption is fair that the play then given was that revived four years later, the 19th March, 1748, at the same house. This was practically Shakespeare with the addition of Lock's music, or the music attributed to Lock, which, of course, involves the introduction of lines from Middleton, and with a dying speech for himself, which, in a spirit of pitiful ambition, Garrick added to his own part. Mrs. Giffard was on the first occasion his Lady Macbeth. The performance can only be regarded as preliminary to that of 1748. " Regulus," a cold, conventional, and declamatory tragedy, of William Havard, the actor, given for the first time on the 21st February, was galvanized into life by Garrick, and ran for eleven nights. Lord Townly to the Lady Townly of Mrs. Woffington, and Biron in " The Fatal Marriage, or the Innocent Adultery," of Thomas Southerne, a play taken from a novel by Mrs. Behn, and at a subsequent date altered by Garrick, followed ; and on the 25th April Garrick played for the first time Zaphna in a version by Miller of Voltaire's tragedy of " Mahomet," then first seen on the English stage. Voltaire's " Mahomet " had been given at the Théâtre Français about eighteen months previously. No further novelty in which Garrick was concerned was produced, and a season concerning the end of which records are meagre then closed.

Garrick's assumption the following season of Sir John Brute in " The Provoked Wife " to the Lady Brute of Mrs. Woffington elicited from Quin, the recognized representative of the part, the grunt " He may possibly act Master Jacky Brute, but he cannot possibly be Sir John Brute." This was a part indeed in which Quin might reasonably expect a drawn battle if not a victory. The question to what extent Sir John is to be shown as a gentleman runs on all fours with that as to how far Lady Teazle is to be shown as a fine lady. Accepting what is taught us by contemporary portraits in Fielding, Quin's reading of this character is as likely to be correct as that of his younger rival. Not until five years later do we obtain any expression of opinion on the subject. Sir John Brute had been one of the great parts of Cibber, whose conception was derived from Betterton, and who shortly after this date resumed the character in antagonism to Garrick. Davies holds that in certain scenes Cibber fell greatly short of Garrick, who in the more boisterous passages was triumphantly riotous, keeping the spectators in continual glee. In the scene, however, in which, when drunk, Sir John discovers Constant and Heartfree in his wife's closet impartiality must, Davies holds, give the palm to Cibber. Both Cibber and Garrick indicated the gentleman behind the rioter and debauchee. This aspect Quin failed to present. Quin wanted moreover in the part, says Davies, " variety, and that

glow and warmth in colouring the extravagances of
this merry (!) rake, without which the picture remains imperfect and unfinished." Another judge,
not less competent, Tate Wilkinson, subsequently
the famous manager of the York Circuit, which
shared with that of Bath and Bristol the reputation
of being the nursery of histrionic talent, held the
balance more evenly. While admitting that no
part could be played in more different style by two
actors Wilkinson opined that if the author had seen
both he would have allowed both to be right. The
opinion that in this part Quin was Garrick's superior
was held with augmenting confidence by those whose
pleasure and self-appointed task it is to elevate mediocrity and to depreciate genius. King John, a
part subsequently abandoned by Garrick for Falconbridge, followed, and was in turn succeeded by
Othello.

Concerning " Othello," first given on the 7th February, 1745, we have a signed contemporary testimony,
a thing of infrequent occurrence at this period of
Garrick's career, though anonymous criticisms were
pressed upon Garrick and carefully preserved by him.
Benjamin Victor, subsequently a historian of the stage,
had written to Garrick expressing a wish to witness
the representation of " Othello," declaring his intention to go to the theatre at five p.m., and desiring
authority to pass into Garrick's dressing-room, where
he appears to have met the Earl of Rochford. On
the 14th Victor wrote a letter declaring that in the
address to the senate Quin, whose merit lay chiefly

in declamation, is surpassed. The performance leaves no doubt in Victor's mind that the " utmost perfection" in the character is within Garrick's reach. Something, however, requires to be done. His pauses are not long enough, and the transitions appear consequently too abrupt. Upon the scene with Desdemona and Emilia Victor passes an opinion which may, since Victor's letters are difficult of access, be quoted :—

" When Desdemona enters to you . . . taking her hand you say,

' Let me see your eyes '—

it is evident the words that follow—

' Look in my face '—

are spoke in anger ; Othello at that instant, observing the attentive eye of Emelia (*sic*) upon him, quits his wife with these words,

'Some of your function, mistress, &c.,'

and pushes her out of the room—you will easily observe this must not be spoken in anger, but in a peevish, smothered, contemptuous tone—and exactly the same when he calls her in and throws the money at her ; this you did last night not only in a wrong tone of voice, but in too much hurry."

As criticism went and still goes this is defensible enough ; the only thing to be said against it being that an opposite view is just as tenable. Continuing, Victor then says :—

" To fix this upon your mind a little closer, give

me leave to observe, that you commit the same fault in your Hamlet (a part in which you excel all within my memory) in the scene with Rosencrass (*sic*) and Gildenstern (*sic*), where they attempt to discover the true cause of your disorder—after Hamlet has ridiculed their attempt, by the stops on the flute, he says—

‘ S’death ! do you think I am easier to be play’d on than a pipe ? ’—

This demands the same tone of contempt, which you spoke in a loud tone of anger, by which the sense is quite mistaken, and the dignity of the character lost.”

He then turns to King John, which he has not seen, and tells Garrick that those who espouse the side of Quin allege,—

“ That by your gestures, you make comedy of that famous scene between King John and Hubert ; and why is this ? the reason is obvious ; your rival shows in his looks and actions, all he feels ; which being little, he expresses little : you, who have a quick conception, aided by a large quantity of spirits, are, perhaps, too apt to run into the contrary extreme. I must confess, for my own part, I could wish, in many places in Othello, your gestures were less violent, because in all parts of distress, there is an extreme point, and there the utmost emotion would appear *naturally* beautiful.”

Not very profound is this criticism. It gives us, perhaps, the most trustworthy opinion obtainable at that period in Garrick’s life, when the first impetus of youthful energy was over, and he was beginning, in popular phrase, to feel his feet. Once more Victor says :—

" As you have the happiness of a most expressive countenance, you may safely trust more to that; which, with your proper and pathetic manner of speaking, would charm more successfully, if those violent, and seeming artful [= artificial] emotions (*sic*) of body were a little abated."

By some means this letter got into print, and appeared in the London *Courant*. The mind of Garrick was much exercised thereby. On the 14th September, accordingly, Victor writes to Garrick, then at Lichfield, a letter containing expressions of regret at the occurrence, and offering to prosecute or pursue any one who can be made responsible for this rude injury. It is hinted that Garrick himself must have been responsible in having shown the letter to some one who had revealed its contents. In the concluding portion Victor writes, " They open Drury Lane Theatre, on Thursday next, and the Saturday following you will certainly be wanted there. I heard you disagreed at the last treaty, but you know a sure method of starving them into your terms."

Garrick would have been less or more than an actor had he accepted without any form of protest Victor's out-spoken criticism. He undertook his own defence, and seems to have maintained that Hamlet and Othello were both angry in the scenes mentioned. Victor maintains his position, and in a letter to Garrick, still at Lichfield, dated the 10th October, repeats his argument. One passage casts light on Garrick's conception of Othello. "What you say relating to emotion in Othello, at the winding up the passion to a statue of horror and despair, is beautiful and strictly true ; that was the point I mentioned in every well-wrote part of distress ; but the error lies in being too *early*, or too *frequent*, in that violence of emotion." In this letter Victor refers to there being some doubt as to Garrick's appearance on the stage this winter. Another passage has a curious interest altogether apart from Garrick, which renders it worthy of quotation on its own account. The Young Pretender was in Scotland, and an invasion of England by the Highlanders was imminent. Victor was one of the earliest to volunteer for service. In reference to the state of England at the time he says :—

"The stage (at both houses) is the most *pious*, as well as most *loyal* place, in the three kingdoms. Twenty men appear at the end of every play, and one stepping forward from the rest, with uplifted hands and eyes, begins singing, to an old anthem tune, the following words :—

> ' O Lord our God, arise,
> Confound the enemies
> Of George our king ;
> Send him victorious,
> Happy and glorious,
> Long to reign over us,
> God save the King,'

which are the very words and music of an old anthem, that was sung at St. James's Chapel for

King James the second, when the Prince of Orange was landed, to deliver us from popery and slavery; which God Almighty in His goodness was pleased not to grant." The *General Advertiser* for the 28th September says, "We hear that Mr. Lacy, master of his Majesty's company of Comedians at Drury Lane, has applied for leave to raise 200 men in defence of his Majesty's person and government in which the whole company of players are willing to engage." Garrick was not one of these heroes. The intelligence received by Victor proved to be correct, and Garrick instead of appearing at Drury Lane revisited Dublin.

Before accompanying him thither, however, some matters may be cleared. Further feuds had arisen, old ties had been broken and new ties had been contracted. Macklin had been received back into favour, and had acted in the same plays with Garrick. Quin remained surly and hostile. He had whenever it was possible challenged comparisons by acting the same characters as Garrick, and had been to see his Othello, upon which he had passed to Hoadly the comic and ill-natured criticism, "Here's Pompey, but where's his tea-kettle and lamp?" Too wise to affect sharp speeches of the kind, Garrick bestowed on the Macbeth of Quin some serious criticism which was not even wholly hostile. On Quin's manner of clutching frequently and spasmodically at the dagger in what is known as "the dagger scene," and on other extravagances, he passed unfavourable comment. He dwelt, however, upon "his slow, manly folding up of his faculties, his body gradually gathering up at the vision, his mind keeping the same time, denoting by the eyes its strong workings and convulsions. He did not dash the goblet to the ground, but let it gently fall from him, as if unconscious of having such a vehicle (*sic*) in his hand." This is perhaps as near an approach to praise as an actor can be expected to afford an enemy and a rival. Upon Quin's comparison of him to Whitefield, the Methodist, Garrick wrote his best epigram :—

> " Pope Quin, who damns all churches but his own,
> Complains that heresy corrupts the town :
> That Whitefield Garrick has misled the age,
> And taints the sound religion of the stage ;
> ' Schism,' he cries, ' has turn'd the nation's brain ;
> But eyes will open, and to church again ! '
> Thou great infallible, forbear to roar,
> Thy bulls and errors are rever'd no more !
> When doctrines meet with gen'ral approbation
> It is not heresy but reformation."

Cibber's occasional reappearances Garrick could afford to neglect. Cibber at the time was near seventy-four years of age, and

> " Looked not like the ruins of his youth,
> But like the ruins of those ruins."

New enemies or what were to develop into such were coming forward. For the implacable animosity of Theophilus Cibber, who was now at Drury Lane, ample excuse, as will be seen, was afforded. Thomas Sheridan's hostility, not yet developed, seems to have been a simple outcome of jealousy. This Garrick must have brought upon himself, since he was the first to invite Sheridan over into England from Dublin, where he was a favourite. In so doing, he appears to have acted with frankness and courtesy. Garrick's letter is not preserved. Its nature is plainly indicated in Sheridan's reply. In this he thanks Garrick for an invitation to spend the summer with him at Walton. With regard to a proposal emanating from Garrick that they should play together, he says, "I am afraid I have too many powerful reasons against it; a well-cut pebble may pass for a diamond till a fine brilliant is placed near it, and puts it out of countenance." Garrick has offered to resign to him any characters he affects. Here, again, he sees a danger. "Richard, Hamlet and Lear, as they are your favourite characters, are mine also; and though you were so condescending to say I might appear in any part of yours, yet I question whether the town would bear to see a worse performer in one of your characters in the same house with you, though they might endure him in another." A curious proposal follows, that they should divide London and Dublin between them, playing alternately one month in each.

Domestic complications had attended Garrick. The tripartite arrangement between Garrick, Macklin and Mrs. Woffington broke down, as has been seen, at the outset. Garrick quarrelled with Macklin, who withdrew from the federation. Garrick and Mrs. Woffington managed to get on for some time, though at the price of an acquiescence in her extravagances,

by which Garrick ran some risk of being compromised. That Garrick loved this most fascinating of creatures is not to be doubted. That she
made an effort in the direction of constancy may,
perhaps, be assumed. But constancy with ladies
of Peg's temperament is a "household virtue most
uncommon." She gave her worshipper cause for no
small amount of uneasiness. Garrick's adoration of
his charmer went so far that he seriously contemplated marriage and, it is alleged, even bought the
wedding-ring. Into the question of Peg's flirtations
and amours it is not edifying to enter. Suffice it to
say that Garrick, who had been accused of conniving
at her intrigues, could stand no more. A rupture
came about accordingly, and letters and presents were
returned. Accepted records of very dubious authority, which give a dramatic account of the final
quarrel, chronicle with much glee a trait of Garrick,
which must be accepted for what it is worth. One
present made by Mrs. Woffington to her lover
consisted of a pair of diamond shoe buckles, said to
have been of considerable value. When all the
pledges of eternal constancy and undying affection
were returned these were omitted. Peg Woffington
waited a month, then sent to demand their restitution.
Garrick, however, wrote back soliciting leave to keep
them as a memorial of old loves and happy hours.
This is one of the stories of meanness that Macklin and
others never tired of telling to the actor's discredit.
That Garrick mourned the loss and was angry, jealous,
and offended, is proved by some verses which Mr.

Percy Fitzgerald has disentombed. A long poem is devoted to the scourging of the fickle fair. The verses are rude, ill-tempered, and ineffective, and compare very poorly with the reproaches heaped upon Peg by his successful rival, Sir Hanbury Williams, which bear a convincing testimony to the power of Peg's fascinations. Garrick's friend, Lord Rochford, seems to have believed in his sincerity. Speaking of the forthcoming reappearance together of Garrick and Mrs. Cibber, he says the news is an agreeable surprise, then asks, "but how will Woff[ington] relish that? or, to speak more properly, how will you relish it? for to tell you my mind, I believe the other party can wean themselves much easier than you can, or I have no skill in woman's flesh." However pained the lover may have been, he did not remain long disconsolate. Another queen was ready to ascend the vacant throne, and the Cytherean Gazette might have announced Cibber promoted vice Woffington resigned.

In that singular mixture of cleverness, impertinence, and romance, "An Apology for the life of George Anne Bellamy," the autobiographer says that Garrick languished to be reconciled to Mrs. Woffington. As this was after the arrival of Sheridan in London, it must be supposed to be about 1745. Miss Bellamy is prudently economic as regards dates. She met Garrick, or implies that she met him, at Sheridan's, and says that Sheridan's hospitality was as well known as Garrick's parsimony. One event is mentioned by the fair chronicler concerning which we should be glad of further information. While she was staying at Teddington with Mrs. Woffington's sister, a performance was given of " The Distressed Mother," Ambrose Philips's adaptation of the "Andromaque" of Racine. In this Garrick was Orestes, Polly Woffington Hermione, and Miss Bellamy Andromache. The occasion was intended for the girls, and Mrs. Woffington and Mrs. Bellamy contented themselves with the rôles of Cephisa and Cleone. The Bellamy we shall meet again; Polly Woffington was prettier than her elder sister Peg, and stole for a time the hearts of elderly managers as well as of young beaux, until her marriage with the Hon. and Rev. Robert Cholmondely, and perhaps later. This appears to have been the only occasion on which Garrick was seen in London as Orestes, though the part figures in the list of assumptions in his forthcoming visit to Dublin.

CHAPTER VI.

THAT Garrick had transferred his affections from Mrs. Woffington to Mrs. Cibber, from Comedy that is to Tragedy, was generally known. A letter signed A. B., and directed to Mr. David Garrick, at his lodgings, at Mr. West's, Cabinet-maker, in King Street, Covent Garden, warns him that the managers are counting upon his love for Mrs. Cibber, and the hazards which, for her sake, he will be prepared to run. The first letter in a long and not particularly interesting correspondence between Garrick and Mrs. Cibber is wholly in the comic vein. On Sunday morning, the 1st May, 1745, she writes to him as follows :—

> "Sir,—
>
> "I am very glad to hear you are better, and, if you dare venture out, shall be glad of your company at dinner. As you are an invalid, pray send me word what you can eat, and at what hour you will dine. I shall send Tom to meet you, and am, Sir David,
>
> "Your most humble friend, and servant
>
> "To command till death,
>
> "MARGERY PINCHWIFE."

Tom, it may be said, is her brother, Thomas Augustine Arne, the musical composer. Margery Pinchwife is the name of the heroine of "The Country

Wife" of Wycherley. She does not use it again. Her correspondence with Garrick is mostly written from Woodhay, the seat of an individual with whom she had lived on terms of intimacy.

Between her and Garrick so strong a resemblance existed that it was sometimes said they might have been brother and sister. She was, like him, short in stature, and she had no beauty to speak of. In symmetry of form and in expression she had no superior. Her voice was musical and her look full of animation. "In grief or tenderness her eyes looked as if they were in tears; in rage and despair they seemed to dart flashes of fire." Intimacy with Garrick was shortly to cease, but the artistic association of the two was maintained until the end of her life. Friendly relations were also kept up, and a scattered fusillade of correspondence was heard to the close. On the 12th July, she addressed him at Buxton, saying, " I must tell you that I hear we are both to be turned out of Drury Lane Play-house, to breathe our faithful souls out where we please. But as Mr. Lacy [the new manager] suspects you are so great a favourite with the ladies that they will resent it, he has enlisted two swinging Irishmen, six feet high, to silence that battery. As to me I am to be brought to capitulate another way." She then jocosely suggests that they should set up a strolling company. " Had you given me timely notice of your going to Buxton, I am sure the landlord of the Hall Place would have lent us a barn, and with the advantage of your little wife's first appearance in the character of Lady

Townly, I don't doubt but we could have picked up some odd pence." The part of Lady Townly she had taken for the first time at Drury Lane on the 16th of the previous March.

Upon his departure for Ireland she chides him for departure without leave-taking, and urges him in earnest to purchase with her the remainder of the patent for Drury Lane, provided that they can get a promise of renewal for twenty years. To this Garrick appears to have given no answer, but he brooded over the scheme of becoming a manager. The opening portions of her letter convey a pleasant impression: "I had a thousand pretty things to say to you, but you go to Ireland without seeing me, and to stop my mouth from complaining, you artfully tell me I am one of the number you don't care to take leave of, and I tell you I am not to be flammed in that manner. You assure me also you sadly want to make love to me, and I assure you, very seriously, I will never engage upon the same theatre again with you, without you make more love to me than you did last year. I am ashamed that the audience should see me break the least rule of decency (even upon the stage), for the wretched lovers I had last winter. I desire you always to be my lover upon the stage, and my friend off it."

Sheridan was now sole manager of the Dublin stage. To his invitation the second visit of Garrick was due. Some coldness had existed between Sheridan and Garrick, while the former was in London. The proposal to Garrick accordingly had some formality. A division of profits was offered with every advantage and encouragement that Garrick could reasonably expect. Nothing, however, Sheridan expressly stipulated, was to be expected from friendship. Garrick at first hesitated. With customary timidity he would rather have had a guaranteed sum, and Sheridan's attitude bred some misgiving. With the comment " this is the oddest letter I ever received in the whole course of my life," he showed it to his friend Colonel Wyndham, who regarded it as manly and straightforward, and advised him to accept. In the disturbed state of the theatres in London, prudence gave similar counsel, and towards the close of the year he started for Ireland, arriving in Dublin the 24th November. According to promise he was met by Sheridan, who repeated the conditions of engagement. Garrick once more expressed his preference for a " lump sum ; " Sheridan then drew out his watch and gave Garrick five minutes in which to decide. Thus forced, Garrick submitted, and the arrangement was made.

A period of trouble and disorder was just over and the promises of the management were fair. Garrick was not unaccustomed to troublous times, since apart from the scene bred of the quarrel with Macklin he had had during the past season to face audiences angry at the alterations that had been made in prices. No opposition was, however, to be dreaded in the presence of the efforts of Sheridan, who, besides getting together the strongest company that had ever been seen in Dublin, had augmented the salaries of

the actors and set an example in all respects of spirit
and enterprise.

A fortnight had to elapse before the appearance of
Garrick, who made his first entry at Smock Alley
Theatre, Dec. 9th, as Hamlet. Earlier in the
season, Miss Bellamy, who was to prove something of a thorn in the side of Garrick, had made her
débuts as Monimia and then as Desdemona. Spranger
Barry and Sheridan were both acting in serious parts,
and in addition to the previous company, including
Ebrington, Nat. Furnival, and Mrs. Glover, Lacy, the
new patentee of Drury Lane, had also been engaged.

The fortnight left at Garrick's disposal was spent
in social pleasures. Garrick's reception by Dublin
society was, with a single drawback, the most cordial
that could be conceived. Lord Chesterfield was at
this time the Lord-Lieutenant of Ireland. Apart
from the service he had sought to render the
stage in his famous speech against the Licencing Bill,
a speech which, with due if transparent employment
of initials, was subsequently printed in Dublin, and
sold for a penny, he was a genuine enthusiast in stage
matters. His habit was to order dramatic representations, for which his personal popularity secured
brilliant audiences. From the first he treated Garrick with studied neglect, the cause of which it is
difficult to conjecture. He was in the habit of
receiving Sheridan at the Castle, whom he welcomed
with much cordiality. When, however, he went
to the theatre on the occasion of Garrick's benefit,
and was ushered, according to custom, to his box

with candles by Sheridan and Garrick, he spoke kindly to the former, and left Garrick's salute unanswered. Davies, while mentioning the fact, tells a story to prove how little Chesterfield's civilities were worth. To Sheridan he intimated that he wished to encourage his plan of establishing in Dublin an academy for the purpose of teaching oratory. His words were, " Never let the thought of your oratorical institution go out of your mind." His contribution to this desirable undertaking, when after his return to London he was waited upon by Sheridan, consisted of a guinea. To this cynical meanness Mr. Percy Fitzgerald aptly likens Chesterfield's treatment of Johnson in regard to the dictionary.

What is absolutely known concerning Garrick's final season in Dublin, is little enough. He played many parts, and added to his repertory Falconbridge, Orestes, and Iago, found the behaviour of Sheridan thoroughly loyal, and returned to London with augmented reputation and fortune. He made the acquaintance and friendship of Spranger Barry, somewhile to become a dangerous opponent, and appears to have advanced him money, and behaved with a kindness and consideration which Barry enthusiastically acknowledges.

From the spirited but untrustworthy apology of Miss Bellamy, who was acting at Smock Alley, we get some further insight. Thus in " The Orphan " Garrick performed Chamont, Barry Castalio, and Sheridan Polydore; and in " The Fair Penitent " Sheridan Horatio, Garrick Lothario, and Barry

Altamont. Barry, who had joined the theatre the
previous season, acted so capitally as Altamont that
"the part seemed as consequential as either of the
others." Miss Bellamy had played many characters,
some of them, she held, very unfit for her. She
worked hard, however, in her early life, and, having
received in Dublin much aristocratic patronage, was
disposed to put a considerable value on herself. Sheridan cast her for Constance in "King John," but
Garrick, anxious to have the advantage of her youthful figure in Prince Arthur, overruled his decision.
Mrs. Furnival was accordingly given Constance, and
the Bellamy took the juvenile rôle. Her anger
at this was excessive, and its demonstrations took,
according to her own account, a form sufficiently
unpleasant to Garrick. Using her influence with the
leaders of Dublin fashion, she induced them to stop
away, the result being a house of less than forty
pounds. When subsequently she was assigned
Constance, Sheridan being King John, and Garrick
Faulconbridge, she removed the interdict—the house
was crowded and numbers were turned away. A
victory so complete as this even failed to placate the
indignant young actress, and when Garrick asked her
to play Jane Shore for his benefit she refused, on the
ground that she was too young for such a part,
this having been the cause alleged by Garrick for
refusing her Constance. With a view to conciliation
Garrick wrote her an epistle, which in a jocose strain
he addressed "To my soul's idol, the beautified
Ophelia." In this he told her that he would write

her a " goody, goody epilogue," which with the help
of her eyes " should do more mischief than ever the
flesh or the devil had done since the world began."
This curious compilation he gave to his servant, who,
having other business on hand, entrusted it for delivery, without first regarding the superscription, to a
Hibernian porter, who was naturally puzzled. In
the end the epistle got into the hands of a newsman,
by whom, to Garrick's mortification, it was inserted
in the public prints.

This was not the only inconvenience, if the
fair chronicler may be trusted, to which Garrick
was subject through the high-spirited Dublin
girl. Mrs. Butler, the wife of Colonel Butler, at
whose house Garrick was a frequent visitor, was a
close friend of the Bellamy, and a great favourite
with Garrick. When Garrick announced to her suddenly his intention of leaving Dublin the following
day, great and general regret was expressed. Animated by a sudden caprice or spirit of fun Mrs.
Butler withdrew, and returned with a sealed packet.
This she put into the hands of the actor with the
words, " I here present you, Mr. Garrick, with
something more valuable than life. In it you will
read my sentiments ; but I strictly enjoin you not to
open it till you have passed the Hill of Howth."
No explanation of the significance of this strange
proceeding was volunteered, and as the lady was
regarded as a prude some astonishment was caused.
" But Garrick," says the mischievous narrator,
" who was conscious of possessing the gifts of

nature to as liberal a degree as any man breathing, took the packet with a significant, graceful air, concluding without hesitation that it contained not only a valuable present (the giver having the power, as well as the disposition, to be generous), but a declaration of such tender sentiments as her virtue would not permit her to make known to him whilst he remained in the kingdom." The contents of the packet, as the lady said after his departure, consisted of Westley's (*sic*) "Hymns" and Dean Swift's "Discourse on the Trinity." Garrick subsequently told Miss Bellamy that so soon as he discovered the trick that had been played him he threw both volumes into the sea. Garrick took good-naturedly all the Bellamy's whimsies, and so soon as he entered upon management sent her proposals for an engagement at ten pounds a week. Speaking of the results of the season, Miss Bellamy says that she does not know what the emoluments of Garrick were, but that report said they were almost incredible.

Upon his return to London Garrick found things no better at Drury Lane. Serious changes had taken place. Fleetwood, his unbridled career having come to an end, had taken refuge in France. Unable to venture home, he had, with a view to paying off the principal incumbrances, sold the remainder of his patent, which was bought for 3200*l.* by Green and Amber, who admitted James Lacy, the actor, as manager to a third. This was in 1745. Garrick, it is believed, had been invited to join them, but, alarmed at the political outlook, had declined, giving, in so doing, much offence to Lacy. When, on the 10th May, 1746, Garrick arrived in London from Dublin, he accepted an invitation from Rich, the manager of Covent Garden, to give a few performances on sharing terms. On the 11th June accordingly Garrick made, as King Lear, his first appearance at Covent Garden. This was followed on the 13th by Hamlet, on the 16th by Richard III., on the 20th by Othello, on the 23rd by Archer in " The Beaux' Stratagem," and on the 27th by Macbeth. By these representations, says Victor, " Garrick added 300*l.* to a great sum gotten the preceding season at Dublin."

Overtures from Lacy for Drury Lane followed his arrival, but Rich had been beforehand, and Garrick was engaged for the rival house. Rich also engaged Mrs. Cibber and Quin, the latter still fuming after his defeat in Dublin, where for the first time he had found his popularity eclipsed, and had failed to reap a golden harvest. It is not more difficult, says Davies, to settle " the covenants of a league between mighty monarchs than to adjust the preliminaries of a treaty in which the high and potent princes and princesses of a theatre are the parties." Garrick and Quin had, however, sufficient shrewdness and regard for money to see that an arrangement was expedient. It was made accordingly, and the division proved fair and satisfactory except so far as it showed to the older actor that his popularity was declining. While the Richard of Garrick drew a crowded house that of Quin was meagrely attended. When, on the 14th

November, 1746, the pair appeared together in
Rowe's "Fair Penitent," Quin being Horatio,
Garrick Lothario, and Mrs. Cibber Calista, much
excitement was caused by the conjunction. The
town had long desired to see the two rivals matched
in characters of equal importance, and loud was the
applause that greeted them when, in the second act,
they were on the stage together. Again and again
the plaudits rose before either was permitted to
speak. Garrick was evidently disconcerted, and
owned afterwards his embarrassment, adding, "Faith,
I believe Quin was as much frightened as myself."
In this instance the result was a drawn battle. Garrick
played with his customary spirit, and Quin displayed
"that emphasis and dignity which his elocution gave
to moral sentiments." Mrs. Cibber, unsurpassable in
Calista, scored a triumph no less pronounced than
that of either of her associates.

During this season Garrick was seen for the first
time as Hotspur, Quin taking the part of Falstaff.
He gave it five times in all, then resigned it never to
be resumed. As Hastings in "Jane Shore" to the
Gloster of Quin, Mrs. Cibber being Alicia and Mrs.
Pritchard, also an admirable actress, Jane Shore,
Garrick altogether out-acted his rival. On the occasion of the first production of his "Miss in her Teens,
or the Medley of Lovers," 17th Jan., 1747, Garrick
succeeded somewhat maliciously in scoring off his
intractable rival. Though not altogether original,
the piece is brisk and enlivening, and Garrick, in the
character of Fribble, designed for himself, Woodward,

the soul of elegance, as Flash, and Miss Hippisley as Miss Biddy commended it warmly to the public. It remained a favourite. Quin submitted at first to play in the piece preceding or succeeding it, but afterwards struck, swearing that he " would not hold up the tail of any farce." Garrick, to whom the speech was repeated, said, " Well then, I'll give him a month's holiday," and tacked it on continually. Not absolutely accurate is this, but it has probably " some relish of salvation in it." At any rate, Quin was obliged to have the objectionable piece played for his benefit, since Garrick, on the plea of illness, declined to play anything else, and Quin was too wise to dispense with an attraction such as Garrick then constituted. Garrick also " created " the character of Ranger in Dr. Hoadly's " Suspicious Husband." This remained one of his favourite parts.

CHAPTER VII.

WHILE performing at Covent Garden, Garrick had been negotiating the purchase of a share in Drury Lane. In consequence, partly, of the run on the Bank of England during the Highland invasion, Green and Amber had failed. Lacy, who supported on his own shoulders the tottering edifice of Drury Lane, applied to the Duke of Grafton for a new patent, which was granted, and made advances to Garrick to participate in management. The terms of agreement are found *in extenso* in the Garrick Correspondence. Garrick, who paid 8000*l.* for his share, was to receive, in addition to 300*l.* each paid to the two partners for the discharge of their function as managers, a further sum of five hundred guineas with a clear benefit as an actor, or higher terms in case such should under the management be given to any other player. The augmented lease, into the possession of half of which Garrick came, extended over twenty-seven years. The purchase was judicious in all respects, and was destined to be fruitful of advan tage to Garrick and to the public.

With his assumption of the reins of management the brilliant portion of his career begins. So great had been his popularity that he had had for the last three or four years virtual control of the stage. At Drury Lane his will had been law ; in Dublin Sheridan, a not too tractable man, had yielded to his every caprice; and at Covent Garden Quin, long the mainstay of the house, had been controlled or jockeyed. Now, however, Garrick was in very sooth the manager, and could carry out his schemes wholly for his own benefit.

Management of a theatre has never been a bed of roses. Subjects more peevish, turbulent and unreasonable than those of the stage-ruler cannot be found. Self-interest, ordinarily a potent factor, is in such cases powerless to contend with vanity, and a month's calm is more, probably, than could be traced by any Asmodeus with power of unimpeded observation. Not far different from those of less favoured mortals in a similar position were to be the experiences of the new manager, who was to find a new interpretation to put on lines he had often spoken—

> Oh ! now for ever
> Farewell the tranquil mind, farewell content !

Fame and fortune were, however, waiting for him. He was to see himself rewarded as no previous actor had been, and to win an intellectual and a social recognition and a position in his art such as to this day move astonishment.

Eminently creditable is the manner in which Garrick set about the discharge of his new functions ; his aim was high, and if, under the strain of temptation, his ambition became more modest, excuses may readily be made. Lacy's functions seem to have been principally concerned with the wardrobe, while in all that regarded acting Garrick was paramount. "Order, decency, and decorum," were the things at which he principally aimed, and his own behaviour set an example of the virtues he sought to establish. Punctuality in attendance at rehearsals was insisted upon, and, most difficult task of all, actors were compelled to play at rehearsals as though the public were present. Those who refused to abide by these rules found themselves omitted from the casts of new pieces.

Before the reins of management were in his hands or the box-seat was mounted, Garrick obtained an experience of the difficulties by which he was hereafter to be beset. Mrs. Cibber's invitation to Garrick to join her in management had not been met. The conjunction would probably have been happy, but under the circumstances it was obviously difficult if not impossible for Garrick to associate her with the direction. An idea, however, that special privileges would be assigned her, got abroad, and on the 11th July, 1747, we find Garrick assuring Pritchard that his wife shall receive fair treatment. "I have not," says Garrick, "engaged Mrs. Cibber as yet, and if I should, you may depend upon it that no such stupid article as playing with her [solely] shall be part of the agreement. If you well consider the falsehood, you may know that such clauses are incompatible with my interest and inclination, and I am sorry they should be thrown out to spoil the harmony I intend

shall subsist in our company." Some following passages are manly, and prove how much in earnest
Garrick was. " I have a great stake, Mr. Pritchard,
and must endeavour to secure my property and my
friends to the best of my judgment. I shall engage
the best company in England, if I can, and think it
the interest of the best actors to be together. I shall,
to the best of my ability, do justice to all, and I hope
Mr. Pritchard and his friends will be the last to im-
peach my conduct, or be uneasy that I should follow
the bent of my judgment in my future management
of the stage."

That he was sincere in his endeavour to secure the
best company obtainable will not be doubted. Barry,
in whom he must have seen the nearest approach to
a rival he was likely to know, one whose virile graces
were a significant advantage, was re-engaged, as was
his old enemy, Macklin. Delane, Havard, the two
Sparkses, Berry, Mills, Yates, Shuter, Woodward,
Neale, and Mozeen, were amongst the men. No
less strong were the women, who were headed by
Mrs. Cibber, Peg Woffington, Kitty Clive, Mrs.
Macklin, Mrs. Mills, and Miss Hippisley, now
Mrs. Green. It may safely be maintained that a more
splendid array of talent never graced the boards of
any theatre. Before the season was far advanced we
find Mrs. Pritchard joining the company after an
absence of five years, and playing parts such as
Æmilia and Lady Macbeth.

Nothing in the shape of opposition was to be
dreaded by the new management, the fortunes of

Covent Garden being at the lowest ebb. Quin, their main support, had retired to Bath in disgust at Garrick's success, and Woodward had retreated to Ireland, and was engaged to join Garrick so soon as he returned. From Bath, as the season progressed, the former wrote to his manager words brief enough for a telegram, " I am at Bath.—Yours, James Quin "— and received the answer: " Stay there and be damned.—Yours, John Rich." Covent Garden was driven to depend in tragedy upon Ryan and the Giffards, and to permit in comedy Theophilus Cibber to play his father's parts. Foote, it is true, appeared as Bayes, but Foote was more an entertainer and a mimic than an actor, and was principally occupied with giving what was known as " Tea at the Haymarket."

A somewhat gloomy opening, taking the conditions into account, was witnessed at Drury Lane. Garrick, on whom had fallen a burden of unwonted responsibility, and who overworked himself in more ways than one—he acted over one hundred times during the season—was more than once disabled. This happened soon after the opening night. It was his wont not to thrust himself too early in the season upon the stage, a kind of prudence well known to actors who are their own masters, and akin to that which prevents the hero and the heroine of a play coming forward until they have been heralded by subordinate characters.

Garrick accordingly did not appear on the opening night of the season, nor until a month later. On

September 15th, 1747, the house opened with the
" Merchant of Venice," the principal characters
being thus distributed :—Macklin, Shylock ; Delane,
Antonio ; Havard, Bassanio ; Mills, Gratiano ;
Neale, Launcelot Gobbo ; Lowe, Lorenzo ; Mrs.
Clive, Portia ; Mrs. Bennett, Nerissa ; and Mrs.
Ridout, Jessica.   Garrick's share in the entertainment
consisted in the recitation of an opening prologue and
the supply of an epilogue to be spoken by Mrs.
Woffington.   The prologue was, as is generally
known, by Dr. Johnson, and has since ranked
as the most masterly production of its class ever
written.   One or two of Sheridan's efforts in the
same direction have sometimes been opposed to it,
but the general voice has been in favour of Johnson.
No prologue, at least, has supplied more familiar
quotations, and the distich—

> The drama's laws the drama's patrons give,
> For we that live to please, must please to live,

may count among the most frequently misquoted lines
in the language.   The entire prologue is too familiar
and too accessible to permit of quotation.   The
epilogue was by Garrick himself, who had a neat
touch in such matters.   In addition to the prologues
or epilogues to his own plays, he had already written
an epilogue to Howard's " Regulus " and a second to
the " Astrologer " of Ralph, an ill-starred author,
whose piece, after waiting for ten years for a chance
of production, had to be withdrawn on the second
night, the theatre being closed for want of an audi-

ence. Both these were spoken by Mrs. Woffington. For " The Suspicious Husband " of Dr. Hoadly he wrote both prologue and epilogue. As a rule, Garrick was happier in the cases in which he had no personal interest at stake, as a tendency to self-consciousness with a consequent unease was a fault of his style. His epilogue for the opening performance is fairly happy. At the foot of the play-bill was printed, " As the admittance of persons behind the scenes has occasioned a general complaint on account of the frequent interruptions in the performance, 'tis hoped gentlemen won't be offended that no money will be taken there for the future." So began an important movement, for which Garrick is wholly responsible, towards the purification of the stage and the elevation of the profession of actor. To this the opening words of the epilogue refer—

> Sweet doings truly ! We are finely fobb'd !
> And at one stroke of all our pleasures robb'd !
> *No beaux behind the scenes !* 'tis innovation,
> Under the specious name of reformation.
> *Public complaint,* forsooth, is made a puff,
> Sense, order, decency, and such like stuff.
>
> .   .   .   .   .   .
>
> Each actress now a lock'd-up nun must be,
> And priestly managers must keep the key, etc.

The whole ends with a not very brilliant nor reverential parody of Othello's speech in farewell to his occupation. Both prologue and epilogue were nightly repeated. On the 22nd, however, when Barry played Hamlet, the epilogue only was given, Garrick being ill. Prologue and epilogue were printed by Cave at the price of 6*d.*, and were announced for sale in the *General Advertiser* of October 8th, with the words, " Mr. Garrick, being disabled by illness from speaking the prologue when it was demanded, hopes the publication will be considered as a proof of his desire to compensate the audience."

On October 3rd, Garrick was sufficiently recovered to speak a prologue to Dryden's " Albumazar," then first given at Drury Lane, and on the 15th he made, as Archer in " The Stratagem," his long-delayed first appearance for the season. Abel Drugger, Hamlet, King Lear, Richard III., Sir John Brute, and other parts followed. Warned, however, by past experience, he left Othello to Barry, and Sir Harry Wildair to Mrs. Woffington. On the revival of " King Henry Vth," given for the first time at Drury Lane, Garrick contented himself with the parts of Prologue and Chorus, and in a revival of " Venice Preserved " he substituted for the part of Pierre that of Jaffier, which he took for the first time. He was also the first Young Belmont in the " Foundling," by Moore, 13th February, 1748. Prologue and chorus, Jaffier, and Belmont were the only new characters he assumed. His Young Belmont was a success, and was given eleven times. In the *Dramatic Censor* it is said that Garrick's peculiar qualifications and happy use of them added amazing spirit to the piece, and gave more consequence to Young Belmont than can well be imagined. Mrs. Woffington was also suited as the heroine, and both Barry and Macklin acquitted themselves well.

Not at all the kind of character the actor of to-day would care to assume is Young Belmont. Having rescued the heroine from violence on the part of a self-constituted guardian, instead of posing as her protector, he seeks by cowardly means to corrupt her, and only marries her on discovering that she is a lady of position. Something had been done since the appearance of Collier's protest towards the purification of the stage, but your beau, or gallant, or man-about-town was still an avowed libertine. In this respect he represented fairly well the ordinary well-bred patron of the theatre. The season was not to pass without affording Garrick an experience of stage mohocks, which in subsequent days was to be greatly enlarged. On the 23rd January, 1748, "a disturbance happened at Drury Lane playhouse, occasioned by two of the principal dancers not being there to dance at the end of the entertainment, whereupon several gentlemen in the boxes and pit pulled up the seats and flooring of the same, tore down the hangings, broke partitions, and all the glasses and sconces," and acquitted themselves generally like lords when "lordliest in their wine." This fact, unchronicled by Garrick's biographers, shows that Garrick, in spite of high aim and promise, was obliged to cater for various tastes. Among the features of the season was a revival of "Macbeth," in which Garrick resumed the character of Macbeth, and played it in a scarlet coat, a silver-laced waistcoat, and an eighteenth-century wig and breeches, as may be seen in Zoffany's picture, now

in the Garrick Club.   Mrs. Pritchard, as Lady Macbeth, rose to the height of her profession.   The
"Tempest" was also given, but it was in Dryden's
version.

Concerning the success of the season, encourag-
ing intelligence had been received in Lichfield from
Garrick's friend, Wyndham.   Garrick had full
houses, was much followed, was in the highest
spirits, and had no competitor.   Some bitter was
there in the cup.   Foote had begun at the Haymarket those mimicries and caricatures in which
Garrick in the ignorant and cruel jubilancy of youth
had indulged, and of which he now knew the taste.
He had, however, too much judgment and caution
not to conceal his sufferings.   In this, as in most
matters, Foote was heartless, craven, and detestable.
Lacy, Garrick's partner in management, had threatened
to break Foote's head, and instead of adopting that
heroic remedy, lodged a complaint with the licenser.
Johnson succeeded in frightening Foote.   In the
immortal "Life," Boswell asks Johnson, "Did
not he think of exhibiting you, sir?"   Johnson's
answer was, "Sir, fear restrained him; he knew I
would have broken his bones.   I would have saved
him the trouble of cutting off a leg; I would not
have left him a leg to cut off" (ii. 95, ed. Hill).
Garrick's plan was to attempt to propitiate.   Dis-
sociating himself from Lacy, he wrote to say that
Foote was "quite welcome."   Foote took care to
avail himself of the permission.   Not at all the sort
of man to be propitiated by courtesy was Foote.

Though a little out of date, his letter to Garrick in the following year, 1749, may here be cited: "Sir," he wrote, "it is impossible for me to conceal a piece of intelligence that I have received this minute from either a friend or an enemy. I am told that on the revival of a comedy called 'Friendship in Fashion' a very contemptible friend of yours is to appear in the character of 'Malagene,' habited like your humble servant. Now, I think it is pretty evident that I have as few apprehensions from the passive wit of Mr. Garrick, as the active humour and imitation of Mr. Woodward; but as we are to be in a state of nature, I do conceive that I have a plan for a short farce that will be wormwood to some, entertaining to many, and very beneficial to, sir, yours, SAMUEL FOOTE.

"If your boxkeeper for the future returns my name, he will cheat you of a sum not very contemptible to you, my five shillings."

This is the letter of a coward and a bully. Not all the wit and capacity of Foote, nor all Johnson's admiration, can palliate the unredeemed brutality of such an epistle. Garrick's answer of remonstrance is admirable in Christian spirit, but is not otherwise satisfactory. Feeling the shoe pinch, he stoops to answer Foote's ill-bred sneer about the five shillings, rebukes Foote for imprudence in calling Woodward contemptible, and assures him that being incapable of engaging with him at the usual weapons of the latter, he has no intention of opposing his wit to that of his correspondent. A letter of this sort was calculated to act as a spur to the indefatigable and venomous satirist, who chuckled over his adversary's meekness, and was not long in proceeding to further excesses.

When the season following—1748-49—opened, Garrick's company had undergone some important losses. Principal among these must be counted the secession to Covent Garden of Mrs. Woffington. Whether Rich, who had been aroused from his apathy by the certainty of ruin, had bribed her with higher terms, or whether, as has been supposed, the reports as to Garrick's forthcoming marriage had caused her vexation is not known. She at least disappeared. With her, or after her, went Delane and Sparks, neither of them an irreparable loss. Macklin and his wife had accepted engagements for Ireland.

With the exception of Mrs. Woffington, none of these departures greatly influenced Garrick's company, which was still strong enough for all requirements. Woodward, who had returned from Ireland, was practically a recruit, and opened the season after an absence of seven years as Marplot in the "Busy Body," which he followed with Lord Foppington in "The Relapse." Mrs. Clive or Mrs. Pritchard was seen almost every evening, and Spranger Barry attracted the town as Hamlet and Othello. Thomas King, another recruit destined before long to rise to the top of his profession, made this season his first appearance upon any stage, under Garrick, playing first the Herald in "King Lear," in which, 8th October, 1748, Garrick and Mrs. Cibber reappeared, and afterwards playing Allworth in " A New Way to pay Old Debts." Many of Garrick's favourite parts were trusted to younger actors, and Scrub even was assigned to Woodward. Garrick's first triumph was as Benedick in " Much Ado about Nothing," in which Mrs. Pritchard was Beatrice. Mrs. Pritchard was voted the equal of Garrick in this play, and every scene between them formed, we are told, part of a continued struggle for supremacy in which the audience found itself nonplussed to decide.

One or two special features mark this season. First of these comes the production of " Romeo and Juliet " in Garrick's mangled version, the earliest of those perversions of Shakespeare's texts which are Garrick's crowning disgrace, and cast something more than doubt upon his much vaunted reverence for Shakespeare. " Romeo and Juliet " had not previously been played at this house, nor did Garrick himself, as yet, appear in it. He left to Barry the part of Romeo, and gave to Mrs. Cibber that of Juliet. Their success in these characters is believed to have led to their secession a couple of years later from the company. Not until 1750 did Garrick print the play. In the preface to the printed version Garrick pleaded that his chief design in the alteration had been to " clear the original as much as possible from the jingle and quibble which were always the objections to the reviving it." For the removal of the character of Rosaline, and the presentation of the hero as faithful from the first to Juliet, he apologized on the ground that his transference of affection was held by many to be a blemish. The making Juliet awake in the tomb before the death of Romeo he justifies because it occurs in Bandello, from whom the story is derived. As the English and French translations "have injudiciously left out this addition to the catastrophe," he supposes Shakespeare not to have heard of it. He pleads also the example of Otway, who, in his "Caius Marius," a tragedy taken from "Romeo and Juliet," has "made use of this affecting circumstance." Excuses of this class beset with wearisome monotony those whose studies lead them to read the stage records between the Restoration and a period within living memory. This alteration of the termination of "Romeo and Juliet" held the stage until within comparatively few years. Portions of the scene which Garrick plumed himself upon adding were taken from Otway, and portions from Congreve's "Mourning Bride." What was Garrick's real attitude towards Shakespeare is shown in a letter included in his correspondence referring to the subsequent mangling of "Hamlet." "I have," he says, "ventured to produce 'Hamlet' with alterations. It was the most imprudent thing I ever did in all my life; but I had sworn I would not leave the stage till I had rescued that noble play from all the rubbish of the fifth act. I have brought it forth without the grave-digger's trick and the fencing match. [!] The alterations were received with general approbation beyond my most warm expectations." Some of the Shakespeare corrupters had the grace to counterfeit shame for their alterations, and

Colley Cibber himself put an extra touch of rouge on his old cheek when he talked of his iniquities. Garrick, it is seen, was unashamed, though he could still call Shakespeare the god of his idolatry.

The second feature in the season was the production of " Mahomet and Irene," as Johnson's tragedy, now known as " Irene," was first called. In all that concerns the historic occasion and in Garrick's general behaviour to Johnson our sympathies are with the actor. The great Doctor preserved to his former pupil something of the air of a pedagogue. Sincerely fond of him and unwilling to hear any censure against Garrick, but his own, he was alternately attacking him and undertaking his defence. Garrick had to put up with a good deal of incivility from men with whom he did not wish to quarrel. So rude were, however, some of the Johnsonian utterances, one cannot but hope that the worst of them were delivered with an air of good-humoured badinage.

Johnson had a genuine dislike of players, attributable in part, according to Boswell, to the imperfection of his organs, but fostered and aggravated by the brilliant triumph of Garrick, who, coming with him to London under conditions scarcely more prosperous than his own, had, at the outset, distanced him in the race after fame as well as in that after fortune. Aware that his own powers were not inferior to those of his ex-pupil, he grew soured and missed no chance at this time or hereafter to talk or write contemptuously of players. An early instance of triumph over Garrick and Giffard is mentioned by Boswell, on the authority of Dr. Taylor, Johnson's schoolfellow and friend. "'The players, sir (said Johnson), have got a kind of rant with which they run on without any regard to accent or emphasis.' Both Garrick and Giffard were offended at this sarcasm, and endeavoured to refute it; upon which Johnson rejoined, 'Well now, I'll give you something to speak, with which you are little acquainted, and then we shall see how just my observation is. That shall be the criterion. Let me hear you repeat the ninth commandment, "Thou shalt not bear false witness against thy neighbour."' 'Both tried at it,' said Dr. Taylor, 'and both mistook the emphasis, which should be upon *not* and *false witness*. Johnson put them right, and enjoyed his victory with great glee.'" Fair enough, if not wholly convincing, is this. It is very different with such retorts as " Punch has no feelings." The low opinion expressed concerning Garrick was, however, mere petulance for the most part. Garrick stood in great awe of his aggressive friend and companion, and found a little cheap and not too noble consolation in mimicking him and his wife behind their backs. In the matter of producing " Mahomet and Irene," Garrick's motives were the best, though the result, unfortunately, was to aggravate such difficulties as had previously existed.

" Irene " is said to have been in Johnson's pocket when he and Garrick made their famous journey to London. So soon as he had the control of Drury Lane, Garrick made advances, which Boswell calls kind and generous, with a view to its production. It is

needless to say that Johnson was as intractable as a
bear, and bristled all over like a porcupine. He
could not bear that a drama " which he had formed
with much study, and had been obliged to keep more
than the nine years of Horace, should be revised and
altered at the pleasure of an actor." Without some
alteration, however, it was impossible. Here Boswell
may again be heard. " A violent dispute having
ensued between them, Garrick applied to the Reverend
Dr. Taylor to interpose. Johnson was at first very
obstinate. ' Sir [said he] the fellow wants to make
me make Mahomet run mad, that he may have an
opportunity of tossing his hands and kicking his
heels.' " Similar phenomena are common enough
to this day in the stage firmament. Johnson, however, was finally appeased, as the author generally is,
and permitted grudgingly some changes, which the
event proved to be inadequate.

Garrick was, in this instance, less moved by vanity
than Johnson had supposed. He did not even pro-
pose to take himself the part of Mahomet. When,
on the 6th of February, 1749, the play was given
for the first time, Barry was Mahomet, Garrick
Demetrius, Mrs. Cibber Aspasia, and Mrs. Pritchard
Irene. Four worthier performers an author could
scarcely desire. The play was ushered in by a
prologue in Johnson's tersest and most vigorous style,
and, for a while, proceeded well enough. Many
accounts of the first performance are preserved, and
all concur in describing it as favourable in the main.

Sir John Hawkins, with what Dr. Birkbeck Hill

calls solemn inaccuracy, speaks of the indifferent
reception of the tragedy. Burney says, " I know
not what Sir John Hawkins means by the cold
reception of 'Irene.' I was at the first representation and most of the subsequent. It was
much applauded the first night, particularly the
speech on to-morrow." From Dr. Adams, meanwhile, Boswell received a somewhat dramatic account.
The prologue, according to this, soothed an audience
which, after the wont of British audiences even up to
to-day, had alarmed the friends of the author with cat-
calls, whistling, and the like. " The play went off
tolerably till it came to the conclusion, when Mrs.
Pritchard, the heroine of the piece, was to be strangled
upon the stage, and was to speak two lines with the
bow-string round her neck. The audience cried out
' *Murder ! murder !* ' She several times attempted to
speak, but in vain. At last she was obliged to go
off the stage alive." After the first representation
this method of putting to death, which was, of course,
new to the English public, was abandoned, and the
death took place behind the scenes. It is easy to
fancy this scene, which has since been repeated
with endless variations. Less easy is it to fancy
the figure of Johnson in unwonted finery which
he considered called for by the occasion, sitting
in a side box in a scarlet waistcoat with rich
gold lace, and a gold-laced hat. He had been
pleased to go behind the scenes during rehearsal, and
had abated somewhat of his prejudice against
actors. He had even to call upon his virtue to

induce himself to abandon the green room, where, as he told David, " the silk stockings and white bosoms of your actresses " excited feelings he felt bound to repress. To Mrs. Pritchard, however, the innocent cause of the misfortune, he showed himself relentless, declaring her a mechanical player, and saying, " It is wonderful how little mind she had." Garrick had himself suggested the use of the bow-string as a means of death, counting, doubtless, upon the novelty as an attraction. He behaved with all possible generosity to Johnson, and kept the play on the bills for nine nights, though it is pretty certain that more attractive entertainments could have been supplied. Johnson's name, it must be remembered, was not at this time an attraction such as it subsequently became.

In his own piece of " Lethe," revived with alterations, with a view to establishing its success, Garrick played three separate parts, the Poet, the Drunken Man, and the Frenchman. The first character did not please the public, and the two others he soon resigned into different hands. He also played, not for the first time, Tancred in Thomson's " Tancred and Sigismunda," and was the original Dorilas, otherwise Eumenes, in the " Merope " of Aaron Hill, which is in a great measure taken from Voltaire.

CHAPTER VIII.

THE summer which followed his second season of management witnessed Garrick's marriage. This event had for some time been expected, and the mere anticipation had caused Garrick some difficulty with the female members of his company, more than one of whom conceived herself to have a lien upon his affections. During the past years Garrick had done his best to establish a species of republic, or to reconcile the actresses to the idea of an intimacy purely Platonic. Mrs. Woffington had, as has been seen, flown off at a tangent. Others had, however, perplexed not a little a manager, recollections of whose past amiabilities were still treasured, and the task to give his little senate laws had been increasingly difficult. Marriage was a wise step on his part, and the experiment that he made proved more judicious than at first seemed probable. The growth and development of Garrick's love are shrouded in some mists which his biographers have as a rule done little to dispel. The account given by Lee Lewes in his Memoirs bears the apparent impress of truth, and is confirmed in some particulars from other sources. The whole truth will never presumably be known, and it is probable that Mrs. Garrick herself was in the dark as to her origin and early history. The romantic story of Lee Lewes presents her as the daughter of the Earl of Burlington and a young Italian lady of position, after whose death in Florence she was compelled to take to the stage as a dancer for a livelihood. Her father had, it is said, looked with care after her education, but the money he forwarded for her use had been misapplied by his agents. As a means of getting her near him, he used his influence to secure her a London engagement, and then induced his legitimate daughter, subsequently the Duchess of Devonshire, to accept her as companion.

A second and not less romantic story represents her as the daughter of a Viennese citizen, called Veigel, a name for which, at the request of Maria Teresa, she substituted that of Violette, the name of Veigel being a *patois* corruption of Veilchen, a violet. She was, however, unfortunate enough to attract the eye of the Emperor, and was hurriedly despatched to England out of his way. This account she herself favoured. She came over to England in masculine disguise, and under the charge of some Germans, and had naturally some stimulating adventures on the way. To deliver himself out of this thicket the reader may take which path he likes! That Eva Maria Violette, as she was known, had had in Florence or in Vienna considerable practice as a dancer is shown by her being able to make an immediate appearance at the Haymarket. Her first performance was attended by the king, and she created a furore in aristocratic circles.

Horace Walpole speaks of her as the finest and most advanced dancer in the world; ladies of rank admitted her to their houses, and her quarrel with another dancer was almost a state affair. A riot at Drury Lane was the consequence of her non-appearance, and the gossip of the middle of the last century is full of her doings. Through all this time the Burlingtons were her greatest patrons. Lady Burlington waited for her at the wings of the theatre, and Lord Burlington was prepared, as he afterwards showed, to give her what was then a considerable dower.

Mr. Fitzgerald, who has taken much pains to verify dates, and to search records, casts grave doubts upon all that is said by Lewes, and regards it as the outcome of ill-natured gossip. Lewes' story has more than a semblance of truth. Garrick had met the dancer at Drury Lane, and does not appear to have been struck with her beauty, which, however, at this time was considerable. It is at least impossible to trace her as the subject of those love songs which he was in the habit of addressing to those by whom he was struck. It was the lady, according to Lewes, who first fell in love with the actor, not at all an uncommon thing in the case of members of Garrick's company. Nothing has ever been advanced against the personal character of Mlle. Violette, and her love for Garrick, like that of Viola, remained untold. Her secret was at length surprised by Lady Burlington, and confided by her to the Earl. Garrick was then fetched, the Earl acknowledged the relationship, and declared his intention of giving her a portion of ten thousand pounds on her marriage. The bait was readily swallowed, and the marriage duly arranged. Six thousand pounds was, according to Murphy, the sum given by the Earl upon the marriage. Lewes' story is pat. Suspicion is cast upon it by the obvious dislike to Garrick which colours his assertion, and by the animated style he gives to conversations he does not even claim to have overheard. One, however, who, on the ground last named, disputed the truth of theatrical anecdote, might as well sweep the whole into limbo. A more serious argument against the truth of Lewes' statement is that Lady Burlington remained long hostile to the proposed union, and that Garrick in contemporary chronicles is depicted as looking very glum and downcast in his attempts to escape her ladyship's supervision, and approach the object of his latest flame. Neither too important nor too edifying is the whole question. In dismissing it another charge of Lewes' may as well be dismissed also. The quarrel soon to break out between Garrick and Spranger Barry is attributed to some rivalry with regard to Mrs. Garrick. As told, the story reflects great discredit upon Barry. Garrick's feuds were seldom, however, personal. Into the motives of theatrical animosities it is wholly inexpedient to enter. Morbid sensitiveness and dislike of rivalry are the most familiar accompaniments of the profession. Garrick possessed both in excess. A well-meaning, upright, honourable, and in some respects generous man, as will hereafter be seen, he yet succeeded in quarrelling with most men with whom in any professional regard he came in contact; his life in this respect being almost as sad as that of Pope.

Garrick was married on the 22nd June, 1749, first at the church in Russell Street, Bloomsbury, and subsequently at the chapel of the Portuguese embassy in Audley Street. Much pother was caused, and squibs and lampoons fluttered in the air. The scandal was noticed by French writers even. In a very curious and almost unknown satire against the Jesuits, " Histoire des Diables Modernes, par M. A——," one of the modern devils says, " J'ai endiabolisé my lord B——n (Burlington), en lui faisant donner sa fille naturelle V——e (Violette), en dépit d'une certaine Majesté (Emperor of Austria), au petit G——k (Garrick), avec une pension considérable sur le pauvre Royaume d'Irlande." Garrick has himself been charged with contributing to the literature of the occasion, some verses published in the works of Edward Moore, entitled " Stanzas to Mr. Garrick, on the talk of the town," being said to be written under his inspiration, if not by himself. They have all the character of his Muse, and are, indeed, just the sort of thing that he would write; witness his " Sick Monkey," of which more anon. Mr. Fitzgerald has unearthed a poem of Garrick's, written on this occasion, which has more grace and less artificiality than ordinarily attend his amorous effusions. It was written in answer to some verses on his marriage, apparently anonymous, which he had preserved. The last two lines of these are—

> " Who is the paragon, the marvellous she,
>   Has fixed a weathercock like thee ? "

To this Garrick replies—

> " 'Tis not, my friend, her speaking face,
>   Her shape, her youth, her winning grace,
>   Have reach'd my heart, the fair one's mind,
>   Quick as her eyes, yet soft and kind.
>   A gaiety with innocence ;
>   A soft address with manly sense,
>   Ravishing manners, void of art,
>   A cheerful, firm, yet feeling heart,
>   Beauty that charms all public gaze,
>   And humble amid pomp and praise." [1]

If there are few of a lover's raptures here, there is a kind of appreciation which is of happy augury for future comfort. After a honeymoon spent in part in Burlington House, Garrick settled with his wife in Southampton Street, Strand. When he re-opened his theatre, further secessions had to be encountered. Mrs. Cibber followed the example of Mrs. Woffington, and refused to act with her faithless manager, though she did not as yet join the rival house. The quarrel was avowedly between her and Garrick. Barry, though he remained a member of the company, was unhappy, and seeking an occasion to break loose. Garrick resigned him one part after another, without being able to root out his discontent. One or two actors quitted Drury Lane for Covent Gar-

---

[1] Life of Garrick, vol. i. 239.

den, in rupture of their engagements, and these Garrick compelled to return. Mills, too, died in the course of the season. Garrick had still Mrs. Clive for comedy, and Mrs. Pritchard for tragedy. Covent Garden had now, however, Mrs. Woffington, in the height of her powers, and Miss Bellamy was, at least, the fashion. Quin, too, had rejoined the house, and the two companies, though they were still far from equal, were more nearly on a level than before. Garrick then sought to strengthen his company by the engagement of Mrs. Ward, whom he is said to have disloyally seduced from Covent Garden. If for the lady Garrick " 'filed his mind," he displayed no more judgment than chivalry. A heavy and unimaginative actress, she was a valueless recruit. Barry refused to accept her as Juliet to his Romeo, and the play was not given.

For his own appearance, 28th September, 1749, Garrick, with characteristic bad taste, chose the part of Benedick in " Much Ado about Nothing," the allusions in which were of course taken up by the audience. He subsequently played King Lear, Mrs. Ward making her first appearance as Cordelia. During the course of an uneventful season he took two new parts. The first was Edward the Black Prince, in W. Shirley's rhetorical tragedy of that name. In this he made no great success, the character being pronounced too cold and tame for his powers. Barry, on the other hand, was received with much favour in Lord Ribemont. The second was Horatius in

" The Roman Father " of Whitehead, a piece imitated from " Les Horaces " of Corneille. Neither of these pieces attracted much attention. On the 9th of February, 1750, for the benefit of the author, Aaron Hill's tragedy of " Merope " was repeated. Hill, who had been unwell for many weeks, died, however, during the same month. Another performance of some interest was for the benefit of Mrs. Forster, granddaughter and only surviving descendant of Milton, when " Comus " was given, and Garrick spoke an occasional prologue by Dr. Johnson. A sum of 130*l.* was handed to a lady so ignorant of theatrical matters that she did not know what was intended when a benefit was offered her. Barry's approaching retirement was meanwhile foreshadowed in a notice which he inserted in the *General Advertiser*, denying the reports circulated to the effect that he had refused to act when his health would have permitted it, and declaring that he scorned to use tricks and evasions of that kind.

Whatever may have been the cause, Barry at the end of this season seceded to Covent Garden. Mrs. Cibber, who had sulked, a feminine Achilles in her tent, joined Rich, and Macklin and his wife, accompanied by Mrs. Elmy, swelled the hostile ranks.

Appalled at the array of talent against him, Garrick sought, according to Tate Wilkinson, to seduce Quin from his allegiance. Quin refused, however, to be bought over, though he succeeded, on the strength of Garrick's application, in extracting from the Covent

Garden management a salary of 1000*l.* a year, the largest then known to have been given.

In point of fact the opposition to Garrick was beneficial, stimulating him to renewed effort. At no period of stage history, indeed, was interest in things theatrical stronger than in the period which began in 1750-1, never was competition more keen, nor, within certain limits, were results more satisfactory. One has only to turn to the magazines of the time to find them overflowing with comment, criticism, eulogy, and epigram. Tate Wilkinson, an independent, disinterested, and competent critic and reporter, says that the general anticipation was that Garrick would be ruined by the powerful competition to which he was subject. His troops, however, were better disciplined than those of his rivals, the comedies he presented were well acted, Shuter was winning acceptance in low comedy, and Palmer, the youngest recruit of importance, in genteel comedy. Add to this, that Garrick was a host in himself, and the combat is seen to be less unequal than might have been expected.

Hostilities were not long in beginning. Though the season at Drury Lane opened September 8th, Garrick did not act until the 25th, which was earlier than his custom. He spoke, however, a prologue of his own composition, in which, after his wont, he took his audience into his confidence. The best lines in this are the following—

> " Strengthen'd by new allies, our foes prepare,
> Cry havock ! and let slip the dogs of war.

To shake our souls, the papers of the day
Drew forth the adverse pow'r in dread array ;
A pow'r might strike the boldest with dismay.
Yet fearless shall we take the field with spirit,
Arm'd *cap-à-pè* in self-sufficient merit.
Our ladies, too, with souls and tongues untam'd,
Fire up like Britons when the battle's nam'd :
Each female heart pants for the glorious strife,
From Hamlet's mother,[1] to the Cobler's wife." [2]

This prologue was repeated for a week.

Barry responded with a prologue in which spitefulness did duty for literary merit. A few of the lines are as follows :—

" When kings allow no merit but their own,
Can it be strange, that men for flight prepare,
And seek to raise a colony elsewhere ?
The custom has prevailed in every age
And has been sometimes practised on the stage ;
For, *entre nous*, these managers of merit,
Who fearless arm—'and take the field with spirit,'
Have curbed us monarchs with their haughty mien
And Herod have out-heroded, within."

Pointing to the green room—

" O ! they can torture twenty thousand ways,
Make bouncing Bajazet retreat from Bayes.
The ladies, too, with every power to charm,
Have felt the fury of a tyrant's arm."

These things were but affairs of outposts. The first pitched battle occurred on the 28th September, when Garrick made his appearance as Romeo, a part he had hitherto shrunk from taking. Miss

[1] Mrs. Pritchard.   [2] Mrs. Clive.

Bellamy, his ancient enemy, was the Juliet, and Woodward the Mercutio. In assuming this part, which was the favourite of Barry, Garrick had with commendable chivalry thrown down his glove. It was gladly taken up, and the same night witnessed the revival of the same piece at Covent Garden. Barry was of course the Romeo, Mrs. Cibber Juliet, Macklin Mercutio, and Mrs. Macklin, the Nurse. In other characters the casts were fairly equal. The struggle was held doubtful, though the verdict leaned to Covent Garden, a fact principally ascribable to the youth and inexperience of Miss Bellamy, which put Garrick at a disadvantage. Woodward, on the other hand, scored a not wholly expected success with Mercutio.

A natural result of these proceedings was to flood the town with epigrams. Pitiful enough for the most part are these, though one which appeared in the *General Advertiser* from Mr. H(ewi)tt had some slight share of wit, and seemed rather in Garrick's own vein.

> " Well, what's to-night? " says Angry Ned,
> As up from bed he rouses ;
> "Romeo again," and shakes his head,
> " Ah! Pox on both your houses."

Most of the so-styled humour rested on attempts to compare the stature of the two exponents of Romeo, it can scarcely be said with the object of belittling Garrick.

> " So reversed are the notions of Capulet's daughters,
> One loves a whole length, the other three-quarters."

Garrick himself mingled in the fray, and put into a different shape the thought embodied in the previous distich, the authorship of which has been attributed to him.

" Fair Juliet at one house exclaims with a sigh,
    No Romeo's clever that's not six feet high ;
Less ambitiously, t'other does Romeo adore,
    Though in size he scarce reaches to five feet (and) four."

As regards the two Romeos no authoritative comparison is preserved. Francis Gentleman, not yet Garrick's enemy, says that Garrick commanded most applause, Barry most tears. Macklin, who detested Garrick, declares that Barry was the best Romeo he had ever seen, while Garrick was nowise qualified for the part. Mrs. Bellamy, also a not unprejudiced judge, states that, except in the scene with the friar, Barry was universally allowed to have carried off the award. To a consensus of opinion such as this we must bow. Barry's noble proportions, fine face, and splendid voice may well indeed in a part of youthful passion have triumphed over the meagre physical gifts of his more intellectual rival.

Amused for a while, the public ended in being angered by the contest, and the consequent dearth of amusement. Rich was the first to retire, the excuse advanced being the illness of Mrs. Cibber, which was pleaded after twelve representations. Garrick was not slow to follow suit, but acted one night more so as to secure the appearance of triumph. This final crowing was accompanied by the delivery by Mrs. Clive of an epilogue of Garrick's composition, per-

haps the poorest he ever wrote. This was an answer
to the charges against him, and especially to
Barry's not very generous implication that he ill-
used his women. A very few lines of such stuff will
suffice.

Mrs. Clive entered hastily as if speaking to some
one who would oppose her—

> " I'll do't, by heav'n I will—pray get you gone;
>   What! all these janglings, and I not make one !
>   Was ever woman offer'd so much wrong ?
>   These creatures here would have me hold my tongue ! "
>
>   *   *   *   *
>
> " I, Catherine Clive, come here t' attack 'em all,
>   And aim alike at *little*,[1] and at *tall*.[2]
>
>   *   *   *   *
>
> " 'Tis true he (Garrick) is of a cholerick disposition,
>   And fiery parts make up his composition.
>   How have I seen him rave when things miscarried !
>   Indeed he's grown much tamer since he married."
>
>   *   *   *   *

Attacking Barry, the epilogue then says—

> " He tells you tales how cruelly this[3] treats us
>   To make you think the little monster beats us.
>   Would I have whin'd in melancholy phrase,
>   *How bouncing Bajazet retreats from Bayes ?*
>   I, who am woman, would have stood the fray,
>   At least not snivelled thus, and run away."

This composition is only curious as showing
Garrick's method of attack when he felt himself
aggrieved. However mild the polemic into which he
suffered himself to be betrayed, it became milder as

---

[1] Garrick.   [2] Barry.   [3] Garrick.

enemies multiplied around him; and his power of making enemies was not small.

Garrick's next step was to carry the war into the enemy's camp by producing a pantomime, otherwise described as a "New Entertainment in Italian grotesque characters, called Queen Mab." Woodward, the author of this unprinted trifle, played Harlequin; Shuter also took part in it. So much success attended this piece that Rich, then regarded as the king of pantomime, began, according to Murphy, "to tremble on his throne." More legitimate experiments were the production of Moore's comedy of "Gil Blas," in which Garrick was Gil Blas, and Woodward, Don Lewis, and the revival of Thomson and Mallet's "Masque of Alfred," in which Garrick was Alfred. The only other new character he assumed was Osmyn, in Congreve's "Mourning Bride," the performance of which elicited from some contemporary versifier the following tribute, which appeared in the *London Magazine*, and is characteristic of a whole literature dedicated at this epoch to the stage:

> "Envy and love for once agree,
>   Bound by coercive merit,
>   T'applaud, to praise and honour thee,
>   But act with different spirit.
> Envy with rage, like Zara, owns thy chains,
> While love in every breast, as in Almeria's, reigns.

At Covent Garden meanwhile, signs of disruption had from an early period been observed. Barry and Quin were at daggers drawn, and could not be always induced to rehearse together. Barry advanced hoarseness as a cause for refusing to play. Mrs. Cibber was genuinely unwell and frequently unable to act. Tired of acting, as she constantly did, as a stop-gap, and seeing at the bottom of the play-bills the name of the tragedian announced in large letters, Mrs. Woffington at length struck and declined to play. She became thus the object of very unfavourable demonstrations on the part of Rich's friends; these with customary courage and resolution she faced, and as she was a genuine favourite she gained the victory. At the beginning of the next season Mrs. Woffington disappeared from Covent Garden; Quin also practically retired, only to play again for benefits, and the most formidable coalition by which Garrick had ever been faced was dissolved.

Garrick's company had meanwhile been strengthened by the addition of Mossop, who made, as Richard III., his first appearance on the English stage, and Ross, who followed suit a few days later, as Young Bevil in the "Conscious Lovers." Both sprang soon into favour. Lee Lewes, whose dislike of Garrick is shown on every possible occasion, hints that the success of these actors caused Garrick annoyance, and says that Taswell, a theatrical courtier and sycophant, came out of the green-room raving against the applause bestowed on two men, one of whom bellowed in unnatural rants, while the other snivelled and whined. He then added :—

> "The Templars they cry Mossop,
> The ladies they cry Ross up,
> But which is the best is a toss up."

With this ebullition, we are told, Garrick was

vastly delighted. Dexter, an actor of some power, also appeared as Oroonoko, and won the applause of Garrick and the public. He had no staying power and soon retired to Dublin.

Kitely, in Jonson's "Every Man in his Humour," altered by Garrick and supplied with a new scene in the fourth act, was a fine performance of Garrick, eclipsed in part by the brilliant success of Woodward as Bobadil. Kitely and Mercour in Dr. Francis's dull tragedy of "Eugenia" were the only two novelties in which Garrick was seen during the season of 1751-52. As an attempt to placate a man of whose brutality he was always in fear, Foote's comedy of "Taste" was given. It ran for three nights only, though Garrick contributed to it one of his briskest prologues.

Foote and Garrick had met in Paris, whither Garrick and his wife had made a summer trip. Concerning Garrick's adventures on this occasion little information is preserved. He was presented to Louis XV., an honour duly chronicled at home, and is said to have been the hero of a sufficiently improbable, but not impossible adventure. Sir George Lewis, with whom he had travelled to Paris, was murdered in the Forest of Bondy, as he was returning burdened with money he had won at a neighbouring château. Garrick suspected an Italian Count, who was arrested, but was on the point of being released when Garrick, made up for the murdered man, appeared and wrung from the assassin an agonized confession.

Not the least of Garrick's afflictions was Miss

Bellamy, whose unintentional or unconscious avowals in her "Apology" show her a very thorn in the flesh, and are far from conveying to the average reader the intended impression. She even, whose accusations, though constantly disproved by more responsible authorities, exercised for a time an unhappy influence over Garrick's reputation, is compelled to make grudging acknowledgment of his abilities, and to own that in the rendering of Alfred, in the masque of Thomson and Mallet so named, Garrick surpassed himself. She adds that when he repeated the line borrowed from the "Athalie" of Racine,

"I fear that God, and know no other fear,"

he appeared to be another Atlas and to carry a world upon his shoulders. Miss Bellamy is, on the whole, ungrateful, since Garrick, though he resented her impertinences and breaches of discipline, put her forward in characters in which she was an accepted rival to Mrs. Cibber. She was thus entrusted with the part of the heroine in Young's tragedy of "The Brothers," which, after being put in rehearsal at Drury Lane in 1726, was not produced until March 3rd, 1753. It owes something to the "Persée et Démétrius" of Thomas Corneille. Miss Bellamy did not score much by her impersonation, to obtain which she had intrigued more than a little, being, as Davies states, unsuited to the part. Garrick played Demetrius, and Mossop, Perseus. It was given for the benefit of the Society for the

Propagation of the Gospel, and Young made the receipts up to 1000*l*. A somewhat ribald epilogue, written by Mallet at Garrick's request, and delivered by Mrs. Clive in her broadest style, caused some coldness between Garrick and Young, who naturally refused to have it printed with the play. A quatrain affords a sample of its merits :—

> " A scheme, forsooth, to benefit the nation,
> Some queer odd whim of pious *propagation !*
> Lord! *talk so, here,*—the man must be a widgeon,
> *Drury* may *propagate*—but not religion."

The previous month (February 7th) another play, destined to become exceedingly famous, had shown Garrick in yet another character. This was "The Gamester" of Moore, a piece towards which Garrick appears to have contributed something more than hints, though, singular modesty on the part of an author, he did not claim a place on the title-page, and which enjoyed the rarely accorded honour of being translated into French. Moore's "Gil Blas" had aroused some opposition, and "The Gamester" was for the sake of prudence assigned to the Rev. Joseph Spence, who, after the fourth night, doffed his vicarious laurels, little to the benefit of the piece. Garrick played Beverly in his best style, and Mrs. Pritchard gave, according to Murphy, "a specimen of the most natural acting that had ever been seen—she did not appear to be conscious of an audience before her—she seemed to be walking about her own parlour in the deepest distress and over-whelmed with misery." During the season Garrick had also played, for the first time, Loveless in Cibber's "Love's Last Shift," for the first appearance at Drury Lane of Miss Haughton, an actress whose promise was never fulfilled. The season was also marked by a quarrel and correspondence between Woodward and Fitzgerald, the latter assumably the same as the subject of Churchill's satire in "The Rosciad," with whom Garrick subsequently was to have a more serious encounter.

At the beginning of the season of 1753-54, Mrs. Cibber, who after her experience of Barry and Rich found that Garrick was not quite so black as she had painted him, returned to Drury Lane and appeared as Monimia in "The Orphan" to the Chamont of Garrick. Old scores were soon settled, and she played Juliet to his Romeo, Ophelia to his Hamlet, Belvidera to his Jaffier in "Venice Preserved," Calista to his Lothario in the "Fair Penitent," and other parts. Her return restored the supremacy of Drury Lane, and left Covent Garden wholly out of favour. Miss Macklin joined the company, as did Foote, who made his first appearance in his own "Englishman in Paris" with the conciliatory and customary addition of a prologue by Garrick. Foote played a round of parts, and gave his celebrated musical entertainment called "Tea," in which, it may be supposed, he did not at this time caricature his manager.

"Boadicea," by Garrick's old friend "Leonidas" Glover, was the first important novelty of the season. In this Garrick was Dumnorix, chief of the Trinobantians; Mossop and Havard, Ænobarbus and Flaminius, Roman captives; Mrs. Cibber, Venusia, wife to Dumnorix ; and Mrs. Pritchard, Boadicea. Though it ran some ten nights and the termination was found supremely touching, and though, it may be added, the cast may be regarded as ideal, " Boadicea " did not fulfil expectations. It was voted a play for the closet, from which, however, if it ever found its way there, it has long been banished, and after it was withdrawn from the stage was never revived.

At the close of 1753, Garrick gave " The Refusal " of Colley Cibber, for the benefit of Macklin, who had announced his intention of retiring from the stage and starting a tavern. Macklin played Sir Gilbert Wrangle, and spoke a prologue, the authorship of which is assigned to Garrick. Foote, with customary cynicism, observed that Garrick wrote the prologue in the hope that Macklin would be as good as his word. His green-room audience declared that an actor capable of giving such a representation could not be spared. Foote then, according to Murphy, replied, " You need not fear, he will first break in trade and then break his word," an imaginary programme which was fulfilled to the letter.

Upon his revival of " King John," 23rd January, 1754, Garrick, leaving the king to Mossop, elected to appear as Faulconbridge, a part usually entrusted to a man of commanding stature. Davies, who credits him with merit in the character, says that Garrick was for some time at a loss for a Robert Faulconbridge who would not shame him by superior proportions,

and hit at last upon a certain Simpson, a favourite
representative of the Apothecary in "Romeo and
Juliet," an actor as insignificant in appearance as in
capacity.

A tragedy on the subject of "Virginia," the solitary
work of Samuel Crisp, miscalled "Henry" in the
Biographia Dramatica, and in the index to
Nichols's *Literary Anecdotes*, and gratuitously
dubbed "Reverend" by Murphy, was the next
novelty, being brought out 25th February. It
was commended to Garrick by Lady Coventry,
but was cold and passionless, and proved a failure.
It served in the character of Marcia to introduce
Mrs. Graham, subsequently famous as Mrs. Yates.
Garrick played Virginius, Mrs. Cibber, Virginia, and
Mossop, Appius. Murphy gives a fairly lifelike,
though ludicrously expanded, account of Garrick in
the scene in which he pleaded before Appius.
Garrick stood "with his arms folded across his
breast, his eyes riveted to the ground, like a mute
and lifeless statue. Being told at length that the
tyrant is willing to hear him, he continued for some
time in the same attitude, his countenance expressing
a variety of passions, and the spectators fixed in
ardent gaze. By slow degrees he raised his head;
he paused; he turned round in the slowest manner,
till his eyes fixed on *Claudius;* he still remained
silent, and after looking eagerly at the impostor,
he uttered in a low tone of voice, that spoke the
fulness of a broken heart, '*Thou traitor.*' The
whole audience was electrified; they felt the im-

pression and a thunder of applause testified their delight."

Whitehead's "Creusa," founded on the "Ion" of Euripides, came out on the 20th April, 1754, with Garrick as Aletes and Mrs. Pritchard as Creusa. As to the reception of this stilted tragedy, authorities differ. Murphy, who commends it as a model of dramatic fable, says that in the pathetic scene Garrick touched every heart, but Davies remarks that the misfortunes of Creusa could not fetch a tear from any eye. Garrick also acted Lusignan in the tragedy of "Zara," but was only seen in it twice.

For some time past, Garrick, absorbed in the double rôle of actor and manager, had neglected his occupation of dramatist, and had confined his literary efforts to the production of prologues and epilogues. During the next season, however, 1754-55, he returned to the task of improving (!) Shakespeare, and turned the "Midsummer Night's Dream" into an opera which he called "The Fairies." The executants included Beard, a famous vocalist, and two Italian singers. In a prologue, in no better taste than the piece, are two lines :—

> "I dare not say WHO wrote it—I could tell ye,
> To soften matters—Signor Shakespearelli."

Garrick had also a hand in altering "The Chances" of the Duke of Buckingham, itself an alteration from Beaumont and Fletcher. His labours were confined to the omission of indecencies, in regard to which, in common with the age, he did not show himself espe-

cially scrupulous.   King George, who recalled Wilks
and Mrs. Oldfield in this piece, expressed a curiosity
to see it again, which Garrick accepted as a command.
Some difficulty was experienced in casting the drama,
as Mrs. Cibber, who insisted on taking the second
Constantia, had now grown matronly, and could not
easily be taken for the double of Miss Macklin, who
played the other Constantia.   Wisdom had tardily
come to Garrick, and he bent to the resolution of
the actress, who took the part, played it on the first
night, 7th November, 1754, failed to please the
public, pleaded illness, and on the 4th December
resigned it to another exponent.   Garrick's Don
John was one of the best of his parts, and Mrs.
Clive and Yates, who also appeared, were warmly
praised by Tate Wilkinson.

Dr. Brown's overpraised tragedy of " Barbarossa "
introduced Garrick as Achmet, Mossop as Barbarossa,
Mrs. Cibber as Zaphira, and Miss Macklin as Irene.
This play obtained a conspicuous success, being acted
sixteen times.   Mrs. Cibber, who at this time was
afflicted with a desire to appear in volatile characters,
in which her abilities were lost, created a great sensa-
tion as the heroine.   It was, indeed, grandly acted
throughout.   Mossop, it is stated, was made for
Barbarossa.   Garrick also acted Don Carlos in " The
Mistake."   The outbreak of a war with France led to
the production of Mallet's masque of " Britannia,"
which acquired much popularity and was revived
during subsequent seasons.   In this Garrick took no
part.   He wrote for it, however, a prologue which

he spoke in the character of " a sailor, fuddled and talking to himself." In this production, of which various versions are in print, Mallet had a hand. It is a curious specimen of what has since been called in France Chauvinisme, containing lines such as,—

> " What ! shall we sons of beef and freedom stoop,
> Or lower our flag to slavery and soup ?
> What ! shall these *parly-vous* make such a racket,
> And shall not we, my boys, well trim their jacket ?
> What ! shall Old England be a Frenchman's butt ?
> Whene'er he shuffles we should always cut," etc.

Portions of it are decidedly effective. So popular was Garrick in it that it was called for even when the play was not to be given, and Garrick, when not acting, was obliged to be dressed in order to be prepared to give it.

CHAPTER IX.

GARRICK, it has been said, "dearly loved a lord." There are few men who, having been born in a position of mediocrity and having risen to eminence, have not prized the recognition which rank at one time had it in its power to bestow. The surest way to approach Garrick with a play was through some aristocratic patron. In the case of Lady Coventry, then the reigning beauty of England, who had brought him "Barbarossa," it would have been more than human on Garrick's part to resist. He was, however, too much disposed, even in the management of his theatre, to yield to aristocratic patronage, and the evenings when he was not acting were not seldom spent in the houses of titled folk. His closest association with the art and literature of his time came later in life. He was not a common visitor even at Johnson's, preferring, not without justification, the compliments and homage that he received in his favourite haunts to the ironical and occasionally churlish greeting of his former companion. Quarrels were already beginning to multiply upon his hands, but the period at which they were to influence and sadden his life was not yet reached. His affection for rank gained him the dislike of the coffee-house frequenters of similar tastes who were unable to obtain his privileges.

Garrick, moreover, was not a formidable antagonist. Kind-hearted, timid, vain, conscientious, vacillating, he receded from a position almost as soon as he had occupied it. A stinging epigram might make his assailant wince, but in presence of a front continuously hostile, Garrick receded. His forgiveness was sublime, and the instances in which he benefited those by whom he had been injured were very numerous. To seek the relative proportions of goodness and of weakness in this conduct would be "to consider too curiously." As yet, however, those subsequently to be his bitterest enemies attacked him with moderation or through his company only. Hill, self-styled Sir John, had already begun attacks on Garrick, of which more will be heard anon, and Rich at Covent Garden was making himself disagreeable in more ways than one, especially by setting his actors to mimic Garrick's peculiarities. Strengthened by the accession of Sheridan, Mrs. Woffington, and Miss, or, as she was now called, Mrs. Bellamy, Covent Garden had been able to make a decent show in spite of the secession of Barry, who, with the sanguine faith in himself not uncommon in his profession, had hoped that his desertion of Rich would ruin the fortunes of the theatre.

Meantime at the Haymarket, Miss Barton, subsequently to render Garrick marvellous service as Mrs. Abington, had made an unobtrusive *début*.

With the opening of the season of 1755-56 Garrick found himself the poorer for the loss of Mossop. Early in the season Garrick had a further experience of the capabilities of the British mob. At the production, Saturday, 8th November, of the " Chinese Festival " the occupants of the gallery, undeterred by the presence of the king, by whom the spectacle was commanded, began a riot on account of the engagement of Noverre and other dancers, whom they assumed to be French, but who were in reality Swiss. Foote refers to these in the *Mirror*, and speaks of the patriot gingerbread-baker in the Borough who would not suffer these dancers from Switzerland to appear, because he hated the French. The disturbance was renewed each time that the " Chinese Festival " was represented. Garrick, however, who had, it is said, spent eighteen months in the preparation of the pageant, which had been designed before the outbreak of war, stood to his guns and was supported by the aristocratic patrons of the house. The mob meanwhile, urged on by misrepresentations such as that the dresses were French and so forth, grew unmanageable.

On the 18th matters attained a climax. The gentry in the house drew their swords and stood in defence of the dancers. They were, however, too few to resist the rioters, who bore down all before them and inflicted, it is said, a thousand pounds' worth of damage on the house. Before logic so irrefutable Garrick bowed his head, and the piece was withdrawn. A proposition to sack Garrick's house had been made, and an attempt, fortunately unsuccessful, to carry out the scheme had followed.

A striking scene, described only by Tate Wilkinson, and passed over without notice by both Davies and Murphy, occurred the following Friday. Dressed for Archer, Garrick made his appearance on the stage. His advent brought murmurs of " Pardon! pardon!" On this Garrick advanced to the front and firmly but respectfully explained his views as to the damage in fortune and reputation he had received from the malignancy of individuals. He acknowledged past favours, but declared that " unless he was that night permitted to perform his duty to the best of his ability, he was above want, superior to insult, and would never—never appear on the stage again." While he was giving dignified utterance to these worthy and honourable sentiments the house subsided into complete silence. The justice of what he said carried conviction, and at the close of his speech " they broke," says Wilkinson, " into such an universal applause as shook old Drury."

Garrick's behaviour was admirable. This was, however, the beginning of the defeats that ultimately drove him from the stage. Wholly irresistible and admirably effective is a reconciliation such as this, and the parties to a quarrel are better friends than before. Heroic measures must not, however, be vulgarized, and alternate quarrels and reconciliations pave the way to final separation.

" The Winter's Tale, or Florizel and Perdita," an adaptation by Garrick from Shakespeare, was the first important novelty of the season. This was produced on 21st January, 1756. It is, like other mangled versions of Shakespeare, included in the collected edition of Garrick's works. Under the title of " The Sheep Shearing " a version by MacNamara Morgan had been given at Covent Garden two years previously. Garrick seems to have been spurred by the success of this to his effort. His adaptation is in three acts, and is fully described in Genest's account of the English Stage.

The words are mostly Shakespeare's, but the greater portion of the first three acts is excised. Garrick, who played Leontes, spoke the prologue, which is brisk and sparkling. He talks of his house—

" You cannot miss the sign, 'tis Shakespeare's head,"

and describes the various liquors to be obtained —champaign (*sic*), French brandy, love potions, etc., for various tastes; then continues, turning to the gallery—

" For you, my hearts of oak, for your regale,
    There's good old English stingo mild and stale
        [the latter a dubious recommendation].
    For high, luxurious souls, with luscious smack,
    There's Sir John Falstaff in a butt of sack :
    And if the stronger liquors more invite ye,
    Bardolph is gin, and Pistol aqua-vitæ.
    But should you call for Falstaff, where to find him,
    He's gone—nor left one cup of sack behind him.
    Sunk in his elbow-chair, no more he'll roam ;
    No more with merry wags to Eastcheap come ;
    He's gone to jest, and laugh, and give his sack at home."

The reference to the retirement of Quin, the accepted representative of Falstaff, involved in the last few lines is particularly generous, and shows how little animosity to a defeated foe Garrick bore. The closing lines of the prologue are :—

> "The five long acts from which our three are taken,
> Stretch'd out to sixteen years, lay by, forsaken.
> Lest, then, this precious liquor run to waste,
> 'Tis now confin'd and bottled for your taste.
> 'Tis my chief wish, my joy, my only plan,
> To lose no drop of that immortal man."

For effrontery these last two lines, employed by one who had allowed, in this piece alone, three acts to " run to waste," cannot easily be surpassed. Garrick, however, only followed the example of his predecessors and betters. Dryden, when he mangled " The Tempest," wrote in the prologue the two lines so audacious in expression,—

> "But Shakespeare's magic could not copied be,
> Within that circle none durst walk save he ; "

and Tate and others followed naturally so illustrious an example, and like the somewhat fanciful highwayman of story, robbed with the utmost politeness and with warm expressions of regret. Paltry enough are Garrick's additions to Shakespeare's text. A misquotation by Mrs. Thrale of a line in a song introduced by Garrick and sung by Mrs. Cibber as Perdita, gave rise to one of Johnson's sneers by which Garrick was greatly mortified. One verse of this song, which, by-the-bye, is most probably not

Garrick's at all, having, it is said, been borrowed by
him from MacNamara Morgan's earlier version,
runs thus,—

> " The giant Ambition we never can dread ;
>   Our roofs are too low, for so lofty a head ;
>   Consent and sweet cheerfulness open our door,
>   They smile with the simple and feed with the poor."

Praising to Johnson Garrick's talent for bright gay
poetry, Mrs. Thrale repeated this lyric and dwelt
with special emphasis on the last line, which she
gave,—

> " I'd smile with the simple and feed with the poor."

Whereupon Johnson broke out, " Nay, my dear lady,
this will never do. Poor David! Smile with the
simple ; what folly is that ? And who would feed
with the poor that can help it ? No, no ; let me smile
with the wise and feed with the rich." Boswell then
continues, " I repeated this sally to Garrick, and
wondered to find his sensibility as a writer not a
little irritated by it." If Garrick did not write
the lines, it was not too loyal of him to leave
their authorship unmentioned. Perhaps, however,
he wrote them and gave them to Morgan, whose
play was published in 1754. They have the stamp
of Garrick's mint. Quite excellent appears to
have been the performance. Leontes, though
miserably abridged, supplied Garrick with opportunities of which he availed himself. Mrs. Cibber's
rendering of Perdita, especially as regards her singing,
kept the town talking. Holland, a young actor of

promise, was Florizel. Mrs. Pritchard as Hermione, and Woodward as the clown were much admired, and the Autolicus (*sic*) of Yates was declared unsurpassable.

On the same day, 21st January, 1756, on which this adaptation was given, a second was revived. This was "Catharine and Petruchio," which had been first given 18th March, 1754, for Mrs. Pritchard's benefit. Then, as now, Woodward was the Petruchio, and Yates the Grumio. Mrs. Pritchard, the original Catharine, was now supplanted by Mrs. Clive; of course there was a prologue by Garrick. Genest somewhat incomprehensibly speaks of this with high praise as perhaps the best afterpiece on the stage. It is, in fact, the most contemptible piece of work Garrick has accomplished, and is responsible for most of the indecencies still permitted when "The Taming of the Shrew" is revived. Woodward overacted, humorously enough, in Petruchio, throwing Mrs. Clive down, and being, according to Davies, more wild, extravagant and fantastical than the author designed. The mock quarrel, indeed, seems almost to have ended in a real rumpus. No love was lost between Woodward and the fair Kitty, and his rude treatment of her stirred her to indignation. Tate Wilkinson declares that the behaviour of Mrs. Clive at the close of the second act almost convinced the audience that "Petruchio was not so lordly as he assumed to be, for Mrs. Clive was so enraged at her fall that her talons, tongue and passion were very expressive to the eyes of all beholders; and it was with the utmost difficulty she suppressed her indignation."

An operatic version of the "Tempest," with a singing Prospero played by Beard, was produced on the 11th February. It is certainly Garrick's and is ascribed to him by Theophilus Cibber, who in his dissertation delivered at the Haymarket in 1756, says, " Were Shakespeare's ghost to rise, would he not frown indignation on this pilfering pedlar in poetry, who thus shamefully mangles, mutilates, and emasculates his plays? The 'Midsummer Night's Dream' has been minc'd and fricasseed into a thing called the 'Fairies,' 'The Winter's Tale' mammoc'd into a droll, and the 'Tempest' castrated into an opera."

Cibber's hard words are not unjustified. Garrick had, however, the grace not to claim the piece, or, at least, not to include it with his collected works. He wrote to it, by way of prologue, a dialogue between an actor and a critic.

Dr. Browne's turgid but not wholly ineffective tragedy of "Athelstan" showed Garrick in the part of Athelstan. He also played Don Carlos in "The Mistake," and Leon in "Rule a Wife and have a Wife" by Beaumont and Fletcher, a part in which his command of contrast was finely illustrated, his assumed simplicity and underlying manliness being shown in excellent fashion.

During this season Barry, who had returned from Dublin, once more tried conclusions with Garrick, by appearing at Covent Garden as Lear. Garrick did not shirk the combat. He had indeed no occasion so to do. Those advantages of face and figure which told in Barry's favour in Romeo were of no avail in Lear, and when it came to acting, Garrick in theatrical slang could act Barry's "head off." Two well-known epigrams remain to attest the interest taken in the struggle; one is—

ON THE TWO LEARS.
"The town has found out different ways
To praise the different Lears;
To Barry they give loud huzzas,
To Garrick only tears."

The second is—

"A king—*aye, every inch a king,*
Such Barry doth appear;
But Garrick's quite a different thing;
He's every inch King Lear."

Theophilus Cibber dealing with the latter owns it is "a pretty conceit," but questions its truth, affirming that Barry beside the loud huzzas never failed to draw a homage of tears. Theophilus Cibber was indeed one of the many hornets who were buzzing round Garrick's ears. These were at this time commencing to swarm. The most persevering of their number was Dr. or Sir John Hill, whose attacks succeeded more than once in wounding Garrick through his ill-worn armour of indifference. Hill was far from a contemptible opponent. He had, however, so many enemies that he could scarcely bestow on Garrick his undivided attention. He was a voluminous writer, and was the author of one book at least concerning which much is heard,

" Mrs. Glasse's Cookery Book," which does or does not contain the memorable advice " First catch your hare." Walpole a little later (3rd January, 1761) speaks of Hill as earning fifteen guineas a week by writing for wholesale dealers, and says he was once employed on six voluminous works of botany, husbandry, etc., published weekly. Among other things he had been an actor. The *Gentleman's Magazine* says that " he acted pantomime, tragedy, and comedy, and was damned in all." Hill made at least three attacks, or what were construed into such, upon Garrick. In a paper which he published, called *The Inspector*, he sounded the praises of Barry at the expense of Garrick, which was of course high treason. Churchill had not yet written the " Rosciad," in which besides praising Garrick he attacked his enemies, and Garrick undertook his own defence. He wrote three satires against Hill, two of them passable enough, but the third clever and pungent :

> " For Farces and Physic his equal there scarce is ;
> His Farces are Physic, his Physic a Farce is."

Hill published, in 1759, two letters to Garrick, one of which he disowned. The second was " To David Garrick, Esq., the petition of I—in behalf of herself and her sisters." From this it appears that Garrick in common with almost all tragedians made havoc with the vowels. Murphy, whose plays Garrick produced and who subsequently became his biographer, took up the cudgels on Garrick's behalf, and used them against all comers. "The Spouter, or the Triple Revenge," a two act farce by Murphy, not owned by him nor included in the collection of his dramatic works, made mirth of Foote, Hill, Rich, and Theophilus Cibber. Garrick, who had a hand in it, in his customary fashion aimed some harmless ridicule at himself. Murphy follows his example and makes one of his characters say, "Ay! that was wrote by M—phy. He's the damn'dest actor, and the damn'dest author. I wonder he'd think of writing such damn'd stuff as that 'Apprentice' (a farce played in the present season) * * * Dapperwit's another fool to think of writing, tho' he's a better writer than M—phy. M—phy's an idiot." Dapperwit is Foote, whom Murphy had every justification for attacking, since Foote had robbed him in the most shameless and cowardly fashion.

To this period belongs a very characteristic and pleasing letter to Hogarth :—

DEAR HOGARTH,

Our friend Wilson hinted to me the last time I saw him, that I had of late been remiss in my visits to you—it may be so, though upon my word I am not conscious of it; for such ceremonies I look upon as mere counters, where there is no remission of regard and good wishes. As Wilson is not an accurate observer of things, not even of those which concern him most, I must imagine that the hint came from you, and therefore, I shall say a word or two to you upon it.

Montaigne, who was a good judge of human nature, takes notice that when friends grow exact and ceremonious, it is a certain sign of coolness, for that the spirit of friendship keeps no account of trifles. We are, I hope, a strong exception to this rule. Poor Draper, whom I loved better than any man breathing, once asked me smiling, " How long is it, think you, since you were at my house ? " " How long? why, a month or six weeks." " A year and five days," replied he ; " but don't imagine that I have kept an account ; my wife told me so this morning, and bid me *scold you for it*." If Mrs. Hogarth has observed my neglect, I am flattered by it ; but if it is your observation, woe betide you ! Could I follow my own wishes, I would see you every day in the week, and not care whether it was in Leicester Fields or Southampton Street; but what with an indifferent state of health, and the care of a large family,[1] in which there are many froward children, I have scarce half-an-hour to myself.

However, since you are grown a polite devil, and have a mind to play at lords and ladies, have at you. I will certainly call upon you soon ; and if you should not be at home, I will leave my card.

Dear Hogarth,

Yours most sincerely,

D. GARRICK.

About this time his carefully preserved correspondence practically begins. Warburton, subsequently Bishop of Gloucester, opens out an animated series of letters. Murphy writes epistles now petulant, again flattering if not subservient.

Garrick's Juliet, upon opening the season of 1756-57, was Miss Pritchard, a lovely girl who seemed an ideal exponent, and whose mother supported her as Lady Capulet. An affecting scene is chronicled by Wilkinson, but the young actress disappointed the hopes that she had raised. Mossop

---

[1] Drury Lane Theatre.

had rejoined the company. Some restorations from Shakespeare were made in " Lear," and Garrick took for the first time what has been thought his greatest comic part, Don Felix, in " The Wonder " of Mrs. Centlivre, a part he subsequently chose for his farewell to the stage. This was the only character that he added that season to his repertory. He was once or twice attacked by illness, and left the principal parts in tragedy to Mossop. Foote also reappeared in his own play " The Author," in which he satirized a Mr. Apreece, who, having influence at Court, obtained from the Lord Chamberlain the suppression of the piece. Garrick produced, 3rd December, 1756, his own " Lilliput," a one act piece extracted from Gulliver, and played by children. On the 24th March was seen " The Male Coquette " of Garrick, at first called " The Modern Fine Gentleman." The trifle was planned, written, and produced, within a month, no very difficult task, says Genest, seeing that some features of the character of the hero, Daffodil, are stolen from Captain Spark, in the " Universal Gallant " of Fielding. Woodward, to whom Garrick gave the play, acted it for his benefit, and was unsurpassed as the hero. In his own play of " Lethe," which he revived, Garrick introduced and played the character of Lord Chalkstone.

" Reprisal, or the Tars of England," a farce satirizing keenly the French, served to heal a long existing feud between Smollett, its author, and Garrick. In " Roderick Random " and " Peregrine Pickle " Smollett had fustigated Garrick unsparingly. His

" Reprisal" was a success.   Some mistake was made in the terms charged him on the performance for his benefit, and Garrick wrote a corroboratory letter which throws some light on the management of the theatre.   It is dated November 26th, 1757, and is as follows :—

> SIR,—There was a mistake made by our office keepers to your prejudice, which has given me much uneasiness. Though the expense of our theatre every night amounts to 90*l.* and upwards, yet we take no more from gentlemen, who write for the theatre, and who produce an original performance, than sixty guineas ; they who alter only an old play, pay eighty guineas for the expense, as in the instance of " Amphitryon."   This occasioned the mistake, which I did not discover till lately.   Though it is very reasonable to take fourscore pounds for the expense of the house, yet as we have not yet regulated this matter I cannot possibly agree that Dr. Smollett shall be the first precedent.   I have enclosed a draught upon Mr. Clutterbuck for the sum due to you.
>
> I am, most sincerely,
>
> > Your most obedient humble servant,
> >
> > > D. GARRICK.

This substantial amount touched to the quick Smollett, who in his reply declared that, in what he had published concerning him in his account of the liberal arts, he had spoken the language of his heart, and that he could not in such a part of his work forbear doing justice to a genius who had no rival. Besides, he thought it actually incumbent on him to make a public atonement " in a *work of truth* for the wrongs done him in a work of fiction."   " Blessed are the peacemakers ! "

At Covent Garden meanwhile one unsuccessful experiment succeeded another, a matter over which Garrick may be forgiven for chuckling. After failing as Demetrius in "The Humorous Lieutenant," Barry essayed Richard III. and broke completely down. His Richard indeed served only as a foil to that at Drury Lane. As Norval in "Douglas" he looked too virile, and Mrs. Woffington as Lady Randolph failed to please. To Covent Garden must be assigned the credit of having produced "Douglas" in London after it had been offered to Garrick and refused. Gray's praise of this tragedy is excessive. He says in a letter to Walpole, "I am greatly struck with 'Douglas,' the author seems to me to have retrieved the true language of the stage, which has been lost for these 100 years; and there is one scene (between Lady Randolph and the stranger) so masterly, that it strikes me blind to all its defects." David Hume, it is known, thought it superior to Shakespeare. Garrick's reasons for rejecting the piece which came from Edinburgh with the cachet of success have been much canvassed. Murphy seemed to think them inscrutable. Genest, however, furnishes a reason for his rejection of both "Douglas" and Dodsley's "Cleone," namely, that let Garrick play what part he would, Mrs. Cibber would certainly have beaten him out of the field. Genest also misquotes from a letter of Victor to Mrs. Griffiths, "As to Mr. Garrick, the tragedy must be a capital one, and a character in it amazingly striking, and that stands forth from the rest, that he takes to himself. We had a tragedy this winter, " Hecuba, from a fellow of one of the colleges at Cambridge, and excellent good writing, but as the subject was a bad one (!) and no character for him, it died silently away and the author, I dare-say, got little or no profit by it. . . . I had rather have a tragedy, at this juncture, acted in Dublin than in London without Mr. Garrick, it would be better supported and performed at Barry's theatre." Garrick's reluctance to appear in plays such as "Hecuba" or "Douglas" is comprehensible enough when the motive of the "leading actor" is taken into account. He regretted more than once his niceness when he saw the tide of carriages rolling to Covent Garden. Before the close of the season Mrs. Woffing-ton retired under very dramatic circumstances. She had been ill while acting Rosalind in "As You Like It," May 3rd, 1757, and had succeeded in reaching the epilogue when her voice broke, she faltered, endea-voured to go on, but could not proceed, she screamed out in a voice of tremor and tottered to the door (query wing rather), where she was caught; "the audience of course applauded till she was out of sight, and then sunk into awful looks of astonish-ment, at seeing a favourite actress struck so suddenly by the hand of death, for so it seemed, in such a situation of time and place." She was then but forty-four and lived till 1760, but only as a skeleton. So vanished Garrick's first stage love, "the most beautiful woman, perhaps," says Tate Wilkinson, "that had ever appeared on the stage," a generous woman, a conscientious artist, and one of the most popular creatures that ever faced the footlights. She left behind her no equal in an entire range of characters, and especially in what were known as " breeches parts," such as Sir Harry Wildair, in which neither Garrick nor Woodward could approach her.

On the 22nd of December, 1757, Garrick produced his adaptation of the " Gamester " of Shirley which he called " The Gamesters." In this he took the character of the hero, young Wilding, who is a gambler, though not the chief representative of the vice. He also supplied a rhymed prologue of no special merit. In his preface Garrick refers to an earlier alteration made by Charles Johnson, produced in 1711, and called " The Wife's Relief." From this piece he has, he boasts, taken nothing, on which one of his critics with more truth than good nature observed that he would have much improved his adaptation if he had. Though far from the best of Garrick's plays, it is fairly spirited. Garrick has indeed animal spirits and appropriateness of speech that recall Colley Cibber and all but do duty for wit. It is amusing to find him printing, as his own, works which he has simply adapted and in part marred. His additions to Shirley are contemptible enough. In the preface, however, he speaks of the whole with a " pride that mocks humility " and with a sincerity of conviction that he is a fine fellow which takes away the reader's breath.

" Agis " by Home was the next novelty. In producing this piece Garrick made mute confession of the error he had committed in refusing " Douglas." It is said, probably with truth, to have been written before that now famous work. As Gray's opinion on " Douglas " has been given, that he expressed upon " Agis " may be read. He says, " I cry to think that it should be by the author of ' Douglas :' why, it is all modern Greek ; the story is an antique statue painted white and red, frizzed, and dressed in a négligé made by a Yorkshire mantua-maker." Garrick did his best to elevate the piece into a success. He introduced " pompous and solemn musical processions " and cast the play with the whole strength of his company. He was himself Lysander, Mossop was Agis, Mrs. Cibber Euanthe, Mrs. Pritchard Agesistrata, and Mrs. Yates Sandane, other parts being assigned to Havard, Holland, and Davies. Home had by this time an influential following. The piece accordingly ran for eleven nights before descending into the limbo of oblivion. It was never, so far as records extend, revived in London.

In a revival of the second part of " King Henry IV." Garrick appeared for the first time as the king to the Falstaff of Woodward. Garrick's figure was un-suited to the character, but " the forcible expression of his countenance and his energy of utterance made ample amends for the defects of his person."

Murphy's farce of " The Upholsterer " enjoyed the rarely accorded honour of being acted so as to please a morbidly sensitive author. Murphy records that " Garrick as Pamphlet, Woodward as the Barber, Yates as Quidnunc, and Mrs. Clive as Slipslop, were sufficient to give celebrity to the piece. A farce so completely acted was never seen before or since."

Murphy's farce is principally taken from the "Coffee-house Politician" of Fielding, produced twenty-eight years earlier. For the season 1757-8, Garrick altered "The Fatal Marriage" of Southerne, published in Garrick's works under the title of "Isabella, or the Fatal Marriage." He omitted all the characters of the comic underplot, justifying this course on the ground that they were not only indelicate but immoral. In the advertisement to the printed edition he makes the somewhat bold statement that the mixed drama of the last age called tragicomedy has been generally condemned by the critic. The close of the advertisement is, "When the passions are violent and speeches long, the performers must either spare their powers or shorten their speeches. Mrs. Cibber chose the latter; by which she has been able to exert that force and expression which has been so strongly felt, and so sincerely applauded." Not exactly a left-handed compliment is this, but it is not wholly convincing. Garrick played Biron, and Mrs. Cibber Isabella, the piece being acted fourteen times.

At the close of the season Garrick lost Woodward, who went to Ireland to join Barry in an ill-starred experiment in Dublin. Woodward, who was valued and occasionally consulted by Garrick, and who was paid a salary larger than any actor in his line had then received, hesitated about taking his departure and offered to stay upon a "consideration" which

Garrick was justified in refusing. Garrick owned his merits, but would make no further advance. Barry, of whom Rich said that he could wheedle a bird from the tree and squeeze it to death in his hand, at length succeeded in beguiling Woodward away. Theophilus Cibber, one of the most inveterate foes of Garrick and the husband of Mrs. Cibber, died in 1758, being drowned in October on his way to Dublin.

CHAPTER X.

To compensate so far as possible for the loss of Woodward, Garrick made one or two new engagements. The first was Fleetwood, a son of the late manager of Drury Lane, who appeared 28th September, 1758, as Romeo, and created a favourable impression, which was not maintained, and who two years later retreated to Ireland. A more important engagement was that of O'Brien, the son of a fencing master, who made his début, 3rd October, as Brazen, in the "Recruiting Officer." In the tuition of this youth Garrick took much pains, and the pupil, thanks to youth, ease and grace of manner, and firmness of style, rose to a position of high favour. For some years he played with conspicuous success, then made an aristocratic marriage, and retired from, and, so far as he was able, repudiated the stage.

A few days later, Foote, accompanied by Tate Wilkinson, the two "exotics" as Garrick called them, appeared in "The Diversions of the Morning," a two act farce by Foote, of which one act was extracted from his own comedy of "Taste," while the second, subsequently altered, was a piece of the "Rehearsal" class, in which imitations of various known actors were given, including a parody of the instruction of Barry in Othello by Macklin. Wilkinson, who in mimicry seems to have been scarcely inferior to Foote, and was known as Foote's pupil, gave imitations of Sparks, Barry, and other actors, and even of Foote, who, at the first mention of Wilkinson's attempts at a parody of himself, uttered violent threats. The success of the entertainment was complete, and the house was nightly crowded. Once more, however, Garrick learnt how sensitive an actor is to anything in the shape of ridicule, and found himself on the horns of a dilemma, with a public insisting on its entertainment, and a company threatening mutiny. Sparks was especially aggrieved, and remonstrated so seriously with Garrick that the imitations, to the great mortification of Wilkinson, were prohibited; Mrs. Clive also rebuked the mimic with far more vigour and feeling, than propriety of language. Wilkinson's cause had powerful advocates in the public, which, disappointed of the promised sport, began a riot. Garrick then changed his plan, and with commendable self-suppression, offered himself as a subject for mimicry, *pour encourager les autres.* His offer was embraced, and Wilkinson included the manager among his victims. How Garrick was treated is not very clear, but a feud between him and Wilkinson followed.

Feuds and difficulties of many kinds had, indeed, begun to beset Garrick. A quarrel with Smollett was happily over, and the recorded opinion of the historian made full amends for the libel on Marmozet, as Garrick was called in "Roderick Random," and for the accusation that he was a parasite "chiefly courted for his buffoonery." In his history Smollett leaves on record that "the exhibitions of the stage were improved to the most exquisite entertainment by the talents and management of Garrick, who greatly surpassed all his predecessors of this, and perhaps every other nation, in his genius for acting, in the sweetness and variety of his tones, the irresistible magic of his eye, the fire and vivacity of his action, the elegance of his attitude, and the whole pathos of expression." Foote even had been in a sense placated. There was no open quarrel. Behind Garrick's back he indulged in constant aspersions, and even to his face he never neglected bringing, with affected bonhomie, the most stinging and venomous accusations. To what extent the charge of parsimoniousness brought against Garrick rests on the stories or witticisms of Foote, can scarcely be judged. It is at least certain that Foote lost no opportunity of making Garrick wince, in whatever company he might find him.

For one enemy that was disarmed, however, three sprang up fully accoutred. Another phase of Sir John Hill's evil disposition was this season to be exhibited.

Before dealing with this, it is necessary to chronicle an attempt of Garrick to rival Woodward. Marplot was a character in which Woodward stood pre-eminent. In the hope to eclipse his deserter Garrick took the part himself. In this attempt he failed. Woodward was able to put on a countenance

so vacant, that all the mischief caused by his interference in the affairs of others seemed the result of
accident.   Garrick, on the contrary, seemed too in-
telligent, and charged the character with so much
intention, that he seemed mischievous or malignant,
rather than stupid.

With a performance of " Zara " for the benefit of
the Lying-In Hospital was coupled the first representation of " The Rout," a farce which was
announced as by a person of quality.   It was· a poor
piece, and the fact that it was by Hill having leaked
out, the enemies of that strange mixture of conceit
and quackery soon drove it from the stage.   Hill
elected to believe that the hand of Garrick was
traceable in this, and the newspaper attacks in which
Hill had previously indulged, recommenced.   Finding
that kindness was wasted on a man of this stamp,
Garrick answered him with his own weapons, and
ultimately drove him from the field.   During this
same month of December, " Cleone," by Dodsley,
was given at Covent Garden, with a success, the chief
responsibility for which is claimed by Mrs. Bellamy.
The fact that the piece had been, for reasons already
indicated, refused by Garrick, had the effect of
enlisting its author in the hostile ranks.

Garrick's next new assumption was Antony, in
" Antony and Cleopatra." This performance has
special interest, seeing that it is the only representation of Shakespeare's play which Genest, in a
chronicle extending from 1660 to 1830, is able
to report.   So popular was " All for Love," an

alteration, for such it must be considered, by Dryden, that it has held from the Restoration, until far into this century, possession, all but undisputed, of the stage. Counsellors are not wanting even now to recommend the substitution of this, Dryden's dramatic masterpiece, for a play of Shakespeare that has rarely held an audience, and has come to be regarded as a vehicle for pageantry. Other adaptations have also been seen. Garrick produced, however, what purported to be Shakespeare's play, and to so much credit he is entitled. No alterations were made except excisions, which were perhaps too numerous.

Not specially strong was the cast, since, except Garrick as Antony, Tate Wilkinson as Canidius, Davies as Eros, Mrs. Yates as Cleopatra, and Miss Hippisley as Charmian, few of the names would now be recognized. New scenery, dresses and decorations were accorded the piece. Its reception can scarcely have answered expectation, since it ran for only six nights.

Garrick next ventured upon an adaptation of his own, in " The Guardian," 3rd February, 1759, a two act comedy extracted avowedly from " La Pupille " of M. Fagan, which Garrick declares is, according to Voltaire and other writers, the most complete *petite pièce* on the French stage. This is not the exact truth. " La Pupille " of Fagan, produced at the Théâtre Français, 5th July, 1734, with music by Mouret, is a one act piece, the idea of which is taken from " L'École des Maris." Garrick owes, however, something to Fagan, and has written a sprightly comedy, which just misses the tenderness of the original. He played Heartly the Guardian, the Ariste of the French piece ; Miss Pritchard was the heroine, and Mrs. Clive, Lucy, her maid.

An altered version of Mallet's tragedy of " Eurydice " followed, Garrick playing Periander, and Mrs. Cibber Eurydice. It was not a success, being acted but four times.

Among those by whom Garrick's peace of mind was at this time most disturbed, was Arthur Murphy, the dramatist. An Irishman, educated at St. Omer, Murphy, though not yet thirty, had had a fairly varied experience. He had tried trade and banking, and had wearied of both, had edited for nearly two years a paper called *The Gray's Inn Journal*, had played tragedy at both the patent houses, and had at length satisfied himself that he could not act. He had then become a political journalist, and after having vainly applied to the Middle and Inner Temple to admit him as a barrister, and being rejected on account of having been an actor, had at length been admitted at Gray's Inn. His chief aim of late had been to obtain success as a dramatist, and with this view he pestered Garrick continuously. It was presumably as a matter of precaution that Garrick preserved the correspondence inflicted upon him. Vain, querulous, petulant, persistent, tricky, Murphy seems to have tried alternate cajolery and menace, or something not far short. Among the pieces which he had shown Garrick, who had already produced a trifle from his pen, was "The Orphan of China," a tragedy drawn principally from "L'Orphelin de la Chine" of Voltaire, but owing something, it is said, to the "Heraclius" of Corneille.

In this play Garrick failed to find anything worthy of his attention. To the protests and overtures of Murphy he remained obdurate, declaring it totally unfit for the stage. Murphy was now one of his declared enemies. At a later date he makes a grudging concession. "A young author could not easily submit to what he thought an act of injustice (!) Perhaps he swelled with too much pride. When he looked back to his own conduct on the occasion, he was willing to pass a censure on himself; but, being encouraged by two friends, on whose judgment and integrity he had great reliance, he began a paper-war. He knew that anxiety for his fame was the manager's reigning foible; on the slightest attack, he was tremblingly alive all o'er. The writer took advantage of that failing, and opened a fierce campaign."

Murphy puts himself out of court by this avowal. He knew too well, however, Garrick's weakness, and the means by which he tried to secure his ends were ingenious. Garrick had met with unruffled serenity the petulance of his correspondent, who wrote now in the first person, now in the third, and addressed Garrick as Sir or Dear Sir, according to the mood of the hour.

When thoroughly roused Garrick could write a manly letter, witness his reply to Dodsley, which, though out of place, may here be given :—

"MASTER ROBERT DODSLEY,—When I first read your peevish answer to my well-meant proposal to you, I was much disturbed at it—but when I considered, that some minds cannot bear the smallest portion of success, I most sincerely pitied you : and when I found in the same letter, that you were graciously pleased to dismiss me from your acquaintance, I could not but confess so apparent an obligation, and am, with due acknowledgments,

"Master Robert Dodsley,

"Your most obliged,

"DAVID GARRICK."

To Murphy, of whose abilities he had a higher estimate, he wrote in milder terms, but still with sufficient vigour and point. In what he labels as "an answer of mine to a wrangling letter," he says to Murphy :—

"As I have really no time, health or inclination, to continue these illiberal wranglings, I hope you will excuse me if I am silent henceforth. I can do no more. I should be very sorry to be forced into any future alter-cation, but if I am called upon so loudly that I must answer, I shall give a plain and just account of our transactions, supported only by undeniable testimonies. Among these I flatter myself that Mr. Murphy will appear in the defence of

"Your obedient, humble servant,

"DAVID GARRICK."

At another period he accepted what seems to be a severance of all ties. This did not suit Murphy, who sought to utilize Garrick, and when away from the hostile influence exercised by his countrymen, had intervals of reason.

According to his own account Murphy had influence enough to induce Fox and Walpole to read his "Orphan of China" and espouse his interests. When dining accordingly at Holland House, Garrick was surprised to hear both Fox and Walpole quote lines from the work. Upon his expression of surprise he was greeted by both with declarations of their admiration for it. Knowing the value of such testimony, Garrick redemanded it and returned it with an expression of his intention to play it next year. He still did not like it. After interminable jangling the piece was submitted to the arbitration of Paul Whitehead, who decided in its favour.

On the 21st April, 1759, "The Orphan of China" was produced. Garrick, who had behaved throughout with commendable magnanimity, and had assisted Murphy with loans of money, acted the part of Zamti the hero. Mandane, his wife, was allotted to Mrs. Cibber, who was unable to play it. The part accordingly was taken by Mrs. Yates, whose reputation it was the means of making. It was a fair success, running for nine nights and being subsequently revived with alterations, but was scarcely worthy of the pother it had caused.

During this season died Mrs. Macklin, unequalled as the Nurse in "Romeo and Juliet," and the Hostess in "King Henry V.," and at its close Mossop finally abandoned Drury Lane. The Drury Lane company was, however, strengthened by the return of King, an admirable comedian, who for ten years had been in Ireland, and by that of Moody, whose first appearance was made as King Henry VIII. Before the season of 1759-60 was over Macklin reappeared.

The first important novelty caused a scrimmage in the theatre, and was the means of bringing about an important reformation in the economy of the stage. This was the production of the famous farce, still occasionally acted, of " High Life below Stairs," at first popularly ascribed to Garrick, but now finally assigned the Rev. James Townley. In the presentation of this the whole comic strength of the company with the exception of the manager was included, the cast comprising Mrs. Clive, Mrs. Abington and Mrs. Bradshaw; O'Brien, Palmer, King, Yates, Packer and Moody. At this time what was called the Footman's Gallery was open gratis to the attendants upon the gentlemen present.

Almost as indignant as the tailors proved themselves when the dignity of their order was assailed on the stage, were these " domestics " at the satire upon their proceedings. On the second night accordingly Love, one of their leaders, came forward and read a letter charged with violent menaces against the actors and the house in case the impertinent production were repeated. So soon as the farce began, a prodigious uproar was heard from the gallery. In the end, the masters and other visitors to the theatre went into the gallery and bundled the malcontents into the streets. The scene is said to have caused the abolition of the privilege that had been abused.

Since he had had to encounter more formidable

opposition, Garrick had abandoned the system of not acting until late in the season. He had thus been seen in many parts before, on the 1st December, 1759, he appeared for the first time as Oroonoko, in an alteration by Dr. Hawkesworth of Southerne's play of that name. Hawkesworth's changes consisted principally of omissions, the whole of the low comedy scenes having been excised. His additions were few and unimportant, and the new version was decidedly inferior to the old. A notice of this play in the *Critical Review* was written by Dr. Johnson. It is a not very convincing apology for the adapter with a prophecy of improvement in subsequent work.

Macklin, who reappeared as Shylock, gave also for the first time his "Love à la Mode," in which he exhibited his famous performance of Sir Archy Mac Sarcasm. A pantomime entitled, "Harlequin's Invasion," *i.e.* his invasion of Parnassus and the territory of Shakespeare, is ascribed to Garrick. It long held possession of the stage, but has not been printed.

Two pieces by Murphy, the production of which was necessarily prefaced by a long and childish correspondence, were given on the same night, 24th January, 1760. "The Desert Island" is a dramatic poem in three acts, the story of which is borrowed from Metastasio. "The Way to Keep Him" is a comedy in three acts, in which Garrick appeared in the principal character, that of Lovemore. In the following season it was enlarged into five acts

according to the author's original plan.   This is a
fairly creditable comedy, preaching the lesson that a
wife should take as much pains to preserve a husband
as to gain him.   " La Nouvelle École des Femmes,"
of Moissy, produced a couple of years previously at
the Théâtre Italien, of which it became one of the
most approved and favourite pieces, supplied Murphy
with the idea which Moissy in turn had drawn from
a tale in the fourth volume of "Amusemens du
Cœur et de l'Esprit."

Home's third dramatic experiment, "The Siege of
Aquileia," was given on the 21st February, 1760,
Garrick appearing in the character of Æmilius, a
Roman consul of the stamp of Brutus.   It is a
dull tragedy, gloomy and depressing throughout.
The liberties it took with history were condemned
in its own day, while its observance of the unities
was lauded.   With its merits and defects alike subsequent times have declined to concern themselves,
and Home's dramatic baggage consists only of
"Douglas."   Garrick then produced but did not
play in Mrs. Clive's comedy of "Every Woman
in her Humour."   In connection with this piece one
or two stories illustrating the weaker aspects of
Garrick's character are told.   Austin, who was cast
for a part, did not appear, and greatly to Mrs. Clive's
annoyance his rôle had to be read.   Garrick took the
matter also in dudgeon, and gave the absent actor
a severe "wigging."   So indispensable was Austin,
however, that Garrick soon reinstated him in favour.
Tate Wilkinson says that Austin's services were

unremunerated, beyond his being occasionally seen walking with Garrick arm-in-arm in the street. When Garrick cast him once for a rôle which he judged unworthy Austin obtained a suit all but identical with that Garrick was going to wear. A comparison, greatly to his disadvantage, between his own figure and that of Austin, induced Garrick to comply with the actor's wish and let him off the part. Garrick spoke during the season one or two of his prologues, and was seen on what appears to have been a solitary occasion as Sir Harry Gubbin in "The Tender Husband" of Steele.

Unable to cope with the opposition against him in Dublin, Sheridan returned to London. Garrick, who recognized his value, though he personally disliked him, and owned that after Barry, Sheridan was the most useful assistant he had ever known, at once secured him on the condition of sharing on the nights on which Sheridan performed. This engagement was loyally carried out, and Garrick resigned to his associate many of his best parts. Nature had not been altogether generous in dealing with Sheridan, whose physical gifts were not remarkable. So conscientious and assiduous was he that he surmounted all difficulties, and the performances of the new comer were followed with scarcely less attention than those of the manager. Among the parts assigned Sheridan, were Hamlet, Cato and Lord Townly. Soon after his accession, George the Third ordered "King John," in which Sheridan played the King and Garrick Faulconbridge.

Once more, if reports are to be trusted, "the fat was in the fire." The King approved of Sheridan, but thought that Faulconbridge was open to improvement. Garrick, of course, heard of the royal criticism and was hurt. The run of the piece was accordingly stopped, though seats had been taken in advance. Murphy says that Mrs. Cibber as Constance eclipsed them both. Genest, while accepting as true Murphy's eulogy, points out that she was not, at the time, in the cast. Garrick's failure as Faulconbridge was the more galling as he had used a good deal of diplomacy to induce Sheridan, who elected to play Faulconbridge, to substitute for it the King.

Two characters only, Oakly in the "Jealous Wife," and Mercutio, were added to Garrick's repertory during the season (1760—1761). The season was not, however, uneventful. "Polly Honeycombe," the first farce written by George Colman without assistance, was produced, as was "The Enchanter, or Love and Magic," a musical sketch ascribed to Garrick.

Henry Brooke's "Earl of Essex," an historical play first produced in Dublin, was given, doubtless at the instance of Sheridan, who played Essex. It was acted nine times. The play is only noteworthy as having given rise to one of Johnson's well-known jokes. Praising Brooke's play in the presence of Johnson, Sheridan quoted the concluding speech of the first act:—

> "I shall henceforth seek
> For other lights to truth, for righteous monarchs,

Justly to judge, with their own eyes should see,
To rule o'er freemen should themselves be free."

Whereupon Johnson, dissenting from the admiration generally expressed, observed that it might as well be said,—

" Who drives fat oxen should himself be fat."

The line thus parodied disappeared from the following edition. Dr. Hawkesworth's fairy play, " Edgar and Emmeline," produced 31st January, 1761, showed to advantage O'Brien and Mrs. Yates. Other novelties of no general importance were given, and Foote made occasional appearances at Drury Lane. At Covent Garden Tate Wilkinson imitated Foote and other actors. Garrick overheard a further imitation of himself, and was so offended that he never addressed Wilkinson again.

It is convenient, though not in strict chronological order, to deal with the two following seasons at Drury Lane, which saw the full development of Garrick's repertory, and ended with his first temporary withdrawal from the stage.

On September 30th, 1761, Garrick produced " Henry VIII." with a coronation spectacle. Coronation scenes were given at both houses. That at Covent Garden, a very gorgeous affair, in which Mrs. Bellamy walked on as the Queen, was included in a representation of " King Henry V." Garrick's show was by comparison pitiful. It included a real bonfire upon the stage by the fumes from which the actors were almost suffocated, and which was in the end omitted, owing to the hostile demonstrations it elicited from the public. Garrick's first important production consisted of his own version of " Cymbeline," one of the most respectable of his adaptations of Shakespeare. In this Garrick played Posthumus, which proved one of his greatest parts. This piece, the alterations in which, according to Garrick's own avouch, consist all but wholly of omissions, is yet printed in what claim to be Garrick's dramatic works. Francis Gentleman, the author of " The Dramatic Censor," has a long description of " Cymbeline " as altered by Garrick, which might earn him a niche in the Temple of Dulness. Garrick speaks of him with profound and justifiable contempt as a " dirty dedicating knave." His time was, indeed, largely occupied in attacking Garrick and sponging upon him. At this moment it is his cue to praise, and he speaks with some warmth of the Posthumus, and says that Garrick's " astonishing talents were never more happily exerted." Those who succeeded him, including Powell, whom Garrick himself promoted to the part, and Reddish, served, according to Gentleman, only as foils.

" The School for Lovers " of the laureate Whitehead was given 10th February, 1762. This is a sentimental and pleasing, but rather heavy and lackadaisical comedy, avowedly taken from " Le Testament " of Fontenelle, a piece not intended for the stage, which puzzled the critics and bored the public. Garrick played Sir John Dorilant, a very lively and self-sacrificing gentleman, and Mrs. Cibber.

who was fifty years of age, won something more than acceptance as a girl of seventeen.

" The Musical Lady," a two act comedy which by Garrick's counsel Colman took from the underplot he had intended for " The Jealous Wife," followed. Garrick's interlude " The Farmer's Return from London " showed him as the farmer, the only other new character he took during the season. It was very popular. An excellent print of Garrick in this character from a painting by Zoffany, was published in 1766.

A favourite scheme with Garrick had been to get rid of the visitors and loiterers on the stage, by whom the action of the drama was impeded, and whose presence was a scandal as well as a nuisance.

Many stories as to the abuses resulting from this practice are current. One which, if it depended only on the testimony of Tate Wilkinson, a man of lively imagination, might be treated as fanciful, is corroborated by Davies. Holland was playing Hamlet, when a sudden gust of wind in the ghost scene blew off his hat. A young lady on the stage felt for the actor thus exposed to " a nipping and an eager air," and seizing the hat stepped gingerly up to Holland and clapped it on. Unfortunately, not being used to that portion of masculine attire, she placed it in a rakish and drunken fashion, with the wrong end foremost, upon the pre-occupied actor's head. Upon the effect of an experiment of this kind it is needless to comment.

Opposition to Garrick's scheme of reformation

was not confined to the idle or dissolute, who resented the loss of a privilege that brought them into proximity with the actresses. Actors themselves found on benefit nights their receipts augmented from those on the stage, and were reluctant to forfeit a source of income. During the summer of 1762 accordingly, Garrick, after a long consultation with his partner Lacy, enlarged the house until the receipts in the portion properly belonging to the audience came to £335, which was as much as the previous house, stage and all, could yield. This important reformation, due to the actor's self-respect, was carried out with less difficulty than had been anticipated, and was shortly afterwards adopted at Covent Garden.

It was from another source, as will shortly be seen, that opposition was to come. When the theatre opened in September, 1762, the company had been once more strengthened, the additions including Jackson, subsequently manager of the Edinburgh theatre and historian of the Scottish stage; William Parsons, a thin and asthmatical man, but a good comedian; and Love, otherwise Dance, actor and dramatist, formerly acting manager in Edinburgh. After producing Shakespeare's " Two Gentlemen of Verona," as altered by Benjamin Victor, in which he did not appear, and a pantomime, Garrick gave, 19th January, 1763, the " Elvira " of David Mallet or Malloch, whom Johnson immortalized in his Dictionary under " Alias," which he defined, " A Latin word signifying otherwise; as Mallet, *alias*

Malloch, that is *otherwise* Malloch." Dennis, angered at Mallet's declamations against Christianity, played on the name, and called him Moloch; and Pope, declining his partisanship, had quoted concerning him Falstaff's words as to Poins, "Hang him, baboon! his wit is as thick as Tewkesbury mustard; there is no more conceit in him than in a Mallet." Mallet had his friends, however; Gibbon watched the rehearsals of his play, and wrote a fairly eulogistic criticism upon it. A political significance was assigned it, the author being supposed to be adulating Lord Bute, and it was consequently unpopular.

Murphy declares it to have been foisted on Garrick in a not very creditable way, Mallet promising to bring into a life of Marlborough, for which he was paid, and of which he wrote not a word, some flattering reference to the actor. It is a translation of the "Inès de Castro" of La Motte, produced 6th April, 1723, at the Théâtre Français. This French piece, written in execrable verse, enjoyed great popularity, but was very roughly treated by the critics. After listening incognito to the censures passed upon it at the Café Procope, La Motte said to a friend, "Allons donc nous encourager à la soixante-douzième représentation de cette mauvaise pièce." Another story concerning it worthy of preservation is that La Motte, who preferred prose to verse, though he wrote this in verse, said to Voltaire concerning "L'Œdipe," "C'est le plus beau sujet du monde, il faut que je le mette en prose," to which Voltaire replied, "Faites cela, et je mettrai votre 'Inès' en vers." Mallet's tragedy was fairly good but ran for nine nights only, though Garrick played Don Alonzo; Holland, Don Pedro; Mrs. Cibber, Elvira, and Mrs. Pritchard, the Queen.

Garrick also played Sir Anthony Branville in "The Discovery" of Mrs. Frances Sheridan, Sheridan, her husband, who was not regularly engaged, appearing as Lord Medway. This bright piece ran seventeen nights. Concerning Garrick's performance Victor says: "Sir Anthony was a character entirely new to Garrick; as in other comic parts he was remarkable for his ease, spirit and expression, in this he seemed utterly to have extinguished his natural talents; he assumed a dry, stiff manner, with an immovable face, and thus extracted from the pedantic object much entertainment for the audience and great credit for the author." A less generous interpretation was placed by Davies upon his conduct. Davies says "that Garrick either did not or would not understand the idea of the author." Garrick's dislike to Sheridan was well known. The direct implication is that he did not intend the piece to succeed.

For the first time during this season, Garrick in reviving the "Fair Penitent," abandoned his famous character of Lothario, which was taken by O'Brien, in favour of that of Sciolto.

CHAPTER XI.

DURING this same season of 1762-63, the results of Garrick's interference with the privileges of the Mohocks, who insisted on sitting on the stage, were shown in an alarming outbreak. The date of this was 25th January, 1763, when for the benefit of Victor, who was responsible for the alterations in the text, a sixth representation of " The Two Gentlemen of Verona" was given. The nominal cause of riot was the refusal of admission at half-price at the end of the third act, a curious practice in the theatres which lingered until a generation ago.

At the head of the movement to resent this was Fitzpatrick, an Irishman of some social position, whose name has already been mentioned in connection with a quarrel with Woodward. Fitzpatrick, who was a dandy and donkey of the first water, had already had some *démêlés* with Garrick. He had espoused with some warmth the cause of Mossop against Garrick, and had, at the gatherings at the " Bedford Tavern," a noted haunt of actors, dramatists, critics, and men of the world, organized an opposition to Garrick's supremacy.

Some tiffs had followed, and Fitzpatrick, who had a large and rather rowdy following, attacked his

adversary.   He is said even to have placed himself
with his companions in the front of the pit when
Garrick was playing, maintaining a " stony gravity "
during the performance of comedy, and laughing
in the most solemn moments of tragedy. Fitzpatrick's
attacks in *The Craftsman* under the signature
X. Y. Z., had been collected into a shilling pamphlet
and issued in 1760, with the title, " An Enquiry into
the Real Merits of a Certain Popular Performer.
In a Series of Letters, just published in *The Craftsman* or *Gray's Inn Journal*, with an Introduction
to D——d G——k, Esq."

David, we are told by his widow, " always wrote
his own criticisms."   He made a strenuous effort to
write his own satires, the satires, that is, on himself.
Many of these survive and cast a curious light on
his character.   He could not obtain a monopoly of
such productions, however, and his own satires carry
far fewer guns than those of his adversaries, and
are altogether less formidable.   Regardless of the
fact that a stalwart champion came to his aid in the
person of Churchill, the author of " The Rosciad,"
Garrick descended into the fray with " The Fribbleriad," which he issued in 1761.

In this the epicene manners of Fitzpatrick, desig-
nated under the name Fitzgig, and his associates, are
amusingly bantered.   Though coarse in parts and
weak in others, " The Fribbleriad " is a fairish satire.
A little ingenuity and industry might discover the
originals of the various characters introduced, but no
good would attend the process.   The caricature of

Fizgig or Fitzgig is able, but its best passages are nowadays scarcely quotable. In place of this, then, let us read a few of the really vigorous lines descriptive of Fitzpatrick which are given in " The Rosciad ":—

> " With that low cunning, which in fools supplies,
> And amply too, the place of being wise,
> Which Nature, kind, indulgent parent! gave
> To qualify the blockhead for a knave;
>
> .   .   .   .   .
>
> Which . . .
> Fawns in the day, and butchers in the night;
> With that malignant envy which turns pale
> And sickens, even if a friend prevail,
> Which merit and success pursues with hate,
> And damns the worth it cannot imitate;
>
> .   .   .   .   ,
>
> A motley figure of the Fribble tribe,
> Which heart can scarce conceive, or pen describe,
> Came simpering on; to ascertain whose sex
> Twelve sage, impannell'd matrons would perplex.
> Nor male, nor female; neither, and yet both;
> Of neuter gender though of Irish growth;
> A six-foot suckling, mincing in Its gait,
> Affected, peevish, prim, and delicate.
>
> .   .   .   .   .
>
> Much did It talk, in Its own pretty phrase,
> Of genius and of taste, of players and plays;
> Much, too, of writings, which Itself had wrote,
> Of special merit, though of little note;
> For Fate, in a strange humour, had decreed
> That what It wrote, none but Itself should read.
> Much, too, It chatter'd of dramatic laws,
> Misjudging critics, and misplaced applause,
> Then, with a self-complacent jutting air,
> It smiled, It smirk'd, It wriggled to the chair.

At the Bedford Fitzpatrick reigned in some such fashion as Garrick and Churchill indicate. He was at the head of a gang of young roughs called " The Town," who, following his mischievous lead, determined to compel the Drury Lane management to admit them at half-price on every night except during the run of a pantomime.

During the representation on the before-mentioned 25th January Fitzpatrick came to the front of the boxes, harangued the audience on the imposition of the manager, and pleaded vehemently the right of the public to fix the prices of admission. Garrick, endeavouring to speak, was received with noise and uproar, and treated by Fitzpatrick and his partisans with the utmost contempt. Not a moment was allowed for deliberation or council. Upon his refusal to concede instantaneously their demands, the benches were torn up, the lustres were broken, and acts of outrageous violence were committed. One madman went so far as to attempt to set the scenery on fire, and was only prevented by the interference of Moody, who seized upon him and dragged him away. The same proceedings were renewed next night, and Garrick found it prudent to comply with the demands of the rioters. A victim was necessary to the mob, and it was found in Moody, from whom an apology was demanded. Thinking to treat the matter as a joke, Moody, speaking in Irish tones, said, " he was sorry he had *displased* them by saving their lives, in putting out the fire." This further inflamed the passions of the rioters, who insisted that Moody should go on his knees. With commendable courage and manhood Moody refused, saying, " I will not, by heaven."

Garrick met him at the wing, embraced him, thanked him for his pluck, said that if he had yielded he would never have forgiven him, but so long as he had a guinea, he should be paid his salary. Garrick was none the less compelled to promise that Moody should not again appear, placing the actor thus in an unbearable position. Moody met the difficulty by making direct application to Fitzpatrick and demanding satisfaction. Davies gives in the life of Garrick the dialogue between the two as it took place at Fitzpatrick's house. Not having been present, he must have drawn on his imagination, after the wont of theatrical chroniclers, or have received the account from Moody. Fitzpatrick tried vainly to ride the high horse, but was compelled to write to Garrick withdrawing the inhibition upon Moody's performances, and promising that when the actor was allowed to reappear he and his friends would attend and contribute to Moody's reinstatement in public favour. The letter in which this statement was made was patronizingly offensive and insulting to Garrick, who, however, was glad at any price to see peace restored.

Animated by the desire to appear to administer equal justice, the rioters attempted the same proceedings at Covent Garden. Beard, the manager, was made of sterner stuff than Garrick, and had some of the offenders arrested and brought before Lord Mansfield, who rebuked their behaviour, and told Fitzpatrick that if a life was lost in consequence of these proceedings, he would have to answer for it with his own.

In the midst of the annoyances to which he was subject, and by which, as will be seen, his conduct was greatly influenced, one event had brought balm and consolation to Garrick while spreading rage and consternation among his fellow actors. This was the appearance of "The Rosciad," of the Rev. Charles Churchill, which in 1761 had come anonymously into the light. This work, an illustrated authoritative reprint of which has just appeared, under the editorship of Mr. Robert W. Lowe, is too well known to call for long comment. It pays a high tribute to Garrick at the expense of most of his rivals, to whom it is often far less than just.

According to its scheme, a competition is held to fill the chair vacated by Roscius. Shakespeare and Ben Jonson are appointed judges. The actors come in turns and exhibit themselves and are described by the satirist. To some few, principally women, the author is lenient, eulogistic even. Mrs. Clive, Mrs. Cibber, Mrs. Pritchard and some others, are treated with more than civility. With the actors it is otherwise. Foote is thus described :—

> "By turns transformed into all kinds of shapes,
> Constant to none, Foote laughs, cries, struts and scrapes :
> Now in the centre, now in van or rear,
> The Proteus shifts, bawd, parson, auctioneer.

His strokes of humour, and his bursts of sport
Are all contain'd in this one word *Distort*."

Concerning Macklin, Churchill says :—

" Macklin, who largely deals in half-formed sounds,
  Who wantonly transgresses Nature's bounds,
  Whose acting's hard, affected and constrain'd,
  Whose features, as each other they disdain'd,
  At variance set, inflexible and coarse,
  Ne'er know the workings of united force," etc.

Of Mossop :—

" Mossop, attach'd to military plan,
  Still kept his eye fix'd on his right-hand man ;
  Whilst the mouth measures words with seeming skill,
  The right hand labours and the left lies still ;
  For he resolved on scripture-grounds to go,
  What the right doth, the left-hand shall not know.
  With studied impropriety of speech,
  He soars beyond the hackney critic's reach ;
  To epithets allots emphatic state,
  Whilst principals, ungrac'd, like lackeys wait," etc.

Of Barry :—

" What man, like Barry, with such pains, can err
  In elocution, action, character ?
  What man could give, if Barry was not here,
  Such well-applauded tenderness to Lear ?
  Who else can speak so very, very fine,
  That sense may kindly end with every line ?
      Some dozen lines before the ghost is there
  Behold him for the solemn scene prepare :
  See how he frames his eyes, poises each limb,
  Puts the whole body into proper trim :—
  From whence we learn, with no great stretch of art,
  Five lines hence comes a ghost, and, ha ! a start."

Quin, Sheridan, Woodward, Shuter, the whole
tribe, including Tom Davies, the actor and biographer of Garrick, to whom is devoted the well-
known couplet :—

> " With him came mighty Davies.   On my life,
> That Davies hath a very pretty wife,"

are described, some of them being very sharply
fustigated,—

> " Last Garrick came.   Behind him throng a train
> Of snarling critics, ignorant as vain.
> One finds out,—' He's of stature somewhat low—
> Your hero always should be tall, you know.'
>
>   .   .   .   .   .
>
> Another can't forgive the paltry arts
> By which he makes his way to shallow hearts ;
> Mere pieces of finesse, traps for applause."
>
>   .   .   .   .   .

Dissenting from such judges, the writer thanks the
gods they have formed him of a coarser kind of
clay :—

> " Nor stung with envy, nor with spleen diseased,
> A poor, dull creature, still with Nature pleased :
> Hence to thy praises, Garrick, I agree,
> And, pleased with Nature, must be pleased with thee."

Shakespeare then, speaking for himself and Jonson,
delivers the verdict :—

> " If manly sense ; if Nature linked with art ;
> If thorough knowledge of the human heart ;
> If powers of acting vast and unconfined ;
> If fewest faults with greatest beauties join'd ;

If strong expression, and strange powers which lie
Within the magic circle of the eye;
If feelings which few hearts, like his, can know,
And which no face so well as his can show,
Deserve the preference ;—Garrick ! take the chair,
Nor quit it—till thou place an equal there."

This is, of course, the expression of an individual opinion, which, however, time has ratified. The appearance of the satire, as may be supposed, fluttered the dove-cotes. The effect has indeed been well, if obviously, compared to the discharge of a gun into a rookery. Not only was

" The winged air darked with plumes,"

it was resonant with " caws;" a chorus of complainings was heard, and a fierce polemic, with which I am in no way concerned, was waged.

Not too discreet was Garrick's reception of this homage. That he was delighted to the heart's core, none can doubt. He walked more perkily, and with an air of loftier triumph, but elected to be indifferent to the homage which was unsought, and, as he indicated, hardly welcome ; and said that the motive of Churchill was doubtless to obtain admissions to Drury Lane. So far as regards his fellow actors, to whose good graces the eulogy he had received at their expense was hardly likely to commend him, this might be policy. He forgot, however, that he had to deal with the vanities of an author, no less exigent than those of the actor. When, for the sake of one man, Churchill had set an entire profession barking at his heels, it was not likely that he should receive with complacency the intelligence that that man was treating him superciliously. An actor in the position of Garrick is surrounded by flatterers and toadies, who bring to him in a distorted state, and with superadded colouring of their own, whatever they may hear said concerning him. It is seldom that a spy does not discharge a double function, and those who carried to Garrick the words of others took back in return his own.

No long time passed, accordingly, before the " Rosciad " of Churchill was succeeded by an " Apology, addressed to the Critical Reviewers," Smollett being the editor of the *Critical Review*. In this, the tone was altered, the actor's profession was assailed in lines as unkind as vigorous, and no exceptions were made. Four lines were supposed to be aimed directly at Garrick :—

> " Let the vain tyrant sit amidst his guards,
> His puny green-room wits and venal bards,
> Who meanly tremble at the puppet's frown,
> And for a play-house freedom lose their own."

The previous lines seem, however, even more personal in their application.

> " But if kind fortune, who sometimes we know
> Can take a hero from a puppet-show,
> In mood propitious should her favourite call
> On royal stage in royal pomp to bawl,
> Forgetful of himself he rears the head,
> And scorns the dung-hill, where he first was bred.
> Conversing now with well dress'd kings and queens,

With gods and goddesses behind the scenes,
He sweats beneath the terror-nodding plume,
Taught by mock honours, real pride t'assume.
On the great stage, the world, no monarch e'er
Was half so haughty as a monarch player.
    Doth it more move our anger or our mirth
To see these things, the lowest sons of earth,
Presume, with self-sufficient knowledge graced,
To rule in letters, and preside in taste?
The town's decisions they no more admit;
Themselves alone the arbiters of wit;
And scorn the jurisdiction of that court
To which they owe their being and support.
Actors, like monks of old, now sacred grown,
Must be attack'd by no fools but their own."

This time, Churchill wounded bigger game. Smollett repudiated the authorship of the attack in the *Critical Review*, of which he was the editor, and Garrick, though careful not to fit on to his head a cap which all thought moulded to the block, made advances to Churchill through his friend Lloyd, the author of the poem "The Actor." Admirable in all respects is the letter in which he shows his hand. After some preliminary matter he continues:—

"I see and read so much of Mr. Churchill's spirit, without having the pleasure of his acquaintance, that I am persuaded that his genius disdains any direction, and that resolutions once taken by him will withstand the warmest importunities of his friends. At the first reading of his Apology, I was so charmed and raised with the power of his writing, that I really forgot that I was delighted when I ought to have been alarmed; this puts me in mind of the Highland officer, who was so warmed and elevated by the heat of the battle that he had forgot, till he was reminded by the smarting, that he had received no less than eleven wounds in different parts of his body. All I have to say, or will say upon the occasion is this : if Mr. Churchill has attacked his paste-board Majesty of Drury Lane from resentment, I should be sorry for it, though I am conscious it is ill-founded ; if he has attacked me merely because I am the Punch of the Puppet-show, I shan't turn my back upon him and salute him in Punch's fashion ; but make myself easy with this thought—that my situation made the attack necessary, and that it would have been a pity that so much strong, high-coloured poetry should have been thrown away, either in *justice* or in *friendship*, on so insignificant a person as myself. In his *Rosciad* he raised me too high, in his Apology he may have sunk me too low ; he has done as the Israelites did, made an idol of a calf, and now *the idol dwindles to a calf again.* He has thought fit a few weeks ago to declare me the best Actor of my time (which, by-the-bye, is no great compliment, if there is as much truth as wit in his Apology), and I will shew the superiority I have over my brethren upon this occasion, by seeming at least that I am not dissatisfied, and appear as I once saw a poor soldier on the parade, who was acting a pleasantry of countenance, while his back was most wofully striped with the cat-o'-nine-tails."

The phrase "The idol dwindles to a calf again," is a quotation, slightly altered, from the poem.

Lloyd's negotiations proved successful, and Churchill until his distressing death in Boulogne, 4th November, 1764, remained an acquaintance of, and to a certain extent a pensioner on, Garrick. Letters from Churchill asking for a loan are to be found. One given by Mr. Fitzgerald is very sad.

"MY DEAR MR. GARRICK.—*Half drunk, half mad,* and quite stripped of all my money, I should be much obliged *if you would enclose, and send by the bearer five pieces*, by way of adding to the favours already received by yours sincerely,

"CHARLES CHURCHILL."

The following letter is, I believe, as yet unpublished. It is curious for the names it introduces, which render it almost historical.

"Mrs. Churchill, that sweetest and best of women, having entertained me with some large and unexpected demands from Gloucester, I should take it as a very particular favour, if you would give me leave to draw on you next week, for between forty and fifty pounds. There is likely to become high fun between Talbot and Wilkes —the immortal Passado. The only thing I like my gown for, is the exemption from challenges. . . . I have seen Hogarth's print, it is much unequal to the previous productions of that master of humour. . . . But Hogarth's are subjects of an Englishman's pen.

"Speedily will be published

"An Epistle to W. Hogarth by C. Churchill.

"Pictoribus et Poetis."

(Forster MSS. x. 61.)

The publication of Churchill's Epistle to Hogarth, July, 1763, assigns to the undated letter an approximate date.

On 12th November, 1764, eight days after Churchill's death, Garrick wrote from Paris to his brother George, stating that Wilkes had told him that Churchill had left money enough for his debts, and "some besides for his *wife*, Miss *Carr*, whom he lived with, &c. You'll do what is proper, but

put in your claim. Churchill, you'll see, paid me
40*l.* (I think) of the note " (Forster MSS. xvii.
151).

In cases such as this, Garrick conducted himself
with a combination of shrewdness and liberality
which is, on the whole, to his credit.

In his treatment by Fitzgerald and the Town, the
iron ate into his soul. His dignity as well as his
vanity was hurt, in having to surrender, almost at
discretion, to rowdyism, ignorance, and presumption. This consideration influenced him in his
temporary retirement from the stage. Another
reason not less potent, though perhaps less readily
owned, even to himself, was the fact that he had
ceased to draw. Sir William Weller Pepys told
Rogers, who records the fact in his "'Table-Talk,"
that Garrick's attraction had much decreased, and
that the pit was sometimes nearly empty. It has
been said that Garrick and Mrs. Cibber had played
to houses of twenty pounds, and once, indeed, to a
house of five pounds. This is comprehensible enough.
People weary of the best, when they have it always
with them, and actors down to modern days have
learnt the lesson, that a temporary absence is not
without its advantage, as a means of reviving a
waning popularity.

That Garrick needed rest has been said, and may
well be believed, acting in his days, when he played
on an average thirty important characters in a season,
being in some respects far more arduous than now
it is. Mrs. Garrick had, moreover, been ordered

change of air. Garrick accordingly determined upon a trip on the continent.

Circumstances had altered greatly since he last went abroad. His reputation had not then extended beyond his own country. Now he was, perhaps, the most popular man of his time. In literary circles, an occasional rebuff might be encountered, chiefly from those whom his astounding success had mortified or perplexed. In aristocratic quarters, however, among those, one of whose chief aims in life is to be amused, he was the most welcome of men. A prized guest at ducal houses, he was allowed to take his wife to the residences of the highest nobility, thanks, no doubt, to her origin. The correspondence which he carefully preserved, and which at the outset is mainly literary and artistic, has by this time become leavened with aristocratic names. In his brother George, he had a representative of unswerving fidelity, in whose hands his interests were safe. With him, however, he associated George Colman, and in Lacy he had a partner whom he could trust. To add to these comfortable conditions, he had discovered in William Powell, a youth, an actor who was able to take creditably his place without, as he believed, inspiring much fear as to future rivalry.

In September, 1763, accordingly, accompanied by his wife, from whom he seems never to have been separated for a day, Garrick started for the continent. The period was well chosen. Things English were at that time in good repute in Paris, and Garrick,

whose reputation had preceded him, was hailed with
enthusiasm. His chosen associates were philosophers
and actors, and it is difficult to say with which he
was the more popular. The most animated report
of his doings is found in the correspondence of
Grimm and Diderot, which, however, is supplemented
by his own letters.

Nothing could be better calculated than the reception accorded Garrick in Paris and on his travels,
to bring balm to his wounded spirits. Everywhere
he was fêted, *choyé,* crowned with laurels. His first
stay in Paris was but short, extending over three
weeks. Brilliant as was even then his reception, he
but sowed the seeds of the harvest he was on his return to reap. He went on the night of his arrival to
the Comédie Française, and saw the "Gouvernante"
of La Chaussée, a piece bearing, in subject, some
faint resemblance to "East Lynne," and received
the freedom of the theatre. Clairon was called
upon, and greeted him with rapture. He saw the
first performance of "Les Amours d'Arlequin et
Camille," a three act comedy of Goldoni, then first
given at the Théâtre Italien, and that also of
" Blanche et Guiscard," a tragedy of Saurin, played
25th September. In this he recognized a translation
of the " Tancred and Sigismunda " of Thomson.
Upon the piece and on Mdlle. Clairon, Garrick kept
a prudent silence, confiding his opinion to a few
trusted friends. Mr. Fitzgerald says that Mdlle.
Clairon, who played the heroine, "was said never to
have done worse." Saurin, at least, thought differ-
ently, when he wrote of her performance,—

"Ce drame est ton triomphe, ô sublime Clairon !
Blanche doit à ton art les larmes qu'on lui donne ;
Et j'obtiens à peine un fleuron
Quand tu remportes la couroune."

Laden with courtesies and compliments, which were to be forgotten after his return in further successes, Garrick started for Italy. He passed by Lyons, and over Mont Cenis to Turin, Milan, Genoa, Florence, Rome, Naples, where he spent Christmas, and stayed nearly three months, returning to Rome by way of Parma to Venice.

His route was one long triumph. Voltaire heard that he was passing near Ferney, and sent him an invitation, placing his theatre at his disposal. From Savoy, on 10th October, Garrick wrote a letter, unpublished as yet, to George, asking him to forward him Churchill's "Ghost" just published, bidding him take care of Hogarth's pictures, and keep them out of the sun, by which they might be spoilt, and telling him that he has had "a most warm invitation from Voltaire," adding "O, the damn'd fellow !" for his depreciation of Shakespeare.

Wherever there was an English colony, it made the most of the actor. In Naples, he was an object of special attention, accompanying Lord and Lady Spencer to Herculaneum, being made much of by Lady Oxford, and asked by the King to be present at an entertainment at the Royal theatre, where, in order to test the powers of improvisation of the actors, he was challenged to frame the scenario of a plot, which the Italians undertook to fill up, and perform within twenty-four hours.

Never had Garrick been so much at his ease. The reserve of great folk, of which at home they could not wholly divest themselves, disappeared under the influence of foreign surroundings, and he remained on terms of perfect cordiality with people of the highest " ton." He is only grieved that reports of his aristocratic doings are indiscreetly sent by somebody—no one, of course, can guess by whom—to the English press, and that the *St. James's Chronicle* has mentioned in print the fact that he danced with the Duchess of Devonshire. Not so absorbed was he in these butterfly proceedings as to forget business, and having heard of the doings of Powell, with equanimity as yet unruffled, he wrote to George, 2nd January, 1763-4, expressing his hope that the young actor has been rewarded by Lacy, and added: " and pray let him doe it handsomely."

In Rome, he associated with the best painters, turning to account for their benefit his facial gifts. Among his intimates was Dance, subsequently known as Sir Nathaniel Dance Holland, who painted a portrait of him as Richard III., now in the possession of Sir Watkin Williams Wynn. Fury, joy, doubt, despair, pity, jealousy, and other feelings or passions were depicted with that marvellously mobile face, and that power of expression, that made Mrs. Clive once say, after contemplating him from the " wings " of the theatre, and finding herself, though angry, unable to resist him, " Damn him, he could act a gridiron." Rome appears to have impressed him most favourably of any foreign city, and he once declares it the place best worth visiting and writing about. Endowed with the collector's mania, he loved pottering about the shops in search of books and antiquities. He describes, of course, his emotion at entering a city where the great Roscius exercised his talents. During a portion of his travels, he followed in the wake of the Duke of York, who was then on a tour among the European courts. In May he was in Parma, where he dined with the Duke of York, meeting the Prince of Parma, Lord Spencer, and other distinguished guests. For his host he recited the dagger scene from " Macbeth,". giving first a sketch of the story, so as to render the scene intelligible. For this, the Prince gave him a snuff-box, then the ordinary form of present. A second was given him by the Duke of Wurtemberg. On his return to London, Holland ungraciously and impertinently referred to these gifts in the Green Room, in the presence of King, saying to Garrick, " So you went about the continent mouthing for snuff-boxes." The liberty was not resented.

Venice allured him for a month, but a home-sickness began to attack him. His wife had accompanied him all through his journey, suffering greatly from sciatica. She derived, however, benefit from the baths of Padua. Garrick himself was the next to be crippled, incurring a violent bilious attack, due to good living, which came upon him at Munich, and laid him up for a month. Mr. Fitzgerald quotes some lines written under the depression thus caused, which are more serious than are ordinarily his verses,

and have some merit as self-estimate.   These he
called his own epitaph :—

> "Though I in frailty's mould was cast,
>   By passions hurried on,
> Though all my days in folly passed,
>   No crime has blackened one.
> Some sins I had—for who is free?
>   Of pride, few mortals less ;
> Not those, I fear, who have, like me,
>   Small merit with success.
> One pride that with myself shall end,
>   That pride the world shall know,
> Much-honoured Camden was my friend,
>   And Kenrick was my foe."

His next visit with a curative design was to Spa,
where he remained until October, when he returned
to Paris.   Very few particulars concerning this long
journey survive.   Garrick began keeping a diary,
but appears to have soon abandoned it, and the
chief information we obtain concerning him, is from
his letters to the Duke of Devonshire, Lady Spencer,
Joseph Baretti, the dictionary maker, and others.
Writing from Munich to Mr. Arden, he describes
with some animation his suffering :—

> "You have read 'Letters from the Dead to the Living,'
> and from the living to the dead, but, I believe, never
> received one before from the half dead to the living—such
> is the case at present ; I am but the shadow of myself,
> that self which at Naples and at Venice made no con-
> temptible figure even at your side, and which was always
> ready and willing to second you in every article of the fat
> and fine ; but alas ! my good friend, all the combustibles

I had long been storing up there and elsewhere took fire at this place, and I have been confined more than a month to my bed, by the most dangerous bilious fever that ever poor sinner suffered, for the small fault of a little innocent society. . . . I am most truly the Knight of the Woeful Countenance, and have lost legs, arms, belly, cheeks, etc., and have scarce anything left but bones and a pair of dark lack-lustre eyes, that are retired an inch or two more in the sockets, and wonderfully set off the parchment that covers the cheek-bones."

The remaining correspondence while he was abroad includes particulars of a proposed purchase by Garrick of early Italian books, an altercation with Jephson, and short and very formal letters between Garrick and Johnson. Johnson writes :—

May 18th, 1765.

DEAR SIR,—I know that great regard will be had to your opinion of an edition of Shakespeare. I desire, therefore, to secure an honest prejudice in my favour by securing your suffrage ; and that the prejudice may really be honest, I wish you would name such plays as you would see, and they shall be sent you by, Sir,

Your most humble servant,

SAM JOHNSON.

To this churlish letter Garrick replied no less stiffly, beginning Dear Sir, and subscribing himself, " Sir, your most obedient humble servant." Little genuine cordiality can have existed between the two men. With the letter of Johnson it is pleasant to compare a warm and delightful epistle of Burke a month later—after Garrick's return :—

Gregory's, Monday, June 13th, 1765.

MY DEAR DAVID,—We have now got a little settled in our new habitation. When will you and Mrs. Garrick come and make it comfortable to us by your company for a day or two? You have promised us, and we are a sort of persevering folks, and will not easily let you off. You shall have fowls from our own poultry yard, and such beef and mutton as our next market-town yields; and to make it complete, we will assure you it is our own feeding, and then you will find it very good. In all sadness we wish, Madam Burke, all with us, and myself, most hugeously to see you, and will take it ill, if you go and see the new Paymaster before us starving proscribed folks. You know the unfortunate are always proud and touchy. We only wish you would give us a day's notice that we may not ramble. Adieu, my dear Garrick, and believe me,

Most sincerely and affectionately,

EDMUND BURKE.

Letters also passed during Garrick's absence between Powell and himself. Powell's letter is very modest and unassuming, and acknowledges gratefully the service received from Garrick. Garrick's reply is too long to be quoted *in extenso*. It is a model of judicious and kind criticism and advice. With pardonable rapture Boaden says that "a copy of it should be worn as an amulet by every young actor of genius 'nearest the heart.'" Here are a few characteristic lines :—

"You have acted a greater variety of characters than I could expect in the first winter, and I have some fears that your good nature to your brother actors (which is commendable when it is not injurious) drove you into parts too precipitately; however, you succeeded, and it is

happy that you had the whole summer to correct the
errors of haste, which the public will ever excuse in a
young performer, on account of his beauties ; but now is
the time to make sure of your ground in every step you
take. You must, therefore, give to study, and an accurate
consideration of your characters, those hours which young
men too generally give to their friends and flatterers. The
common excuse is, ' They frequent clubs for the sake of
their benefit ;' but nothing can be more absurd or
contemptible,—your benefits will only increase with your
fame, and should that ever sink by your idleness, those
friends who have made you idle, will be the first to
forsake you. When the public has marked you for a
favourite (and their favour must be purchased with sweat
and labour,) you may choose what company you please,
and none but the best can be of service to you."

We have here a clue to Garrick's own conduct,
always sagacious, prudent, and a little calculating.

CHAPTER XII.

IT may be doubted whether any other theatrical record
is so wholly pleasant and edifying to read as that of
Garrick's stay in the French capital. For once, and
for once only, it seems as if the jealous susceptibilities
which are the curse of the actor's profession were laid
to sleep. For once too there was apparently no gall
in the cup. Everywhere that Garrick presented
himself he was the subject of the most honouring
attentions. The intimacies moreover ripened in
almost every case into friendship, the correspondence he maintained with celebrities was constant
and enduring, and for once a people it is the custom
to regard as fickle and volatile, proved themselves
capable of enduring affection. Years afterwards
visitors to Paris found the name of Garrick one with
which to conjure.

Very untrustworthy is most theatrical anecdote.
The details will bear investigation no better than
those of most " ghost " stories, and scene and time
vary in every different record of the same event. In
the main, however, the stories told concerning
Garrick may be accepted at least so far as regards the
broad facts. It must interest students of the stage
to know that it was à *propos* of the visit of Garrick,

and a pamphlet which his visit produced, that
Diderot seems first to have enunciated the views that
were subsequently developed in his " Paradoxe sur le
Comédien." The title of the pamphlet is " Garrick,
ou les Acteurs Anglais; ouvrage contenant des
réflexions sur l'art dramatique, sur l'art de la
représentation et le jeu des acteurs ; avec des notes
historiques et critiques sur les différents théâtres de
Londres et de Paris; traduit de l'Anglais, 1769."
According to Barbier ("Dictionnaire des Ouvrages
Anonymes," ii. 522), the author was Antoine (*sic*)
Fabio Sticotti.[1] This work Diderot lashes with
severity. The gist of the views expounded is found
in the following phrases : " L'acteur est las, et vous
êtes tris ; c'est qu'il s'est démené sans rien sentir,
et que vous avez senti sans vous démener : s'il en
était autrement, la condition d'un comédien serait
la plus malheureuse des conditions. Heureusement
pour nous et pour lui, il n'est pas le personnage, il le
joue : sans cela, qu'il serait plat et maussade ! Des
sensibilités diverses qui se concertent entre elles pour
produire le plus grand effet possible ! Cela me fait
rire. J'insiste donc, et je dis : C'est la sensibilité qui
fait la multitude des acteurs médiocres ; c'est la
sensibilité extrême qui fait les acteurs bornés ; c'est
le manque de sensibilité qui fait les acteurs sublimes.

---

[1] Sticotti's work was translated and adapted from " The
Actor : a Treatise on the Art of Playing " (1750), published
anonymously, but probably by Sir John Hill, which was, in its
turn, translated and adapted from " Le Comédien," by Rémond
de Sainte-Albine (1747).

Les larmes du comédien descendent, celles de l'homme sensible montent ; ce sont les entrailles qui troublent sans mesure la tête de l'homme sensible ; c'est la tête du comédien qui porte quelque trouble passager dans ses entrailles."

How these views were subsequently elaborated by Diderot and formed the basis of a dispute which still rages is well known. It is pleasant to Englishmen to find the whole originating in the visit of Garrick.

Three months after the return of Garrick to London we find in the correspondence of Grimm and Diderot many particulars concerning his stay. Diderot, supposing it be he that writes, tells us that Garrick has kept his promise and spent six months in Paris on his return from Italy. Garrick, he opines, would be ungrateful if he did not feel some regret on quitting France, where he has enjoyed the most distinguished reception. His chosen intimacies have been with the philosophers, whose regrets he carries with him, and whose manners and views he cherishes.

Garrick is described as of mediocre stature, inclining to little. His physiognomy is agreeable and *spirituelle*, and he has a wonderful play of the eye (un jeu prodigieux dans les yeux). His vivacity is extreme. He has much esprit, great finesse and correctness, is a born mimic (naturellement singe) and can imitate anything. He is always graceful. By a profound study of nature, and by researches full of finesse and sublimity (a curious phrase), he has perfected his great natural gifts. Perpetually mingling with the crowd, he surprises nature in all her originality and naïveté.

Returning on horseback in company with Préville, a reigning actor of the Théâtre Français, from the Bois de Boulogne, Garrick said, " Let us both imitate drunkenness." This was done while passing through the village of Passy. Not a word was spoken, but the village emptied itself, to see two intoxicated cavaliers. Young folk derided them, women cried out for fear they would fall from their horses, and old men shrugged their shoulders in pity, or burst into laughter, according to their temperaments.

" How have I acquitted myself, O Master? " said Préville, as they issued from the village. " Well, very well," said Garrick; " but you were not drunk in your legs." In this, the narrator found proof how close was Garrick's perception of nature.

He heard in Ireland of a father, who playing with his child, had the misfortune to let the child drop out of a window, and saw the little life crushed out upon the pavement. Some years after the accident Garrick saw the father, who had lost both speech and reason. To his French friends, Garrick gave an imitation of the scene, which made all around him shudder. This well-known story, which is used in " Doctor Davy " and in other pieces, is told in many ways. This record, if the tamest, seems also the most trustworthy.

Garrick is then declared to be a great admirer of Shakespeare. He will never forgive Voltaire for the manner in which he has spoken of the English poet on various occasions, and, in fact, the writer thinks, certain criticisms reflect little honour on the

taste or the good faith of Voltaire. This injustice
does not hinder Garrick from estimating Voltaire as
the greatest tragic poet the French have possessed.
Of Racine, so fine, so enchanting to read, he holds
that he is unsuited to the stage (ne peut être joué),
because he says everything, and leaves nothing for
the actor to do, and because the harmony of Racine's
verses requires a species of chaunt, which is far
removed from true declamation.

Not very convincing seem now, some of these
assertions. They carried conviction, however, to the
French hearer, and appear indeed to have been a sort
of anticipation of the romantic movement, which was
to follow sixty years later. We are here, says the
writer, a small flock of believers, and are in accord
with Roscius Garrick on all these points. We
recognize Homer, Æschylus, and Sophocles, for the
law and the prophets, we intoxicate ourselves with
the gifts of genius wherever we find them, without
regard to tongue or nation. The English Roscius
is our religion and our church.

One or two other statements from this warm
admirer deserve to be quoted. Mr. Garrick enjoys
a considerable fortune. He has fully fifty to sixty
thousand francs a year, reckoning what he receives for his management of one of the Royal
theatres of London. Our clever folk (gens à talent)
do not make similar fortunes. Garrick is believed to
be fond of money (Il passe pour aimer l'argent). He
has been attacked in Munich with a malignant fever,
which threatened his days, but the air of Paris has

re-established him.   It is doubted, however, whether
he will long continue to play.   The manner in which
he is possessed by his rôles (il s'affecte de ses rôles)
would destroy the most robust temperament, and he
is not strong.   Master of a great fortune, satiated
with glory, cherished, esteemed by his compatriots,
illustrious throughout Europe, he can retire, when
he chooses, to a pretty country house, which he
possesses near London.   He married, near seventeen
years ago, a German, born in Vienna, a Catholic, by
whom he has no child.   She has accompanied him in
his travels.   We maintain that he was born jealous,
and he does not dispute the truth of our assertion.

Not in the least highly coloured is this account
of Garrick.   It conveys, however, the idea of a
splendid triumph.   To have captured the entire
salon of the Baron d'Holbach, and to have converted
into disciples the leaders of thought in Paris was
an unparalleled accomplishment.   Garrick's triumphs
did not end here.   Actors, dramatists, artists, were
all carried away by his vivacity and charm.   It
was always worth while in Garrick's view to captivate
the best, and by such a fisherman the large fry
were as easily captured as the small.   A record of
his friends is a mere list of the celebrities of Paris.
Beaumarchais, Marmontel, Crébillon fils, De la
Place, Marivaux, Ducis, Paradis de Moncrif, Favart,
are a few only of those who have left tokens
of their admiration.   To De la Place is owing a
further story concerning Hogarth's portrait of
Fielding.   This, it is said, was painted from Garrick,

who made up his face as Fielding, and so was
responsible for the likeness. When narrated by De
la Place, this story caused some incredulity. To
convince the most sceptical, Garrick once, more
personated Fielding, in a manner that won instant
recognition. French literature of the time is full of
records of his doings, and the terms used are always
those of affection. Mrs. Garrick also comes in for
much respectful homage. Messages to her followed
from many of her associates, and it was not until
after Garrick's death that a word was said against her,
and that word was only an imputation of stinginess,
which was probably no more merited in her case
than in Garrick's.

Garrick was, however, anxious to get home. If
there was on the horizon the smallest cloud, it was
or should have been so tender, diaphanous, and
fleecy, as to be an attraction the more in his heaven.
The news from Drury Lane was, if possible, too
good. Powell had caught the public, and was as
great a draw as Garrick himself. The houses
were nightly crammed, and there was no reason
whatever for Garrick's return. To one who had
left home for the purpose, in part, of showing
the public that it could not do without him; one,
moreover, in whom the fires of ambition were not
even smouldering, having been fanned into a fierce
flame by the adulation he had experienced in the
artistic capital of Europe, the intelligence that London
was getting on capitally in his absence, was not un-
reservedly comforting. It was too late to come

back for the present season. Powell must enjoy his rather puzzling honours, and next season must be reserved for a contest, if contest there must be. On the 25th April, 1765, accordingly, Garrick reached London.

Before his return he was guilty of a characteristic piece of trickery. The choice of a word is difficult here. Garrick's fondness for anonymity is not an heroical trait; the only question is whether it can justly be called mean as well as tortuous. It was, at any rate, in keeping with his very nervous and excitable nature to send before him a species of *avant-coureur*, that, if it did not forestall other satires, might at least set people talking about him. Having, it is said, been reading La Fontaine, he determined to give this piece the character of a fable. This precious production he sent to George Colman, who had it put into type. Immediately upon Garrick's return, accordingly appeared " The Sick Monkey, a fable," with the motto " Thursday afternoon, David Garrick, Esq., arrived at his house in Southampton Street, Covent Garden. *Public Advertiser*, April 27th, 1765."

Never did a damper squib go out with a feebler fizzle. As satire it is milk and water, as literature it is contemptible, and as an imitation of La Fontaine it may almost be called dishonouring. Such point as it possesses is coarse, and it has indeed no claim upon attention, beyond the fact that it furnishes an insight into Garrick's strange and composite individuality. Its story even is too poor to be told.

The following are, perhaps, the most presentable passages :—

> " Garrick ! thou mighty chief of kings and queens,
>   Despotic tyrant of the scenes !
> Think'st thou all human race to mock,
>   In buskin and in sock?
>   And will not fools
>   Thy mock'ry ridicules,
> From Chalkstone's Lord, to dainty Fribble,
>   Rave, chatter, write,
> In various ways display their spite?
> For all can talk, and some can scribble.
>   Others again
>   Take up the pen,
> In panegyrick's gaudy colours paint thee ;
>   As humour flows
>   Now friends, now foes,
>   In prose and verse, and verse and prose,
>   Bedevil thee, and saint thee."

One feels disposed on reading this fable, to say with Rosalind,—

> " Patience herself would startle at this *matter*,
> And play the swaggerer ; bear this, bear all
>
> .　　　.　　　.　　　.　　　.　　　.
>
> Why, 'tis a boisterous and a cruel style,
> A style for challengers."

It missed fire, as has been said, and those even who were most anxious to please the stage-king knew not what line to take in dealing with it. Another anonymous production for which one of his biographers, Boaden, holds him responsible, is wholly creditable. This is " Extract of a letter from an

English gentleman at Paris to his friend in London." It supplies a long, elaborate, ingenious and highly favourable estimate of the capacity and talent of Préville, and is an admirable piece of stage criticism. Upon Préville's excellences, the writer dwells with gusto. It would be pleasant to think that praise so frank, outspoken, and ungrudging of a fellow comedian belongs to Garrick. The only external evidence, its discovery among his papers, is unconvincing; internal evidence, however, points to him as the author.

During Garrick's absence death had been busy among his friends, several of whom had departed. The most serious loss he had experienced was that of Hogarth, news of whose death grievously affected him. Churchill, his champion, had died during his absence, as had the Duke of Devonshire, whose kindness had been unremitting. Intelligence of Hogarth's death had been received while he was ill, and had been for some time kept from his knowledge by Mrs. Garrick. Intimacy between the two began soon after Garrick settled in London. At the time when Churchill was writing his "Epistle to Hogarth," Garrick wrote with admirable loyalty, though without success : "I must entreat of you by the regard you profess to me that you don't tilt at my friend Hogarth before you see me. . . . He is a real and original genius. I love him as a man and reverence him as an artist." When the epistle appeared, Garrick pronounced it "the most bloody performance that has been published in my time," and expressed himself as being much hurt at it. Garrick and Hogarth had been associated in work. Many pictures of the actor from the hand of the painter are in existence, the most celebrated perhaps being that of Garrick and his wife, sold in Mrs. Garrick's sale, now in the Royal Collection at Windsor. For a portrait of Garrick, as Richard II., painted in 1746, exhibited at the Grosvenor Gallery in 1888, and now in the possession of Lord Feversham, Garrick said that Hogarth received two hundred pounds, " which was more than any English artist ever received for a single portrait." A third picture, representing Garrick in the Green Room, sketches of Garrick and Quin, a portrait of Mrs. Garrick, and a picture of Garrick's Villa, are described in Mr. Austin Dobson's admirable " William Hogarth," 1891. Garrick was the purchaser of some of Hogarth's works, wrote the descriptive verses to the two prints, " The Invasion, or France and England," and allowed himself, it is said, to be drawn in one of them as a rustic whose height is being taken by a recruiting sergeant. The last service he was to pay this friend, with whom he never seems to have had a misunderstanding, was to write the epitaph placed on the monument erected in 1771 in Chiswick Churchyard. It is as follows :—

> " Farewell, great Painter of Mankind !
>   Who reach'd the noblest point of Art,
>   Whose *pictur'd Morals* charm the Mind,
>   And through the Eye correct the Heart.

> If Genius fire thee, Reader, stay ;
>> If Nature touch thee, drop a tear ;
> If neither move thee, turn away,
>> For HOGARTH'S honour'd dust lies here."

Johnson suggested an alteration :—

> " The Hand of Art here torpid lies
>> That traced the essential form of Grace ;
> Here death has closed the curious eyes
>> That saw the manners in the face."

When Garrick came back, his announced purpose was not to act. He purposed living in retirement at Hampton House, now known as Garrick Villa. Garrick became tenant of this famous spot in January, 1754, and six months later purchased the estate. A year or two afterwards he altered the house, giving it a new front, adding to the grounds, and building an octagonal temple to receive Roubillac's statue of Shakespeare, for which Garrick sat, and for which he paid the sculptor three hundred guineas. Here he placed his pictures by Hogarth and Zoffany, and here he gave the dinners and garden parties with allusions to which the gossip and memoirs of the day overflow. Writing to Bentley 4th August, 1755, Horace Walpole states that he met here at dinner the Duke of Grafton, Lord and Lady Rochford, Lady Holderness, the crooked Mostyn, the Spanish minister, and other people of condition. Here every 1st of May Garrick regaled the village children with cakes and wine, and gave parties with variegated lamps, converting it into an aristocratic Vauxhall. And here too, when he first contemplated all the magnificence around him, Johnson said rebukingly, "Ah, David, it is the leaving of such places that makes a death-bed terrible." Here Garrick lived until his death, adding as he could to the grounds, and here his wife lived after him for forty-three years.

In the arrangement of his new books and curios, and in the continued exercise of hospitality, he would find employment enough, and the "loathed stage" should see him no more. Some there were whom these protestations took in, and Hoadly congratulated Garrick on his resolution. An ingenuous nature was necessary to accept such declarations. The wires were being dexterously pulled, and a royal puppet at length removed all Garrick's scruples. Mr. Garrick must not retire, said George the Third. Would he not re-appear at royal command? What could so loyal a subject as Garrick do?

On the 14th November, 1765, accordingly, as Benedick in "Much Ado about Nothing," Garrick returned to the stage. During his absence Powell had made his first appearance as Philaster, 8th October, 1763, and had won high commendation, acting the part sixteen times during the season. He had played also Posthumus, Lusignan, Henry IV., Castalio, Lord Townly, Alexander the Great, Othello, Leon, Oroonoko, the Ghost in "Hamlet," and other parts, growing steadily in public estimation, and becoming before the end of the season the most formidable rival, after Barry, that Garrick had known. Holland, King, Yates and O'Brien had been often seen, and the last-named had retired from the stage, having married a daughter of the Earl of Ilchester, and been provided with a place. Colman had produced his own " Deuce is in Him," and Garrick's adaptation of " A Midsummer Night's Dream." Mrs. Sheridan's " The Dupe " had failed in spite of some admirable acting by Mrs. Clive. These were the principal events of the first season of Garrick's absence. In the season of 1764-65 there is little to chronicle except the complete ascendency over the town obtained by Powell and the production of new plays of no great importance by Lloyd, Mrs. Griffith, and other writers of no special reputation.

Garrick had not wholly neglected his theatre during his absence, having negotiated with foreign dancers and the like, and taken constant note of such improvements as he had seen in continental theatres. The result of these was shown at the outset of the season of 1765-66 in the new method of lighting. For the circular wooden frames, each furnished with a dozen candles, were substituted lights invisible to the audience. Before his re-appearance Garrick scrutinized closely the list of parts in which the rapidly acquired reputation of Powell had been obtained, and discarded from his own repertory those characters in which, on the strength of physical gifts, the younger actor was seen to have the advantage. Whether this course was heroic may be doubted. It was at least careful. Lusignan, Lothario, and Leon were the only characters in which comparison was challenged. As from this time forward he took no character in which he had not previously been seen, the task of following his representations is simplified.

The Beatrice to his Benedick was Miss Pope. From the first moment that he appeared, doubt as to any deterioration of style or power was at an end. Strengthened indeed by observation and experience, and emboldened by the honours accorded him in foreign countries, Garrick began what is practically the most distinguished part of his career. Most comment upon his performances that survives and has influenced his successors belongs to the period following his return. The conquest of the town was both complete and final.* From this period to his retirement, he had no further complaint to make of neglect or disparagement. Men of highest position were wont to bribe the attendants to admit them, probably so as to escape the conflict at the doors.

Upon his first appearance he spoke the inevitable prologue. Neither in expression nor in taste is this very happy. It furnishes, indeed, a marvellous illustration of his fidgetiness and want of repose, in which respects it may almost compare with the "Sick Monkey." Like that too, it includes a fable. Here it is :—

> " Permit me to repeat
> What late I heard in passing through the street :
> A youth of parts, with ladies by his side,
> Thus cock'd his glass, and through it shot my pride :
> ''Tis he, by Jove ! grown quite a clumsy fellow ;
> He's fit for nothing—but a Punchinello.'

O yes, for comic scenes, Sir John—no further,
He's much too fat—for battles, rape, and murther."

In the mood in which it then was the town
tolerated everything, and the prologue was frequently
called for and repeated.

For this season Garrick had engaged Cautherley, Dodd and Mrs. Fitzhenry, formerly Mrs.
Gregory. The two latter were valuable acquisi-
tions. The former, with whom he took special
pains, proved " little more than a walking gentleman." Garrick was to experience during the season
the greatest loss he ever knew in the death of Mrs.
Cibber. They had corresponded to the last on formal
but agreeable terms, addressing one another as Dear
Sir and Dear Madam, but venturing on little proofs
of intimacy in the body of letters, as when she owns
that his praises have made her " as conceited as the
very Devil." Her name appears in the bills for the
last time 13th December, 1765, when she played
Lady Brute to the Sir John Brute of Garrick. She
died on the 30th of the following January. Her
death wrung from Garrick the exclamation, " Then
Tragedy is dead on one side." He made also a
gracious allusion to her and to Quin, who died in the
same month, in his prologue to his own and Colman's
" Clandestine Marriage."

Among the Forster MSS. is some business correspondence between Garrick and Lacy and Mrs. Cibber
with regard to deductions from her salary in consequence of her seldom acting through illness. She
there states that her engagement is for seven hundred

pounds for the season and a benefit free of all charges.
This was at that time a very high salary ; Mrs. Cibber•
was worth it however.   For parts at once tragic and
sympathetic she left no equal behind her.   In comedy
her gifts were less high, but she had a great reputation for the delivery of prologues.   Quin had so long
retired from the stage that his death caused little
comment.   During late years he and Garrick had
been on friendliest terms.   For Quin's tomb in Bath
Cathedral Garrick wrote the epitaph, a moderately
successful composition :—

> " That tongue, which set the table on a roar,
>   And charm'd the public ear, is heard no more !
>   Clos'd are those eyes, the harbingers of wit,
>   Which spoke, before the tongue, what Shakespeare writ.
>   Cold are those hands, which living, were stretch'd forth,
>   At friendship's call, to succour modest worth.
>   Here lies James Quin ! deign, reader, to be taught
>   (Whate'er thy strength of body, force of thought,
>   In nature's happiest mould however cast),
>   To this complexion thou must come at last."

Some of Garrick's lighter compositions concerning
Quin, chiefly dealing with his reputation for gourman-
dise, are in a much happier vein.   Quin's supposed
soliloquy on seeing Duke Humphrey at St. Albans
is perhaps the best epigram Garrick wrote.   It
belongs to 1765 :—

> " A plague on Egypt's arts, I say !
>   Embalm the dead ! on senseless clay
>   Rich wines and spices waste !
>   Like sturgeon, or like brawn, shall I,
>   Bound in a precious pickle, lie,
>   Which I can never taste ?

Let me embalm this flesh of mine
With turtle fat and Bordeaux wine,
    And spoil th' Egyptian trade !
Than Humphrey's duke more happy I—
Embalm'd alive, old Quin shall die
    A mummy ready made."

The " Plain Dealer," altered by Bickerstaffe, was produced 7th December, 1765. The event of the season was the production, 20th February, 1766, of " The Clandestine Marriage," a comedy by Garrick and George Colman, founded upon Hogarth's " Marriage à la mode." Garrick's share in this piece has been much disputed. So much better is " The Clandestine Marriage " than any other comedy in which Garrick had a hand that one is justified in supposing the lion's share to belong to his coadjutor. According to the *Biographia Dramatica*, the authority of which is disputed by the younger Colman, Colman declared that " Garrick composed two acts, which he sent to me, desiring me to *put them together*, or do what I would with them. I did put them together, for I put them into the fire, and wrote the play myself." Garrick was, moreover, credited with the invention of the character of Lord Ogleby. So nearly related is this character to his own Lord Chalkstone that the moderate exercise of talent involved in the alteration needs scarcely have been denied him. Denied him it was. A letter from Colman to Garrick begins abruptly, " Since my return from Bath, I have been told, but I can hardly believe it, that in speaking of ' The Clandestine Marriage,' you have gone so

far as to say, 'Colman lays a great stress on his
having penned this character on purpose for me—
suppose it should come out that *I wrote it*.'" Here
a charge of disloyalty and false assumption is
obviously brought. Matters were sufficiently serious
to beget a quarrel between the two collaborators.

When both were dead a third claimant appeared.
A Mr. Robardeau, who married the daughter of
Townley, the author of " High Life Below Stairs,"
states in his "Fugitive Verse and Prose," 1801, that the
characters of Lord Ogleby, Sterling and Brush are
stolen from a piece by Townley called " False Con-
cord," which was acted by Woodward for his benefit
on a single occasion only, 20th March, 1764, at
Covent Garden. Garrick was at that period out
of England. As the play, moreover, is not
printed it is impossible to judge of the extent of the
obligation.

The quarrel between Colman and Garrick was due
to the refusal of the latter to play the part of Lord
Ogleby, which was intended for him. This was
regarded by Colman as a sacrifice of his interest;
Garrick had, however, made up his mind to play no
new part, and stuck to his determination. The piece
did not suffer, since King's Lord Ogleby, besides
making the reputation of the actor, had conspicuous
success, and was held one of the finest pieces of acting
on the stage. Garrick thought otherwise. After he
had quitted the stage he said to Cradock, " I know
that you all take it as granted that no one can excel,
if he can equal, King in Lord Ogleby, and he cer-

tainly has great merit in the part; but it is not MY Lord Ogleby, and it is the only character in which I should now wish to appear."

The quarrel meanwhile between the two dramatists was not allowed to continue. The interests of both lay in the same direction, and they had a genuine regard for each other. Their acquaintance had begun pleasantly enough in an obligation conferred upon Garrick. In a pamphlet of which he was the anonymous author, entitled " A Letter of Abuse to David Garrick, Esq., 1757-58," Colman had contrived, while affecting to espouse the cause of Garrick's assailants, to render them ridiculous. Subsequently he had addressed to Garrick his " Critical Reflections on the old English Dramatic Writers." A warm correspondence had been kept up, and Garrick had addressed Colman by the affectionate diminutive of Coley, employed to him by his supposed father, Lord Bath. During Garrick's tour Colman had been his most trusted correspondent, and it is from the letters between them that we get the best picture of Garrick's continental impressions and adventures. A very " pretty quarrel " while it lasted was that between two men, both well-meaning and peppery. Negotiations were, however, undertaken by joint friends, and before long Garrick was addressing his dear Coley as before. Concerning one contribution to "The Clandestine Marriage " on the part of Garrick no doubt is possible. Garrick wrote the prologue and the epilogue. The latter is a short play in itself in Garrick's own line, showing a combination of aristocratic noodles, male and female, to damn the play.

Garrick's appearances during the season were few. He acted Benedick three times, Sir John Brute, Lusignan and Lord Chalkstone twice each, went to Bath in March, and after his return acted Kitely in "Every Man in his Humour." This was for the benefit of the Drury Lane fund for the relief of actors obliged by infirmity to retire from the stage. He also spoke an occasional prologue. Of the above-mentioned fund Garrick, who was angered at the Covent Garden fund having been started in his absence on the continent, was a munificent patron. His entire contributions to it have been estimated at four thousand four hundred pounds. Among the not very interesting dramatic productions of this season stands out "Falstaff's Wedding," a play extracted by Kenrick from a previous and more ambitious work with the same title. It is not destitute of merit. The adapter, as has been seen, was an enemy of Garrick. Kenrick indeed had nothing but enemies.

Garrick's first speculation of interest in the following season was the production of "The Country Girl," 25th October, 1766, his own rendering of Wycherley's "Country Wife." This adaptation of a play which, even in Garrick's time, when play-goers had no superfluous squeamishness, could not be produced, has some merit and long held possession of the stage. As usual in the alembic of adaptation, the wit went off in company with the indecency.

Garrick, moreover, took, in debonair fashion, liberties with his original, introducing, in addition to very commonplace matter of his own, songs, scenes and situations from other works. Garrick did not act in it. He assigned the principal parts to Moody and Dodd, and supplied with an epilogue Miss Reynolds, who made, as Miss Peggy, her first appearance at Drury Lane. He took much pains with her coaching. His labour was not wholly in vain, since she afterwards showed some touches of humour acquired from him. She soon disappeared from London and ruined herself by drink.

Another piece assigned to Garrick was " Cymon," a dramatic romance, in five acts, founded on the "Cymon and Iphigenia" of Dryden, and produced 2nd January, 1767. King as Linco, Parsons as Dorus (a magistrate), and Mrs. Abington as Fatima obtained a great success in a play devoid of a single claim upon consideration. It is amusing to find the long-suffering editors of the *Biographia Dramatica* roused to protest. They call it justly "a wretched production, equally devoid of wit, humour, and poetry," and add, "To the scene painters and the vocal performers it was indebted for its success, which (to the shame of taste and common-sense) was considerable." Criticism such as this is uncommon in their pages.

Other new pieces played during the season include " The Earl of Warwick," a poor adaptation by Dr. Franklin of " Le Comte de Warwick " of Laharpe, produced three years previously in Paris ; " The

English Merchant" of Colman, a rendering of
" L'Ecossais " of Voltaire, and " Dido," a tragedy by
one Reed, a rope maker, for which Garrick wrote a
prologue. Not very strong was Garrick's faith in
the piece last named. To his brother George he
writes, " And does Dido please? Good God! And
will they come twice to see it? Good God! It is
time to leave the stage, if such a performance can
stand upon its legs. Good God! "` In the same
letter, dated 5th April, 1767, he mentions meeting
Colman, and says, " We pulled off our hats, but did
not smile. Our friends here will stir heaven and
earth to bring us together : make the best of it, it
will be but a darn." In another letter to the same
faithful friend and servant, undated, but of about
the same time, we get a small glimpse of a domestic
interior. "My wife desires you to write a note
the night you receive this (Saturday) to our maid
at Hampton, Nancy Hetherington, to prepare some
mutton and a pudding, with some asparagus, for our
dinner on Tuesday, about five o'clock, or rather
six."

In addition to the parts he played in the previous season, Garrick had been seen, generally by
desire, in Abel Drugger, Hamlet, Lothario, Ranger,
Bayes, Oakly and Leon. He took matters easily,
however, acting only about twenty-two times in the
season. A dispute with his partner, Lacy, is heard
of, but came to nothing. A quarrel with Arthur
Murphy, the dramatist, gave rise to a very lively
correspondence. Garrick also wrote to Foote in a

very friendly tone upon the accident which had deprived that ungracious mimic of a leg, and received a civil answer. Foote had at the time engaged Barry and Mrs. Dancer for the Haymarket, where they were in much favour.

CHAPTER XIII.

BEFORE the next season began Covent Garden had changed masters. Beard, the son-in-law of Rich, sold his patents to Harris and Rutherford, two business speculators, who were joined by Colman and Powell. In the case of the last two of this quartett, the opposition to Garrick was manifest. Powell was engaged at Drury Lane, and could only go to Covent Garden by breaking his contract, and incurring a forfeit of a thousand pounds, on which the Drury Lane management very reasonably insisted. Colman yielded—very unfortunately for himself, as the event proved—to the glamour of theatrical management. The step seems to have been intentionally hostile to Garrick, who kept discreetly his temper, and gave Colman sensible advice. More than one of his company, notably the Yateses, had gone over to the opposition. Mrs. Clive was no longer young; Mrs. Pritchard was to retire at the end of the season, and shortly afterwards to die, her death being preceded by that of Palmer. Mrs. Abington had sprung into high favour, and was a most winsome creature. Powell was difficult to replace, and Garrick, who cherished against the offending actor very great wrath and indig-

nation, took a bold step, and re-engaged Barry
and Mrs. Dancer, subsequently Mrs. Barry. He
also engaged Reddish and James Aikin, two fairly
competent actors.

The accession of Barry and Mrs. Dancer took the
wind out of the Covent Garden sails. The news of
their engagement ran like wildfire through the town.
Mrs. Dancer appeared 14th October, 1767, as
Sigismunda, to the Tancred of Holland, and Barry a
week later as Lear. A round of tragic parts was
played by the two actors, and was followed with
enthusiasm. Garrick himself acted more frequently
than in the previous season, reappearing in Ranger,
Archer, and Macbeth. When he played Lusignan
in "Zara," Mrs. Dancer was his Zara. The
choice of new pieces was influenced by the conditions of rivalry between the two houses. After
" The Widow'd Wife " of Kenrick had been given,
" False Delicacy," the first dramatic work of Hugh
Kelly, was put on the stage. Kelly, a young Irishman, was the author of " Thespis, or a critical
examination into the merits of all the principal
performers belonging to Drury Lane Theatre," in
which he had shown a distinct capacity and disposition
to sting. Satirists were the bane of Garrick's life,
and were by any means to be reconciled or slain.
Kelly's "Thespis" was indeed quintessentially
vulgar, speaking of Mrs. Clive's "weak head and
execrable heart," and calling Mrs. Dancer "a
moon-eyed idiot." This second-hand Churchill
Garrick had determined to take up, moved partly

by the desire to conciliate a possible foe, and partly in the hope of securing a rival to Goldsmith, the production of whose play, " The Good-Natured Man," was a feature of the season at the rival house. Always seeking to make friends of " the best," and it may be added, of the best alone, Garrick troubled himself little about individuals of secondary importance, unless they forced themselves upon his attention by some form of annoyance or menace. Goldsmith was in his opinion not of " the best," and had never succeeded in impressing him favourably. A certain jealousy of Goldsmith, which Garrick manifested, was reconcilable with a low estimate of the man who had more than once contrived to nettle him, and who had indeed reflected on his management. An anonymous pamphlet by James Ralph was, curiously enough, the cause of estrangement between Garrick and Goldsmith. The title of this pamphlet, which appeared in 1758, was, " The case of Authors by profession or trade stated. With regard to booksellers, the stage and the public." It was a mere growl on the part of a would-be dramatist, whose ability was not commensurate with his ambition. A capable pamphleteer and a respectable historian, a man moreover at one time associated with Fielding in the management of the Haymarket, Ralph, who is the object of a savage attack in the notes of the " Dunciad," and is mentioned in the poem itself, had no poetic or dramatic power. Garrick, as has been said, produced Ralph's " Astrologer," which was a failure, spoke the prologue, wrote the epilogue, lent the author money, and procured him, if Davies is to be trusted, a pension of 200*l.* from Pelham. Unimportant in themselves, the sneers of Ralph in this pamphlet at the management of Garrick acquired some value from the approval they obtained from others. As a supposed champion of Ralph, Goldsmith was a *persona ingrata* to Garrick, who seems in regard to him to have been superfluously sensitive. So unamiable was his mood, that when a personal application by Goldsmith was made for his vote, for the vacant secretaryship of the Society of Arts, Garrick said that " Mr. Goldsmith having taken pains to deprive himself of his assistance by an unprovoked attack upon his management of the theatre in his ' Present State of Learning,' it was impossible he could lay claim to any recommendation from him." Not thus would Garrick have treated Goldsmith if he had been visited by a prophetic glimpse of his coming greatness. Goldsmith's blunt reply, " In truth he had spoken his mind, and believed what he said was very right," was not likely to mend matters between them.

After this ill-starred encounter Garrick and Goldsmith appear to have remained strangers until they were brought together by Sir Joshua Reynolds, with a special view to the production of " The Good-Natured Man." Very little exercise of the imagination is necessary to grasp the situation. Both men were overwhelmed with a sense of their importance. Garrick was more than a little given to patronage, and here was an opportunity for the display of his loftiest consideration. After a long experience of neglect, Goldsmith had at length won recognition, and his estimate of the value of the goods he had to offer was high. Like two big dogs, to use a familiar, but as regards the dimensions of the heroes, not wholly applicable metaphor, the two regarded each other, and parted discontented, if not angry. The victory leaned, however, to the side with the bigger ordnance. Goldsmith was poor and burdened with debts, Garrick rich, and glad to disburse cash for which he got a consideration. The piece was accordingly put into the hands of the manager, who advanced the writer money upon it, and, not without some *malice*, proceeded to justify the strictures of Ralph and Goldsmith by insisting on alterations. Whether Garrick was quite honest in this matter, or whether he was enjoying the wrigglings of the victim on the hook, cannot be told. One thing is certain, the alterations proposed were such as Goldsmith could not possibly accept. They were such also as Garrick was assumably indiscreet, to use no stronger word, in demanding. From the deadlock thus created, the issue was found in the change of management at Covent Garden. Colman took charge of Goldsmith's piece, and produced it, with what result there is no need to concern ourselves.

In opposition then to Goldsmith, Garrick in a not too happily inspired moment, took up Kelly. Financially, " False Delicacy " was at the outset as great a success as " The Good-Natured Man." It ran for many consecutive nights, was played eighteen or nineteen times in all, and brought sentimental comedy into vogue, until Foote turned the genus into ridicule in his "Piety in Pattens." It was even revived in 1782. It is a rather lackadaisical play, with one or two brightly conceived characters, but it failed to gain its author the reputation of a Goldsmith. Murphy meanwhile had forgotten his grievance against the manager, and was again, through the agency of Bickerstaffe, for a brief while on the friendliest terms. His "Zenobia," played 27th February, 1768, was the chief tragic production of the season. It is an adaptation of the "Rhadamiste et Zénobie" of Crébillon, produced 23rd January, 1711, and regarded as that author's masterpiece. It is conceivable that the piece, which remained in the répertoire of the Théâtre Français, was seen by Garrick, and recommended by him to Murphy.

On 24th April, 1768, as Lady Macbeth to the Macbeth of Garrick, Mrs. Pritchard took her farewell of the stage, speaking a pleasing and natural epilogue. She died the following August. Few more competent or better graced actresses· have been seen, though Johnson, who had reasons for disparaging her, speaks of her in ordinary life as "a vulgar idiot." A portrait of her and Garrick in the dagger scene in "Macbeth," by Zoffany, occupies a prominent place in the Garrick Club. A second in the same club shows the same actors as Ranger and Clarinda in "The Suspicious Husband." Garrick as Macbeth wore a modern suit richly embroidered

with gold lace.   The last night of the season Garrick
played Hamlet for the Theatrical Fund.   In August
and December he gave, by special desire, performances
of six different characters for the King of Denmark,
with a scratch company, including Woodward and
Mrs. Bellamy.

The Covent Garden managers were already at
loggerheads, and the legal proceedings which followed,
resulting in a victory for Colman, lasted until 1770.

The following season, 1768-69, was to witness
another formidable breach in Garrick's ranks in the
retirement of Mrs. Clive, almost the last of his "old
guard."   She was to live for some years to come on
terms of delightful intimacy with him.   Had she
died he might almost have varied the remark he made
on the death of Mrs. Cibber, and said, "Then Comedy
is dead on one side."   Of all Garrick's actresses she
was the most interesting and in a sense inspired.   Her
orthography is execrable even for her times, but to
her merits as a comedian unanimous testimony is
borne.   She frightened Garrick almost out of his
wits, and was the person of all others who could best
keep him in order.   She might have remained on the
stage for many years, for in the class of parts she
now took no one came near her.   " If ever there was
a true comic genius she was one," says Victor; "she
was never equalled in her walk by any preceding
actress, and will in all human probability never be
excelled—she was always inimitable . . . . and the
spirit, roguery, and speaking looks of her chamber-
maids, accompanied with the most expressive voice

that ever satisfied the ears of an audience, made her
an irreparable loss." Davies and Tate Wilkinson
bear testimony no less flattering to her abilities,
which those who read her correspondence will readily
believe. She was, as Lacy her manager said, "true
game," and would "have died upon the spot" rather
than give in. Garrick she constantly challenged
to a contest, which he as studiously avoided. In his
lordliest moods Garrick feared her, and the knowledge of this was a constant source of delight to her.
For her sake he relinquished his carefully guarded
stage discipline, and a whispered joke would render
him incapable of remaining serious. Her adieu took
place 24th April, 1769, as Flora in the "Wonder"
to the Don Felix of Garrick and the Violante of Mrs.
Barry, and as the Fine Lady in "Lethe." The
house, though the pit was all turned into boxes, was
not half big enough for the public that sought to
attend. Walpole and not Garrick in this case wrote
the farewell address.

In a letter to Garrick dated 14th April, 1769,
beginning "Dear Sir" and signed "Your most sincere
friend and humble servant"—more familiar and affectionate terms of address had not yet begun—she
conveys a notion scarcely reconcilable with that of a
woman about to retire. "When I heard you was in
such great pain, I was most sincerely sorry. In the
next place, to be sure, I am *glad* you are well for
the sake of my audience, who will have the pleasure
to see their own Don Felix. What signifies fifty-
two? they had rather see *the* Garrick and *the* Clive

at a hundred and four than any of the moderns; the ancients, you know, have always been admired. I do assure you, I am at present in such health and such spirits, that when I recollect I am an old woman, I am astonished."

Havard, a sound and judicious actor, who had long been before the public both in tragedy and comedy, also retired. In general respects the season was not specially noteworthy. Bickerstaffe was rewarded for his attempts to reconcile Garrick and Murphy by being allowed to produce (17th November, 1768) the "Hypocrite," a workmanlike version of the "Nonjuror" of Colley Cibber. Bickerstaffe introduced for the sake of Weston the character of Mawworm, which is not in the original. This sprang into immediate popularity, which it long retained, and has coloured much subsequent satire extending even to present days. Old Lady Lambert, a part taken by Mrs. Bradshaw, was an introduction from "Tartuffe." Charlotte, an admirably designed coquette, was played in inimitable style by Mrs. Abington. "Zingis," a tragedy by Alexander Dow, followed (on 17th December) with no great success. Mrs. Griffith's comedy of "The School for Rakes," adapted from the "Eugénie" of Beaumarchais given two years earlier at the Comédie Française, had better fortune, as had Home's tragedy "The Fatal Discovery."

Garrick was still discontented with the behaviour of Lacy, who seems to have resented the manner in which he was effaced by his more brilliant partner, and to have taken various small methods of wounding, or at least irritating, him. He professed himself anxious to get rid of George Garrick, drawing from Garrick, in so doing, the declaration that when George went he should follow him. The threat of retirement seems to have generally brought Lacy, who knew on which side his bread was buttered, to his senses. It was on Garrick's part less of an empty menace than it appeared. During the time when he was laying the foundation of his fortune Garrick was always careful not to let his aristocratic inclinations interfere with his work. He was now independent. Acting had lost a portion of its attraction, and he had begun to take a pleasure in intellectual and aristocratic enjoyments, with which the necessity to be on the stage continually clashed. His reception in Paris had enlarged his sense, never small, of his importance. It had given him also "immortal longings," and his aspiration to be in the intellectual "swim" dates from his return. Not wholly wise, from his present point of view, was the step he was now about to take. In both England and France he posed as the great defender of Shakespeare, oblivious of the fact that he had continually, with no feeling of shamefacedness, promoted his own kitchen drudge of a muse to occupy the same eminence with the muse of Shakespeare, and though he had not once given a play of Shakespeare as it was written, he had always assumed the position of a guardian of the great dramatist. In France he had given himself airs with regard to Voltaire on the subject of Shakespeare, and had refused to meet men whose criticisms upon the poet seemed to him unworthy. With Ducis, whose so-called translation was responsible for the ignorance concerning Shakespeare that long prevailed in France, he had no feud. Ducis' conduct was too like his own. Now, however, he was to make capital out of his self-constituted guardianship. Very pardonable is this affectation, as evidently are all the affectations of Garrick. When he takes himself too seriously, as he is perversely inclined to do, one is amused with Walpole rather than cross with Johnson. His latest scheme for identifying himself with Shakespeare was to give a jubilee commemoration at Stratford-on-Avon, the scene of Shakespeare's birth. The little Warwickshire town was not as yet a place of pilgrimage. Such indeed, except in the case of celebrated universities or religious shrines, are of modern growth. A few scholars and antiquaries had visited Stratford in a bungling and inefficient quest after relics. Since the days, however, when Jonson and Drayton, if report is to be trusted, went down to see Shakespeare, and by prolonged festivities brought about his death, no record or tradition of any pilgrimage of interest is preserved. The inhabitants none the less took a certain pride in the fact that the most distinguished of Englishmen had been born in their midst, and the authorities, at least, had a dim notion that something might be derived from a privilege so exceptional. No ten cities warred for the honour of Shakespeare's birth; the claims of Stratford were uncontested. When accordingly a certain Reverend Mr. Gastrell purchased the house and gardens of Shakespeare and cut down, because it overshadowed his dwelling and rendered it damp, the famous mulberry tree which Shakespeare was said to have planted, a wail of lamentation and execration went forth against the perpetrator of the deed. After the unsentimental parson had been hounded out of the midst of a populace which vowed never to allow one of the same, fortunately not very common, name to reside in Stratford, the mulberry tree, like other objects of veneration, was turned to practical account. In a box made from the wood of the sacred tree the Corporation of Stratford enclosed to Garrick the freedom of their town, requesting in return his portrait together with some bust, statue or picture of Shakespeare from his collection, which they would place beside it in the Town Hall. A request so flattering, so modest, so devoid of all possible regard for self-interest, could not do other than win from Garrick a sympathetic response.

No long time, one may be sure, elapsed before the town possessed the news of the compliment that had been paid the actor. It was a rhyming and pasquinading age, and verses satirical, bantering, eulogistic, poured forth, while the idea of what use was to be made of the opening provided was taking shape in Garrick's mind. At the close of the season of 1768-9 he had decided on a Jubilee commemoration in Stratford.

To this idea, which had previously been canvassed, he gave formal expression on the last night of his acting, when, with customary loyalty to the fund for decayed actors, he gave the profits to that institution. On this occasion, after the expected promise in the epilogue to come again next year, he continued, bowing to the audience :—

> " My eyes, till then, no sights like this will see,
>   Unless we meet at *Shakespeare's Jubilee !*
>   On Avon's *Banks, where flowers eternal blow !*
>   Like its full Stream our Gratitude shall flow !
>   Then let us revel, show our fond regard,
>   On that lov'd Spot, first breath'd our *matchless* Bard ;
>   To Him all Honour, Gratitude is due,
>   To Him we owe our all—to *Him* and *You*."

Poor enough, apart from a certain conventional neatness of turn, are these lines.   They furnished an occasion however for Gray to praise Garrick's happy knack at epilogue.

The comparison of gratitude to the full stream of the Avon was less happy than it sounded.   Prominent among the misfortunes which attended the celebration was the over-fulness of the ungrateful stream in question.

During the summer, arrangements with a view to the commemoration progressed.   These are fully described in the supplement to the " History of the Theatres " by Benjamin Victor, who was present. Prominent among these was the erection of an amphitheatre on the model of the famous Rotunda at Ranelagh.   As the Rotunda itself, which had been in existence for twenty-seven years, had been projected by Lacy, Garrick's partner, the design may have been his. This was decorated by Garrick's work-people in the best style of stage adornment. Transparencies presenting the great characters, tragic and comic, in Shakespeare's plays were exhibited through the Town Hall windows, and a large transparency showing the sun struggling through clouds to enlighten the world enveloped Shakespeare's house. The church, though closely connected with Shakespeare and enclosing his bust, seems for some reason to have escaped similar honours. Perhaps the clergyman objected. Very little assistance was to be derived from the inhabitants, whose share in the proceedings, scientifically administered, consisted in fleecing the visitors. The most commonplace and indispensable preliminaries had been neglected, and Garrick found himself compelled to do almost everything by his own agents, who seem to have been regarded in the town with little favour.

On the 6th of September, 1769, what, if done at all, should have been a summer festivity, began. The public, at least, had been true to Garrick, and people of wealth and distinction flocked in from London, from the neighbourhood of Stratford, and from adjacent counties to take part in an ill-starred entertainment. Nothing very specially Shakespearian distinguished the first day's proceedings. Victor, even, special apologist and laureate as he is, seems in doubt as to the appropriateness of all that was done, and an occasional hiatus in his account is filled up from outside sources.

Wednesday, the 6th, opened with the firing of

cannon and the singing of " waits," who in masquerade habits serenaded the principal visitors. Programmes of the entertainment, of which Garrick was elected the steward, were circulated. At nine o'clock there was a public breakfast at the Town Hall, followed by a procession to the Church, at which at eleven the oratorio of "Judith" was sung. Thence to the amphitheatre, where, after a chorus (*sic*) of vocal and instrumental music, there was at three p.m. an ordinary for gentlemen and ladies. At five a further concert was given of " new songs, ballads, roundelays, catches and glees, etc.," and a ball followed at nine. Before the breakfast the magistrates and corporation had assembled and presented Garrick with a medal of Shakespeare carved on a piece of the mulberry tree and set in gold, and with a speech. To the latter Garrick replied, while the former he fastened on his breast. The various processions were accompanied by music, to which Garrick supplied the words. Dr. Arne conducted the service in the Church. At night the houses were illuminated, and country dances were kept up in the amphitheatre until three in the morning.

Much more resplendent were to be the proceedings of the second day. After another public breakfast there was to be, if the weather permitted, a pageant, and an ode " upon dedicating a building and erecting a statue to the memory of Shakespeare " was to be " performed." At four was to be an ordinary, at eight fireworks, and at eleven a masquerade.

Unfortunately the weather did not permit. Un-propitiated by all the fine things said about her, the Avon invaded the spot set apart for feastings and pleasures, while the rain coming down in a deluge put an end to all thought of pageantry. Garrick's famous ode was however given, the author speaking the recitative and standing in the front line, with the female singers alongside of him. He then made a speech lamenting that the task of writing the ode had not fallen into more capable hands, and delivered an oration in eulogy of "the Bard." At the close of this he asked if any of the company had anything to say against the supposed object of the day's ceremony, whereupon King, dressed as a Macaroni, came forward and made a mock attack, giving Garrick opportunity for a crushing reply and for further verses. At dinner a turtle weighing one hundred and fifty pounds was served. The fireworks were soaked with rain and would not go off. The masquerade was, however, a success. Lady Pembroke, Lord Grosvenor, Mrs. Bouverie and Mrs. Crew(e) were conspicuous in splendour. Most conspicuous of all was Boswell—Johnson's Boswell—who, as the well-known friend of Paoli, appeared in a Corsican habit with a scarlet waistcoat, a stiletto in his belt and a musket at his back, and in a cap with a blue feather, and the legend around it in letters of gold "Viva la Libertà." He had written a poem which he intended to speak, but the crowd would not suspend its diversions to hear him. The list of dukes and other noblemen, friends of Garrick, who were there, may be read in Victor.

The third and last day began with the customary breakfast, followed by a horse race for a jubilee cup of fifty guineas, duly won. Further feasting and music at the amphitheatre followed. Fireworks this time were let off, and a ball brought the whole to a conclusion.

In the midst of these farcical proceedings Garrick strutted. He had spent much money and was entitled to some recompense in the way of airing his vanity. It is doubtful whether the whole was not as joyless as it was dishonouring. Beyond extortion in charges the townsfolk took little part in the business, while, except King, we hear of no actor of importance having any share whatever in the proceedings. Garrick must have had an uncomfortable prevision that difficulties would ensue. For him, with so many enemies as he possessed, anything short of a complete success must be a failure. He had had matters all his own way. What he did not write, his factotum, Bickerstaffe, did, and no one but himself and Boswell appears to have scored. Some praise has been bestowed upon Garrick's ode and upon his share generally in the literature of the ceremony. As a whole, however, it is sorry stuff. One song concerning Shakespeare has enriched us with a quotation still occasionally used. It is that, separate verses of which end " For the wag of all wags was a Warwickshire wag," " the lad of all lads was a Warwickshire lad," etc. Warburton, spoiling a few lines of Dryden, compared the ode disparagingly with the odes of Cibber, and said that Cibber's nonsense occasionally verged on sense, but that "this man's sense, when he does deviate into sense," was always like nonsense, which observation itself is indeed remarkably like nonsense.

Of Foote Garrick had, not without cause, the liveliest apprehension. When Garrick, upon his return, sought to make a profit out of the whole business by bringing the Jubilee in little upon the stage of Drury Lane, Foote, who had waited for an opportunity to justify an assault upon Garrick, saw it. For two days out of the three Foote had been in Stratford. One of his sharpest witticisms is indeed connected with his visit. A country gentleman had challenged an encounter of wits, and addressed Foote, who, after some peaceable conversation, learned that his adversary came from Essex, and, with unsurpassable insolence, said, "Indeed, who drove you?"

Foote's purpose was to bring out a mock procession, introducing, as the principal figure, a man dressed for Garrick as steward of the jubilee, with "his wand," white topped gloves and the mulberry tree medallion. Some ragamuffin of the troupe was then to heap on the simulated Garrick the most unctuous flattery, to which the answer was to be Garrick's flapping his arms like a cock and crowing Cock-a-doodle-doo!

At the news of this scheme Garrick perspired with terror. In the end a nobleman, a friend of both, who saw how miserable Garrick was, prevailed upon Foote to abandon the scheme. As if by chance the two actors met at dinner. Descending at the same time from their "chariots," they stood opposite each other. " Is it war or peace ? " said Garrick. "Oh! peace, by all means," replied Foote, and the difficulty was over. Those who did banter the scheme remained unforgiven by Garrick, and to one friend who perpetrated a harmless piece of waggery on the subject Garrick never spoke again. Steevens was among those who turned it into ridicule. The general impression, however, seems to have been that it was a failure as well as a mistake.

Before the season of 1769-70 began, Garrick had lost one of the two opponents whom the town had for a while elevated into the position of rivals. William Powell, next to Garrick and Barry the best actor of his day, an affecting and natural tragedian and a man of much sensibility in comedy, died in Bristol on the 3rd July, 1769, at the age of thirty-four. So affected were the actors at the Bristol theatre at the news of his death they were all but unable to play, and were exonerated from performing the final farce by a sympathetic audience. Powell was buried in Bristol Cathedral Church in presence of Colman, who wrote the epitaph, and of Holland, the great friend of Powell, who only survived five months. Holland's epitaph in Chiswick Church is by Garrick, who writes concerning him with unfamiliar warmth of eulogy. All indeed speak of him as a competent actor and a worthy man. Foote even, who had a good word or a favourable verdict for few, praises Holland, though with customary irreverence he calls his vault the family oven, in allusion to Holland being the son of a baker, a fact Holland made no effort to conceal. Holland however, though his death is naturally mentioned in connection with that of Powell, took part in Garrick's coming season, 1769-70.

Of this season the first novelty was the delivery, on 30th September, by Garrick, of his Stratford Ode, with the musical accompaniments. Garrick, it may safely be assumed, had heard of Colman's intention to be beforehand with him in producing a jubilee pageant, and as his own was not ready, thought he would discount it by giving the ode. His delivery of it incurred some condemnation, and the ode itself, published 4to, 1769, was the subject of parodies, attacks and vindication.

Not until the 14th October was the pageant produced at Drury Lane. Garrick personated Benedick, Miss Pope Beatrice, King (who spoke the prologue) Touchstone, Holland Richard III., Brereton Romeo, Cautherley Hamlet, Love Falstaff, Reddish Lear, Aikin Antony, Mrs. W. Barry Portia, Vernon Apollo, Mrs. Barry the Tragic Muse, and Mrs. Abington the Comic Muse. It was a great success, and was played throughout the season. Garrick's introduction was never printed, and the MS. was burnt in the fire at Drury Lane in 1809. The pageant at Covent Garden was, with the purpose of forestalling Garrick, given on the 7th October in the course of Colman's comedy then first acted, "Man and Wife, or, the Shakespeare Jubilee;"

Mrs. Bellamy was the Tragic and Mrs. Mattocks the Comic Muse. A full description of the Drury Lane pageant may be found by those curious in such matters in the *London Magazine*, October, 1769, pp. 497-8, and in the Notes to Davies's " Life of Garrick," 1808, vol. ii., pp. 238-244.

Thanks to the success of the Jubilee the season ran on into June without the production of more than one novelty of anything approximating to importance. This was " A Word to the Wise," by Hugh Kelly, a piece which was given on Saturday, 3rd March, 1770, for one night only, and was to enlarge Garrick's unenviable experience of English theatrical rowdyism. Kelly was doubly unpopular. In the political world he was regarded as a Government hireling, in histrionic circles he was known as the author of the ill-natured and ill-bred satire of " Thespis." At the head of a party determined to damn the play at all hazards was Wilkes, whose political animosities overpowered his friendship for Garrick. Kelly had also a strong party in his favour. A battle royal was the natural result. Kelly's piece was, in fact, above the average of its time. By dint of hurrying through their parts the actors succeeded in bringing the performance to a conclusion, and the piece was announced from the stage for the following Monday. The riot now attained such proportions that Kelly consented to the withdrawal of his play, and " Cymbeline " was promised in its stead. What placated one portion of the audience annoyed the other. A demolition of the house was threatened if the original scheme were not carried out. Garrick was out of town, and Hopkins, the prompter, on behalf of Lacy consented. Kelly now, at Garrick's suggestion, waited on his friends and vainly urged them to recede from the position they had taken up. They would not suffer the pleasures of the town to be sacrificed to party pique, and insisted that the piece should be heard.

For three hours on Monday the riot was maintained. Kelly came forward, requesting once more that his play might be withdrawn, and was once more refused. A compromise was at length arranged. The money was returned, and it was agreed that "False Delicacy," Kelly's earlier comedy, should be given on Tuesday for his benefit. On Tuesday, "False Delicacy" was played amidst much confusion, the actresses being insulted. The scrimmage then closed. Kelly published the piece by subscription at a crown a copy, and sold enough to compensate him for any pecuniary loss he had sustained through its withdrawal from the stage.

CHAPTER XIV.

AMONG the correspondents of Garrick at or about
this period is Thomas Gainsborough, who writes to
him with great familiarity and with a use of exple-
tive which Boaden, the editor of "The Garrick Correspondence," feels bound to condemn. Gainsborough
is the painter of the portrait of Garrick in the Stratford Museum. One letter, written from Bath, tells
of the death of Mrs. Pritchard, and, speaking of
Stratford, pronounces Shakespeare's bust in the church
"a silly, smiling thing." A letter from Mrs. Clive
is docketed in Garrick's own hand, "A love-letter
—the first I ever had from that truly great comedian
Mrs. Clive." In it she writes, "How charming you
can be when you are good. . . . I shall certainly
make use of the favour you offer me; it gives me
a double pleasure—the entertainment my friends
will receive from your performance, and the being
convinced that you have a sort of sneaking kindness
for your Pivy.[1] I suppose I shall have you tapping
me on the shoulder (as you do to Violante), when I
bid you farewell, and desiring one tender look before
we part, though perhaps you may recollect and toss

[1] Clivy Pivy, a term of intimacy and affection used by
Garrick to her.

the pancake into the cinders. You see, I never forget any of your good things." Among his correspondents are Burke, always writing the friendliest letters, Mrs. Montagu, and Joseph and Thomas Warton, the last-named borrowing books from Garrick's fine collection for his " History of English Poetry."

During the following seasons to the close of Garrick's career Drury Lane may be said to have rested on its laurels. Garrick played infrequently, though always to good houses. He was chary of changing his characters often even in the limited repertory to which he confined himself. Barry and Mrs. Barry took the lead in tragedy, supported by Mrs. Egerton, who joined the company in 1770. Mrs. Abington, Mrs. Baddeley, and Miss Pope with Bannister (from Dublin), Moody, Dodd, and Parsons were foremost in comedy. " 'Tis Well it's no Worse," a comedy from the Spanish by Bickerstaffe, an adaptation, says the " Biographia Dramatica," of " El Escondido y la Tapada" of Calderon, was given 24th November, 1770, with a success that was greatly augmented when it was subsequently cut down into a farce called " The Pannel." " King Arthur," a dramatic opera extracted by Garrick from Dryden, followed on the 13th of the next month and was played twenty-one times, a fact for which spectacular splendour was wholly responsible. Madame Celesia, often spelt Celisia, a daughter of Mallet, married to a Genoese, supplied " Almida," 12th January, 1771, a translation of the " Tancrède" of Voltaire. Cumberland's " West Indian," played 19th January, was the feature of the season. It is by general consent Cumberland's best play, and retained possession of the stage for thirty years. Mrs. Abington obtained conspicuous success as Charlotte Rusport, and rendered the character a lasting favourite with following actresses; and King, Moody, and Mrs. Baddeley were greatly approved.

Garrick's next contribution to the stage consisted of the "Institution of the Garter, or, Arthur's Round Table Restored," an alteration of a dramatic poem of Gilbert West, included in Dodsley's "Collection of Poems." It was written for the sake of introducing a procession at the installation of the Knights of the Garter, Garrick having now learnt the value of pageantry. His calculations were right, but the piece was more remunerative than creditable. Cumberland's "Fashionable Lover," though a favourite with the author, failed to maintain the reputation he had acquired with the "West Indian." Better fortune attended Murphy's "Grecian Daughter," which revealed great tenderness and power in Mrs. Barry, and has been frequently acted in the present century. In December, 1772, O'Brien, the retired actor, gave at Drury Lane "The Duel," a translation of "Le Philosophe sans le savoir" of Sedaine, which, though judged unworthy of being produced at the French Court, had had seven years previously a great success at the Théâtre Français. Garrick himself gave to the stage the "Irish Widow," an adaptation of "Le Mariage Forcé," in two acts, which was favourably received. The 18th December, 1772, witnessed Garrick's gravest mistake in dealing with Shakespeare. On that day he gave a version of " Hamlet" in which he took unpardonable liberties with the disposition of the scenes and the text. So much had been told him of the illumination that he cast upon Shakespeare, and he had heard himself so often described as the best of the commentators, that he once more took himself seriously and endeavoured to justify the opinion expressed by his flatterers. For this weakness he incurred, as he deserved, a rap on the knuckles so smart that, contrary to his wont, he did not print the piece, and announce it as his own. So careful became he, indeed, that Tate Wilkinson, moved by an ambition, subsequently carried out, to rival his exploit, could not obtain from the theatre a copy of the alterations. What these are is known in part only. The grave-diggers' scenes disappeared ; the plot between the King and Laertes to slay Hamlet was cahnged, and the character of Laertes was sentimentalized. Osric was banished; the Queen, conscious of guilt, was led off the stage in a state of insanity ; and the duel of Hamlet with Laertes was followed by another with the King, the monarch, when assailed by Hamlet, seizing a sword for the purpose of defending himself.

These alterations could not well escape censure. Testimony to Garrick's marvellous histrionic power is afforded in the fact that the adaptation was popular and was used after Garrick's retirement and, apparently, for a short time after his death. In this version Henderson made, 30th September, 1777, his first appearance at Drury Lane.

It is too much, perhaps, to hope that an actor so steeped in adulation as Garrick, and so ready to be misled by eulogy, will ever perceive, until the lesson is forced upon him, the difference between the interpretative functions of criticism and those of stage exposition. Garrick's impertinence, for such must be held the tampering with a masterpiece like "Hamlet," was forgotten in the beauty of his performance. He had, it is true, given no actor a chance except himself, and when a dying speech which he wrote for Laertes was received with applause, he withdrew it from Aikin, the exponent of that character, and incorporated it in his own part. He had intended to print his rendering, and had even accepted a preliminary acknowledgment from the booksellers. More prudent counsels prevailed in the end, the "consideration" was returned, and the play was never published. Curious proof of the almost irresistible influence of vanity is afforded in the fact that in his later days Garrick, though liberal, when not himself playing, in furnishing opportunities to the actors of his company, sought on other occasions to monopolize interest and sympathy. The editors of the "Biographia Dramatica" charge him with having altered "Hamlet" in the spirit of Bottom, the weaver.

Home's tragedy of "Alonzo," produced 27th February, 1773, was galvanized by Mrs. Barry into a semblance of vitality, ran for nine nights and then departed into the limbo of vanities. Among the other novelties Garrick produced before his retirement few call for mention. "The School for Wives," 11th December,

1773, is a clever comedy, which Hugh Kelly, knowing his unpopularity, produced under the name of Addington, deluding thus the pit into accepting it "A Christmas Tale," 27th December, an entertainment in five acts, by Garrick, with music by Dibdin, is perhaps the most inept piece with which the memory of Garrick is associated. It was subsequently curtailed into three acts, and after incurring general censure from the press was at last hissed off the stage. Previous to the production of this he gave Drury Lane an alteration of "The Chances," in which he reappeared as Don John, a second of "Albumazar," and a third of Mallet's "Alfred." So slight is his share in these that it is scarcely necessary to burden him with the responsibility. His chief function, when in his later years he prepared a piece for revival, was to give himself the required supremacy. He had within recent years been deprived of the services of his literary factotum, Isaac Bickerstaffe, who had executed for him much drudgery, and had more than once helped him seriously at a pinch. Bickerstaffe's last contribution to Drury Lane was "The Sultan," a farce played by Mrs. Abington with success 12th December, 1775. Three years previously, however, he had abandoned England and taken refuge in France. His life, though he came of a respectable family and had been admitted into good society, appears to have been shameful from the outset. So recently as 1769 he had dined at Boswell's, other guests being Johnson, Garrick, Goldsmith, Sir Joshua Reynolds, and Murphy. In 1772 he fled to escape a capital charge,

and lived under a false name in France, where he
survived until 1812 if not later. To Garrick he
made a despairing appeal. A letter dated St. Malo,
June 24th, 1772, unsigned and addressed to Garrick,
is one of the very saddest of human documents. Its
opening words are :

> "Monsieur,—Si votre cœur a conservé jusqu'à
> présent la moindre trace de cette prévention que vous
> avez autrefois avouée pour un homme qui est aujourd'hui
> le plus malheureux qui soit sur la terre ; je vous
> supplie de me le faire connoître par trois ou quatre
> mots adressés pour M. Burrows, chez M. Vagries fils,
> Libraire, au côté du Cathédrale, à Saint Malo, Bretagne,
> France."

Silence is promised and asked in a letter which
claims to come from a dead man to a living. The
place of his retreat is a matter of the greatest consequence, on no account to be revealed. Harrowing as
is the utterance, it found Garrick presumably obdurate.
It remains in the correspondence endorsed in Garrick's
own hand, " From that poor wretch Bickerstaffe ; I
could not answer it." His reticence was not, however, to save him from a charge which of all others
ever brought against the most abused man of his day
caused him most pain and humiliation. From this
he was immediately and finally absolved, and the
entire infamy of the transaction fell upon the malignant, obscene, and leprous creature by whom it was
brought. Though all obtainable under the circumstances, the consolation was slight. Not a spot in the
character of Garrick's assailant was there on which
further infamy could rest.

William Kenrick had been from the first a libeller of Garrick, as indeed of most men with whom he had been thrown into any form of association. More than once Garrick, who classed Kenrick among those whom he thought worthy of conciliation, had made advances to him. On the flight of Bickerstaffe, Kenrick saw an opportunity to sting, he does not appear to have had any definite purpose beyond. In the same year accordingly, 1772, appeared "Love in the Suds; a town Eclogue, being the lamentation of Roscius for the loss of his Nyky" (Isaac). This was the first of a series of insults and retractations concerning which those curious in such matters may consult Mr. Lowe's "Bibliographical Account of English Theatrical Literature." Further investigation into this matter is not to be counselled. The charges brought against Garrick of sharing the offences of Bickerstaffe have not won a single adherent. Garrick had, indeed, only to treat the matter with contempt or to set seriously in motion the agencies of the law. He did neither. With characteristic timidity and vacillation he tried to steer a middle course, the result being that he presents himself in a repellingly unheroic aspect. The obvious course was to place the conduct of an affair of this class in the hands of loyal friends with whom he was surrounded. He is found on the contrary indulging in language of alternate menace and appeal. Proceedings were taken, and what had to be accepted as an apology was made by Kenrick, who told Thomas Evans, the publisher, that he had never believed in Garrick's guilt, "but did it to plague the fellow "; after hearing which Evans did not speak to him again.

Garrick even contemplated a duel, as though by any theory of social life a being such as Kenrick could be entitled to the " satisfaction of a gentleman." A letter is extant and endorsed by Garrick, " This note sent to that scoundrel, Dr. Kenrick. . . . It was judged best not to answer any more of Dr. Kenrick's notes, he had behaved so unworthily." It is perhaps the most marvellous piece of imbecility Garrick ever wrote. Painful as they are, a few words from this are indispensable to a grasp of Garrick's invertebrate mind. " Sir," he wrote, " I am really sorry for the figure you made in the late transaction with me. Could not you have finished a little better, for the sake of that honour which so readily drops from your pen ? What ! talk of dangers and attacks whicn were never conceived, and which even you would not be frightened enough to believe. Your suggestion about Becket is a poor tale. . . . Do you imagine I could have risked my reputation to have acted unlike a man, even to him who has been ungratefully vilify-ing me ? No, sir. I would have honoured you by giving the satisfaction of a gentleman, *if you could* (as Shakespeare says) have screwed your *courage to the sticking place* to have taken it." As if this was not inconceivable enough, he then begins to apologize for the non-performance of a play by Kenrick, in which he sees the cause of the outrage, and says, " He would have acted it had it been sent him in time." Here is poor David to the life. With little sense of personal dignity he thinks less of what damage a man may have done in the past than of what further shafts may be in his quiver.

Kenrick gave himself innumerable airs, was said to be walking about with lethal weapons and bragging everywhere that Garrick was afraid to meet him. He had himself a wife and children, but if Garrick would settle half his fortune on his (Kenrick's) family, he, Kenrick, would meet him in arms. Sorry matter is all this with which to have to deal. From the lips of one, in every full sense a man, comes, however, one half-conciliatory moral. After the flight of Bickerstaffe had confirmed the rumours of his guilt, Thrale told Johnson that Bickerstaffe had long been a suspected man. " By those who look to the ground, dirt will be seen, sir," was Johnson's virile reply. " I hope I see things from a greater distance."

An enemy even more formidable and not very much less scrupulous had for a time put Garrick in a trepidation which probably was the most serious he ever experienced. Jubilantly elated at his own importance and success, Garrick threw himself across the path of Junius. From Woodfall, the printer, he heard that Junius would write no more. Garrick at once sent this announcement to the King, by whom it was discussed. Garrick received accordingly a letter to the following effect: " I am very exactly informed of your *impertinent inquiries*, and of the information you so busily sent to Richmond, and with what triumph and satisfaction it was received. I knew every particular of it next day, through the indiscretion of one, who makes it a rule to betray everybody that confides in him. *Now mark me, vagabond!* Keep to your pantomimes, or be assured you shall hear of it. Meddle no more, thou busy informer! It is in my power to make you curse the hour in which you dared to interfere with Junius."

Terms of so withering contempt would have aroused some spark of manhood in Garrick if there had been any to rouse. Consternation is the one feeling stirred in his mind. Some protest there is against the employment of unkind language, some declaration that in his vindication he will use neither violence nor abuse. But the cheek is turned to the smiter. He writes to Woodfall : " I beg you will assure Junius that I have as proper an abhorrence of an informer as he can have, that I have been honoured with the confidence of men of all parties, and I defy my greatest enemy to produce a single instance of any one repenting of such confidence. I have always declared that, were I by any accident to discover Junius, no consideration should prevail upon me to reveal a secret productive of so much mischief; nor can his most undeserved treatment of me make me alter my sentiments." The letter ends with a very half-hearted assumption of courage : " I beg you will tell all you know of this matter, and be assured that I am with great regard for Junius's talents, but without the least fear of his threatenings, your well-wisher and humble servant, David Garrick."

Very proper and becoming, no doubt! The one thing I want, however, in the case of Garrick is a little generous indignation. If Garrick could once tell Junius or Kenrick or Murphy or any of the thousand and one people at whom he is always "nagging" to "go to the Devil" I should be content. Unregenerate is, without doubt, such a wish, but the conciliatory ways of Garrick in the case of men of mark beget a rebellious spirit, a strong disposition towards contempt.

" Matilda" and " Braganza " were among the uninteresting novelties of 1774-5, the former a dull and rhetorical tragedy by Dr. Thomas Francklin, a Court Chaplain, concerning whom Churchill says,—

> " 'Twas known
> He sicken'd at all triumphs but his own,"

the second a respectable and conventional drama by Captain Robert Jephson, M.P., popularly known by the curious sobriquet of the " Mortal Momus." New comedies included General Burgoyne's " Maid of the Oaks," which was played twenty-five times; Cumberland's "Choleric Man," which is derived from the " Adelphi " of Terence, but might from its title be supposed a piece of autobiography; and Garrick's comedy of " Bon Ton," 18th March, 1775, an excellent little piece which Garrick lent King for his benefit. Lacy and Smith joined the company, the latter playing Richard III. and Hamlet in Garrick's alteration, the former appearing as Alex-

ander in " Alexander the Great," altered from Lee's
" Rival Queens."

Another so-called rival of Garrick had meanwhile
died in poverty, it may almost be said in despair. This
was Henry Mossop, the Irish manager and tragedian.
Garrick befriended him through life and until death,
and reaped a customary harvest of ingratitude.
One of Garrick's worst quarrels was with David
Williams, a Welsh dissenting minister, who on the
strength of his intimacy with Mossop wrote " A
letter to David Garrick on his conduct as a principal
manager and actor at Drury Lane Theatre," a somewhat stinging satire on Garrick's eccentricities and
condemnation of his treatment of other actors. It
turned out, however, to be little more than an attempt
at *chantage*. As such it was almost a success since
Garrick contemplated buying off his enemy. Mossop
before his death made ample amends, owning that he
had done Garrick grievous injustice, and bringing
Williams also on his knees. Proofs of Garrick's
good nature and readiness to oblige abound. In
Forster's MSS. xxxiii. 207, Sir Grey Cooper
mentions his having obtained through Lord North
a commissionership in the Customs for a certain
Charles Hort, in whose favour Garrick had interceded.
Sir Grey also speaks by report of Garrick's performances, saying : " We learn that you never were so
great, that the whole theatre fell into tears, and that
you were in the full exercise of your dominion over
the passions." What part Garrick had played we
are not told. He had to this time maintained his

habit of taking juvenile characters, though now con-
siderably over fifty years of age. The feat was
rendered easier of accomplishment since his figure
remained slender. Tate Wilkinson says that Garrick
" acted young parts to the last without impropriety
—he was a most lucky instance for retaining his
spirits and the use of his limbs, with the face growing plump instead of sharp ; when dressed there was
not the least mark of age about him to the end of
his theatrical career." Williams, it is true, says in
the pamphlet before-mentioned that Garrick speaks
through his nose, has lost the power of pronouncing
many English words, and in young characters looks
" like an old doating, shrivelled beau." Among
those who at this moment repaid Garrick's assistance
with insult was Charles Dibdin, who wrote, September,
1775 : " I retort your charge of falsehood, and tell
you that you shall not dare, when you know it is as
false as ungentlemanlike, to accuse me of it ; and
as to ingratitude no man can be ungrateful to you;
he can have no obligation to you, but on the score
of money, and that you ever take care to cancel by
upbraiding him of it. The world, for my comfort,
is kind and candid, and it shall be acquainted with
every circumstance of your *kindness*, from the
hamper of wine to the present transaction." This
letter, quoted by Mr. Fitzgerald from the Bullock
MSS., is endorsed by Garrick, " Dibdin's Consummate Impudence, Folly and Ingratitude." Dibdin had
indeed been more than once saved by Garrick from
ruin. Garrick was receiving at this time 800*l.* a

year as actor and 500*l.* as manager.   After him on
the pay list came Mrs. Yates.   Mrs. Abington we
find near this date, 16th September, 1772, complaining in an unpublished letter that she has hitherto
provided herself with clothes, as those found by the
management were not sufficient, and stating that
she is "exceeding distressed in the article of
clothes."   Her "circumstances are no longer equal
to the expense," so she begs the management to
grant her 60*l.* a year extra, and she will (still)
provide herself with clothes.

The last season of Garrick's conduct of a theatre has
now been reached. He had long been weary of the toils
of management and the importunity to which, partly
owing to his weakness, he had been subject.   An
unpublished letter of Lord Camden, unfortunately
undated so far as regards the year, shows that Garrick
had been seriously thinking of retirement.   It is
equally honouring to both parties.

"October 11th, ——.

"DEAR GARRICK,—I was pleased with the warmth of
your letter, which sympathizes with my own feelings.
Speak no more of the honour of my friendship : we are
perfectly equal, being both private gentlemen, with this
difference only, that your talent is in full exercise and
living, and mine (if it ever was any) is silenced and
forgot ; but when you retire, as you sometimes threaten,
then we shall be quite upon a par—Garrick and Camden
instead of Roscius and the Chancellor.   At present you
have the advantage.   But no more of this stuff.   We
shall be happy to see you and Mrs. Garrick next Saturday se'nnight.   I wish it was earlier, but the acquisition

of a favourite bit of ground in the country is of more importance than a hundred visits here.

"Yours most sincerely and affectionately,

"CAMDEN."

Drury Lane, which had undergone some alterations, reopened September, 1775, with a musical prelude by Garrick entitled "Theatrical Candidates," which, though slight to triviality and feeble to inanity, had some success. Garrick played Kitely in "Every Man in his Humour," October 6th; and on the 13th Mrs. King, from York, made her first appearance as Rosalind, playing subsequently Lady Macbeth, Lady Lurewell, Ruth in "The Committee," and other characters. "May-Day, or The Little Gipsy," a musical trifle attributed to Garrick, was acted on the 28th October, and served for the introduction to the stage of Miss Abrams, a young Jewish singer.

On Friday, 29th December, as "a young lady, her first appearance," Mrs. Siddons made her courtesy to a Drury Lane audience as Portia. She had been recommended to Garrick by the Rev. Henry Bate, "The fighting Parson," afterwards Sir Henry Bate Dudley. She played during the season Epicene and other parts with no very distinguished success, and in subsequent years, besides grumbling over the salary paid her, charged Garrick with keeping her back through discreditable motives, among which jealousy of her superior talent was naturally included. No justification for any charge against Garrick seems to exist. Mrs. Cowley's comedy, "The Runaway," was produced 15th February,

1776, with less success than it merited. For a first piece, it has high merit. Emily, the heroine, was played by Mrs. Siddons. A copy of Mrs. Cowley's letter asking Garrick to produce it is still in MS., and contains some clever coaxing and one or two interesting statements. Here is a portion of her own estimate of her piece : " If any of my characters have a claim to originality, it is that of Lady Dinah, and in hers I have left all the finishings to the judgment of the performer. In an age in which all women are well bred, in which every woman reads and converses, there can be no very striking difference in their language or their sentiment ; character must, therefore, be expressed by manner. I meant her to be pedantic, haughty, and resentful. The Justice owes his existence in this piece to the comic capabilities of Mr. Weston, Bella I drew from Mrs. Abington, Harriet from Miss Younge. Allow me to add that in Jarvis and Susan, I thought of Mr. Palmer and Miss Pope."

After declaring that she will not seek a recommendation to him from the great, but will owe everything to him, she tells Garrick she has formed a design on his heart, to make an impression on which, she continues,

> " I would show you three little cherubs, who, if they could talk, would tell you their future welfare depends in great measure on your acceptance of their mother's labour; they should promise you their infant love and their maturer gratitude. My little Betsey would in five minutes smile you into all the sentiments I could wish.

"The title of an author, I assure you, Sir, I am not at all ambitious of, nor could vanity have induced me to attempt making my name public. This attempt is a sacrifice to those for whose benefit every effort in my power is a duty. I think thus much necessary by way of apology for having stept out of that province which is prudently assigned to my sex.

"I have conceived a thousand fanciful ideas about the character I should assume to myself in this epistle, but I cannot discover which would be most likely to effect my purpose. I must therefore conclude with entreating you, Sir, to imagine me whatever would in your judgment render me most worthy your protection. In twelve or fourteen days I beg to be allowed the favour of waiting on you to receive your opinion of my performance."

[Unsigned] Forster Add. MSS. xxvi.

Garrick's last season was not to pass over without a riot of the kind with which he was familiar. This came *à propos* of the production of the Rev. Henry Bate Dudley's musical farce, "The Blackamoor Washed White." In the previous season Garrick had played the "Rival Candidates" of the same author. Besides being a rowdy and a fighter, the reverend gentleman was a sufficiently unscrupulous journalist, and as such was held in much disesteem and contempt. In the *Morning Post*, a scurrilous paper of the epoch, he had heaped abuse upon gentle and simple, and the audience damned "The Blackamoor Washed White," out of dislike to the author. Ladies were politely told to leave the theatre, and the spectators then hissed the play off the stage. This was on its fourth performance, when Garrick,

knowing that a row was probable, had tried to stop
it by himself playing Sir John Brute earlier in the
evening.   With this exception, however, the season
was, in the main, the most peaceful, as well as the
most brilliant, of Garrick's career.

Many reasons had conspired to drive Garrick into
retirement.   Among these illness occupies a prominent
place.   He was subject to gout, stone, and kindred
complaints, and suffered agonies when, during a
representation, he had to fall or use any violent
exertion.   His partner in management, Lacy, had
died in 1774, leaving as his successor his son
Willoughby, a young man far from easy to manage,
on whose judgment Garrick had no very firm
reliance.   His leading women were a source of
perpetual trouble to him.   Miss Pope, with more
firmness than he ordinarily exhibited, he drove for a
time from the theatre.   Miss Younge and Mrs.
Yates wearied him with affectations and pretences;
and for Mrs. Abington, perhaps the cleverest of the
lot, he conceived a positive loathing.   Her letters
are indeed those of a jealous, conceited, nagging
woman.   Garrick calls her in one place "that
worst of bad women, Mrs. Abington," and again
speaks of "that most worthless creature, Abington,"
adding, "she is below the thought of any honest
man or woman; she is as silly as she is false and
treacherous."   Few of her letters are without some
marginal comment, derisive or contemptuous, as,
"Another fal-lal from Mrs. Abington."   This difficulty with his actresses, probably the least potent

reason of all, was advanced with waggish persistency in the press as the foremost, and humorous poems were written likening Garrick to Orpheus. Mr. Fitzgerald quotes a distich to this effect:—

> "Three thousand wives killed Orpheus, in a rage,
> Three actresses drove Garrick from the stage."

There remains the excuse of age. This in Garrick's case was not excessive. Men older than he by a score years have continued on the stage. Garrick, however, continued to the end to play youthful parts, and for such his age began to incapacitate him. He was sore on the subject. Like others of his profession, he tried to keep his years a secret. To a man of position who had, with singularly bad taste, written to Garrick to ask his age, as the means of settling a wager, he wrote, " My age, thanks to your Excellency's proclamation of it, has been published with a proper certificate in all the papers, so that I am obliged to resign all the love-making and ravishing heroes. The ladies, who are very quick in these matters, sit now very quietly in the boxes, and think that *Mrs. Sullen* and *Mrs. Strictland* are in no great danger from *Archer* and *Ranger,* and that *Jane Shore* may easily escape from a *Lord Hastings* of *fifty-six.*"[1] Some genuine signs of age weighed upon Garrick. Not only could he not study a new part, he was unable without extreme difficulty to learn a few lines even that were not his own composition.

[1] Fitzgerald, ii. 380.

When once the resolution was taken and announced, Garrick obtained a brilliant aftermath of popularity. The house was nightly crowded with a rapturous audience, the applications for seats on the part of the "great unpaying" became clamorous, and new quarrels were begotten by Garrick's inability to satisfy the wishes of all who thought they had a claim upon him. Not until the 7th March, 1776, had Garrick told the public of his intention to retire. He then, in a prologue which he wrote to Colman's farce, " The Spleen, or Islington Spa," through the mouth of King, who played Rubrick, a bookseller and dealer in quack medicines, said,—

" The master of *this shop*, too, seeks repose,
  Sells off his stock-in-trade, his verse and prose,
  His daggers, buskins, thunder, lightning, and old cloaths."

His adieux practically extended over the period between this date and 10th June, when he made his last appearance.

He had acted frequently during the season, having been seen in Kitely in "Every Man in His Humour," Lusignan in "Zara," Sir John Brute in "The Provoked Wife," Benedick, Abel Drugger in "The Alchemist," Archer in "The Stratagem," Leon in "Rule a Wife and Have a Wife," Hamlet, and Sir Anthony Branville in "The Discovery," the last a part in which he had not appeared for twelve years. On 7th March, however, Lusignan was announced as played for the last time; on the 11th April he played Abel Drugger for the last time;

on the 25th Kitely, on the 30th Sir John Brute; on 2nd May Leon, on the 7th Archer, on the 9th Benedick, and on the 30th, for the benefit of the Theatrical Fund, Hamlet. Ranger was given for the last time on 1st June; on the 3rd Richard III. was announced for the last time, but it was given again "by command" on the 5th. King Lear was played on June 8th, and the final farewell of the stage was taken as Don Felix in "The Wonder," on the 10th.

Some glimpses of the manner in which these farewell performances were received are obtained from the behaviour of the audience when he was seen for the last time as Abel Drugger. Garrick says that he thought they were cracked, and that it almost turned his brain. Curwen, an American clergyman, notes in his diary under 7th May, 1776, "Attempted to get into Drury Lane Theatre to see Mr. Garrick in the character of *Archer*, but the crowd so great, that after suffering thumps, squeezes, and almost suffocation, for two hours, I was obliged to retire without effecting it." [1] His women tormentors seem under the influences that prevailed to have relented somewhat. Indeed, with the exception of Mrs. Abington, their gravest faults appear to have been due to nothing worse than conceit and caprice. A touching scene was presented at the close of the performance of "King Lear." Garrick then addressed Miss Younge, one of the most constant offenders, who

---

[1] Fitzgerald, ii. 394.

played Cordelia, and, calling her his " dear daughter," expressed a hope that the blessings he had invoked on the stage might fall on her in real life, whereupon the mutineer, now penitent, prayed him to give her his real blessing, which Garrick did with much solemnity.[1]

Garrick had originally intended to take his leave in Richard, the character in which his first success was obtained. In the end he substituted for the part the less arduous character of Don Felix in " The Wonder."

The following unpublished letter from Sir Giles Rooke, concerning Garrick's Richard, and its effect on those who witnessed it, though necessarily in the language of compliment, conveys a good idea of Garrick's powers, and furnishes a pleasant picture:—

> MY VERY GOOD SIR,—You have obliged and astonished me beyond measure by enabling me to see the incomparable Richard so commodiously last night. Say what you will of your fever and inability, you never discovered greater powers, nor exerted them more completely to the satisfaction of the public, than in that wonderful performance. I, who have seen and admired you in it even from my boyish days, never was so sensible of its excellence as last night; it was like magic or enchantment to me. The young lady and her aunt are in raptures with you ; the latter says she could hardly refuse her daughter Elizabeth to such a wooer ; the former (whose name is Anne) believes she should have been as unable to resist your suit as the lady her namesake. By-the-bye, the little jade insists upon it that I give her love to you and thank you, and add further that she lives only in the hope

---

[1] Fitzgerald, ii. 394.

of seeing you in Lear. . . . Excuse me, dear sir; I write in the warmth of my heart, and under the orders and auspices of a fair lady to whom, if you were to see her, you could refuse nothing. However you may dispose of us at Lear, the obligations you have already conferred on me demand the most cordial acknowledgments from your very constant and sincere admirer, frequenter, and friend,

GILES ROOKE.

Inner Temple, 6th June, 1776.
(Forster MS. ii. 121.)

Garrick's last performance was ushered in by a rhymed prologue of the class of which he had an overflowing supply. Anxious, it may be assumed, to avoid such premature and needless indulgence in sentiment as should incapacitate him for performing, or anticipate the final tenderness of farwell, he avoided in this all but the slightest reference to existing conditions, and made it a simple appeal to the charity of those present on behalf of the Theatrical Fund, to which, with remarkable generosity, for the second time in a season, he gave the receipts. The opening lines of this include one of the most familiar of subsequent quotations:—

> "A vet'ran see! whose last act on the stage
> Intreats your smiles for sickness and for age.
> Their cause I plead; plead it with heart and mind;
> A fellow feeling makes one wond'rous kind."

Not devoid of humour is what follows, though it is disturbed by that morbid self-assertion by which Garrick was beset:—

> "Shan't I, who oft have drench'd my hands in gore,
> Stabb'd many, poison'd some, beheaded more,

> Who numbers slew in battle on the plain,
> Shan't I, the slayer, try to feed the slain?
> Brother to all, with equal love I view
> The men who slew me, and the men I slew."

Under circumstances such as existed, Garrick's acting could scarcely fail to be at the highest point, and accounts concur in representing his performance as excellent. When the close was reached, Garrick spoke in prose. He owned that his thoughts had turned in the direction of the customary rhymed epilogue. He felt, however, that the " jingle of rhyme and the language of fiction " would not suit his feelings. His address, the delivery of which was disturbed with tears, was quiet and effective, and was, of course, well received. At the close, Garrick quitted for ever the stage, the brightest ornament of which he had been.

CHAPTER XV.

WHATEVER may be thought of Garrick's general character, behaviour, and management, the circumstances attending his retirement were wholly honouring. How anxious people of rank and fortune were to take part in the closing ceremony is abundantly testified in the correspondence. His presentation of the entire receipts to the professional charity was heroic. Garrick's contributions to the Drury Lane Theatrical Fund are indeed munificent, and are in themselves enough to vindicate him from the charge of meanness or stinginess. That the inception of the idea was not his was a subject of mortification to him. The scheme of a theatrical fund was started at Covent Garden in 1765 by Thomas Hull, the occasion that gave it birth being the poverty of Mrs. Hamilton, an actress of some capacity, who had been thrown on the private charity of the actors. Aided by Mattocks, and supported by Beard and others, Hull carried out the scheme, and the society was, in 1776, incorporated by Act of Parliament. When the movement originated, Garrick was abroad. After his return he founded the Drury Lane Theatrical Fund, in which he took a keen and continuous interest. Aided by Lacy, he paid down a considerable sum at the establishment of the fund, and gave an annual benefit at which he rarely if ever failed to act. In 1776, Garrick paid personally the expenses of an Act of Parliament legally establishing the fund. The following particulars, now first printed, concerning this have some interest. Under the date 12th March, 1776, Nathaniel Barwell writes to Garrick from the House of Commons concerning the Act of Parliament incorporating the Drury Lane performers, and says, " I beg you would not give yourself any trouble about paying my bill. I am not in any want of money at this time, having much more by me than I have any occasion for. . . . The expense of your Act (exclusive of printing) is 111*l.* 19*s.* 10*d.*" Elsewhere the separate items of expense are given, including the sums paid to various officials of the House of Commons. The addition to this of the printer's bill, 4*l.* 10*s.*, brings the whole to 116*l.* 9*s.* 10*d.* The bill is endorsed, " Received 11th April, 1776, the contents in full by me, Nath. Barwell."

Many other contributions were made by Garrick, the entire amount with which Davies supposes him to have enriched the institution being near 4500*l.* Knowledge of the fact that Richard Brinsley Sheridan, Thomas Linley, and Richard Ford were to become possessors of Garrick's share in Drury Lane, oozed out in January, 1776. Of the sum which Garrick received, Sheridan contributed 15,000*l.*, and the others 10,000*l.* each. Willoughby Lacy was dissuaded by Garrick from selling his share, but ultimately did so, the purchaser being Sheridan, who appears at this time to have had command of large sums of money.

Garrick's sale of his share did not involve a stoppage of his interest in the theatre. He still supplied prologue and epilogue, and volunteered advice which the managers as a rule were prudent enough to accept. For the remainder of his life, accordingly, his name remains associated with Drury Lane, and the influence of his judgment or his prejudices is distinctly visible. The opening piece for the season of 1776-77 was an occasional prelude by George Colman, entitled " New Brooms." In this, to which Garrick contributed a prologue, Colman contrived to compliment Garrick by quoting in regard to him from " Richard II." :—

> " As in a theatre the eyes of men,
>   After a well-graced actor leaves the stage,
>   Are idly bent on him that follows next."

Miss Pope, whom Garrick had mercilessly snubbed, and whose applications for forgiveness had been granted at the warm request of Mrs. Clive, reappeared at the theatre. The letter in which Mrs. Clive congratulates Garrick on his retirement from the stage, is one of the most delightful in its class that Garrick or any manager ever received, and is so enchanting that a quotation of the greater portion will be more than pardoned. It is dated from Twickenham, 23rd Jan., 1776, and begins :—

" DEAR SIR,

   " Is it really true that you have put an end to the glory

of Drury Lane Theatre? *If it is so*, let me congratulate my dear Mr. and Mrs. Garrick on their approaching happiness. I *know* what it will be ; you cannot yet have an idea of it ; *but* if you should still be so wicked not to be satisfied with that *unbounded*, uncommon degree of favour you have received as an actor, and which no other actor ever did receive, nor no other actor ever *can* receive, I say, if you should still long to be dipping your fingers in their theatrical pudding (now without plums), you will be no Garrick for the Pivy. [Clivy Pivy Garrick called her.]

" In the height of the public admiration for you, when you were never mentioned with any other appellation but the Garrick, the charming man, the fine fellow, the delightful creature, both by men and ladies ; when they were admiring everything you did, and everything you scribbled—at this very time, I, *the Pivy*, was a living witness that they did not know, nor could they be sensible, of half your perfections. I have seen you, with your magical hammer in your hand, *endeavouring* to beat your ideas into the heads of creatures who had none of their own. I have seen you, with lamb-like patience, endeavouring to make them comprehend you, when that could not be done. I have seen your lamb turned into a lion. By this your great labour and pains the public was entertained ; *they* thought they all acted very fine, they did not see you pull the wires.

" There are people now on the stage to whom you gave their consequence ; they think themselves very great ; now let them go on in their new parts without your leading-strings, and they will soon convince the world what their genius is ; I have always said this to everybody, even when your horses and men were in their highest prancings. While I was under your control, I did not say half the fine things I thought of you, because it looked like flattery, and you know your Pivy was always proud ; besides, I thought you did not like me then, but *now*

I am sure you do, which makes me send you this letter.

* * * *

" Now let me say one word about my poor, unfortunate friend, Miss Pope. I know how much she disobliged you, and if I had been in your place, I believe I should have acted just as you did. But, by this time, I hope you have forgot your resentment, and will look upon her late behaviour as having been taken with a dreadful fit of vanity, which for that time took her senses from her, and having been tutored by an affected beast, who helped to turn her head; but pray recollect her in the other light, a faithful creature to you, on whom you could always depend, certainly a good actress, amiable in her character, both in her being a very modest woman, and very good to her family, and to my certain knowledge has the greatest regard for you.

" Now, my dear Mr. Garrick, I hope it is not yet too late to reinstate her before you quit your affairs there; I beg it, I entreat it; I shall look upon it as the greatest favour you can confer on your ever obliged friend,

" C. CLIVE."

This charming letter is endorsed by Garrick, " My Pivy, excellent." Who can wonder that in presence of such solicitation and such eulogy Miss Pope was reinstated?

On December 10th, 1776, Mrs. Robinson, afterwards famous as Perdita, made her first appearance as Juliet. Garrick, who had great belief in her powers and attractions, was especially pleased with her voice, which recalled to him that of Mrs. Cibber. He exhausted himself in teaching her Juliet, and sat in the orchestra to watch her performance, which was successful. The great event of the season

was, of course, the production of " The School for
Scandal," May 8th, 1777, which brilliant comedy
was so well acted that it stamped with the seal of
general recognition all who took any part in it. It
has since been said that " no new performer has ever
appeared in any one of the principal characters that
was not inferior to the person who acted it originally."
Garrick's known share in the production is confined
to a not very happy or brilliant prologue, spoken by
King. To Covent Garden he had also contributed
an address spoken by Mrs. Barry in " Douglas," after
the death of her husband, Spranger Barry, and an
epilogue spoken by Mrs. Mattocks after the performance of Murphy's " Know your own Mind,"
February 22nd, 1777. Prologues and addresses in
plenty were indeed contributed by him at this
time, not only to the two patent houses, but to the
Haymarket, and even, it is conjectured, for his
special aversion, Mrs. Abington, to be delivered
July 4th, 1778, at the Theatre Royal, Dublin. 'To
Hannah More's tragedy of " Percy," produced on
December 10th, 1777, at Covent Garden, he supplied
both prologue and epilogue, the former spoken by
Mrs. Bulkeley, and the latter by Lee Lewes. He
could do no less since Hannah More was his latest
friend, and his most enthusiastic admirer. To her
opinion upon his performances there will be occasion
to recur. Garrick, moreover, had much influence in
commending her plays. There is nothing very noteworthy in either of these productions, except that a
reference in the prologue to the Chevalier d'Éon

appears to have nettled that gentleman—or lady. To Fielding's posthumous play, "Fathers, or the Good-natured Man," Drury Lane, November 30th, 1778, Garrick also contributed both prologue and epilogue, these being the last he appears to have written. The prologue, which was admirably spoken by King, introduces not unhappily the principal characters in "Tom Jones." Allworthy makes the last appeal to the "leaders of the taste and fashion."

> " Departed genius left his orphan play
> To your kind care—what the dead wills, obey;
> O, then, respect the Father's fond request,
> And make his widow smile, his spirit rest."

This prologue elicited some very sensible criticism from Garrick's great friend, Lady Spencer. The epilogue, which is commonplace, was spoken by Miss Younge.

After his retirement to Hampton, Garrick had abundant occupation. He was an assiduous correspondent, and Hannah More alone must have taken up no inconsiderable share of his time. None of the pleasantest were the business communications he received from Lacy and the other managers of Drury Lane, the uneasiness they gave him as regards the security of his mortgage being quite justified. There was also the task of accepting or declining the invitations thrust upon him. Concerning his social popularity no doubt can be entertained. Best among his friends seem to have been the Spencers, whose invitations are constant and cordial. Not to the very close of his life, moreover, was Garrick to be free from threatening letters written by the most loathsome and detestable of their race. One such was hanging over his head at the time of his death. A certain Curtius, who demands an answer to be sent to H.L.T.X., to an address in Globe Court, Shoe Lane, wrote to him a letter full of horrible insinuations. It is dated November 21st, 1778. Here are a few lines from the precious production :—" The public have hitherto seen you only in the polished mirror of a parasite's adulation, the flattering gloss hath shown its figures falsely ; but, in the position wherein Curtius will place it, the public will perceive it neither magnifies nor diminishes. Yet the exact reflection will astonish ; for the universe [!] will see its mistake, and Garrick's nature must be humbled in the dust. Indeed, sir, my Lord North will scarce blacken under my pen like the man, who for many years has enjoyed the *idolatry of affection* without meriting one single sentiment of *sufferance* abstracted from his mimical talents." A letter such as this might waken in the meekest one spark of virility. But no. Garrick writes a long letter intended to soothe and to disarm. He quotes his best Shakespearean phrases, and even tells the reptile that he would rather have " his praise than his blame." Was ever such a comment upon Goldsmith's famous lines?

> " Of praise a mere glutton, he swallowed what came,
>   And the puff of a dunce, he mistook it for fame."

Something worse than the puff of a dunce—the

praise of a hired libeller—seemed worth stooping to obtain. A further letter, dated January 12th, 1779, tells Garrick that Curtius has heard of his illness, and postpones further action or menace until Mr. Garrick shall be in a condition or "state of body to answer any public charges." Such a state of body was not to be reached. While superintending rehearsals at the theatre Garrick had caught a cold which he was unable to throw off. When paying a customary Christmas visit to Althorp he was attacked by his old illnesses, gout and stone, complicated with herpes. Leaving that hospitable house, he by easy stages reached London, arriving at the Adelphi on January 15th. Certain symptoms inspired uneasiness, and his apothecary, Laurence, called in Dr. Cadogan, who advised Garrick to settle his worldly affairs, and was told that this had been done. Fresh advice was taken, Dr. Heberden, Dr. Warren, and Dr. Schomberg being called in. Rousing from the kind of lethargy into which he had sunk, Garrick hailed the last named, and took him by the hand, exclaiming, "Though last not least in love." To succeeding physicians he was less complimentary, quoting after their arrival the lines of Horatio in the "Fair Penitent":—

> "Another still succeeds,
> Another, and another after that,
> And the last fool is welcome as the former."

To one of his physicians he confided that he "did not regret being childless, for he knew the quickness of his feelings was so great, that, in case it had been his misfortune to have had disobedient children, he could not have supported such an affliction." Other stories concerning his last days are told by Davies, a not wholly unprejudiced authority, but the best to be had. On Wednesday, January 20th, 1779, Garrick, who appears to the last to have anticipated recovery, fell back at 8 o'clock in the morning and painlessly expired. An examination revealed unsuspected disease of the kidneys, which had been mistaken for stone. So, sanguine and hopeful to the last, surrounded by friends and weighed down with honours, Garrick passed away out of the reach of the actresses who tormented him, the dramatists who alternately coaxed and menaced him, and the Kenricks and Curtiuses who sought to prey upon him. So came about the death which Johnson said " eclipsed the gaiety of nations," justifying afterwards the use of the word " eclipsed," which did not mean extinguished, and that of " nations" by reckoning the Scotch as a separate nation.

The funeral took place in Westminster Abbey on February 1st, 1779, the line of carriages extending over the length of the course from Adelphi Terrace to the Abbey. A full account of the imposing spectacle is supplied in the appendix to the latest edition of the life by Davies. George Garrick, the faithful friend, brother, and servant, survived but a few days, and was now on his death-bed. Garrick was always " wanting " him, and when the cause of George's death was asked, the touching joke was

made, " David wanted him." Some of Garrick's
nephews were among the family mourners. Seldom
has so princely an array of talent and rank been seen.
Drury Lane sent King, Smith, Yates, Dodd, Vernon,
Palmer, Brereton, Bensley, Moody, Aickin, Baddeley,
Parsons; Covent Garden, Mattocks, Clark, Aickin,
Baker, Hull, Lewis, Wroughton, Reinhold, Lee
Lewes, Whitfield, Quick, Wilson. The Literary
Club chose as representatives Lord Althorp, Hon. T.
Beauclerk, Sir Charles Bunbury, and Edmund Burke.
Sheridan was chief mourner, and in the crowd con-
stituting the procession were, to mention a few only,
the Duke of Devonshire, Lord Camden, Lord
Spencer, Lord Palmerston, Lord Ossory, Johnson,
Percy, Gibbon, Charles James Fox, Sir Joshua
Reynolds, Colman, and Joseph Banks. Guardsmen
and mounted horsemen also took part, the Bishop of
Rochester read the funeral service, and the Dean and
Chapter of Westminster took one hundred guineas
of the 1500*l*. which the pageant is alleged to have
cost.

Garrick's will, a creditable document, also given
in extenso in Davies's " Life," bequeaths to the
trustees of the British Museum, after his wife's
death, his statue of Shakespeare and his noble
collection of old English plays. It makes a fine
provision for Mrs. Garrick, to be diminished should
she elect to reside beyond sea, and leaves handsome legacies to his brothers and their descendants.
The monument to Garrick in Westminster Abbey
was not erected by Mrs. Garrick—who, seeing

that the funeral expenses were not paid in 1782, and the undertaker was ruined, seems indeed to have merited the charge of penury often brought against her husband—but by a friend, Mr. Albany Wallis, who entrusted the execution of the monument to Webber, and the epitaph to Pratt. Garrick, it may be stated, had previously erected a monument in the Abbey to Albany Charles Wallis, a Westminster scholar, son of the before named, who was drowned in the Thames in his fourteenth year. Garrick is buried at the foot of the statue of " his beloved " if much desecrated Shakespeare. Webber's meretricious monument with Pratt's lines is on the opposite wall. The two provoked from Charles Lamb the expression of an uncustomary sentiment. " Taking," says he, " a turn in the Abbey the other day, I was struck with the affected attitude of a figure, which, on examination, proved to be a whole-length representation of the celebrated Mr. Garrick. Though I would not go so far, with some good Catholics abroad, as to shut players altogether out of consecrated ground, yet I own I was a little scandalized at the introduction of theatrical airs and gestures into a place set apart to remind us of the saddest realities. Going nearer, I found inscribed under the harlequin figure a farrago of false thought and nonsense." An inscription by Burke was offered, but was declined as too long. To the same place followed, October 25th, 1822, his wife, aged, it was said, ninety-nine, and described as " a little bowed-down old woman who went about leaning on a gold-headed cane, dressed in deep widow's mourning, and always talking of her dear Davy."

Her own death was curious. She was on the point of going to see some alterations made by Elliston in Drury Lane, and chid somewhat testily the maid-servant who handed her a cup. "Put it down, hussy; do you think I cannot help myself?" she said, tasted the tea, and expired. Many actors called to see the old lady, and one, Edmund Kean, received some encouragement from her. She was devoted to the memory of her husband, as she had every occasion to be, seeing that during their married life he had never spent a day entirely away from her. In compelling her to live in England, however, Garrick knew her well. Her money that she had saved she left to her German relatives. She allowed the Hampton residence—where she was visited by Queen Charlotte, who found her peeling onions, and is said to have joined her in her occupation—to go into disrepair, and she took, in 1807, proceedings in Chancery with a view to benefit further under her "husband's" will, which brought on her the charge of greediness. On the whole, recollections of her are pleasant, and the pictures presented of her in her later years in diaries and the like are generally agreeable.

CHAPTER XVI.

ABUSE, much of it superfluous, has been lavished on the early biographers of Garrick, who are charged with prejudice and injustice. Cumberland and Davies had both had dealings with Garrick, and both thought themselves aggrieved. On the points on which they were sore the verdict of the great continuous session of literature is against them. Not wholly imaginary are, however, their grievances, since they are those of almost every dramatist with whom Garrick was thrown into association, and a chorus of complaint heard from all sides must be accepted for something. Individually Garrick may have been better than any one of his assailants; he can scarcely have been so much better than the whole of them as to be placed on a pedestal at the foot of which they lie. Two classes of vanity came into collision. The immediate triumph was with the actor manager. The clamour of the dramatists was louder than his, and they forced a hearing. Now, when both are mute, the side generally espoused is Garrick's. The fact remains that Davy was a difficult man with whom to deal, and the most honouring intimacies he made were those in regard to which he showed himself most subservient. There are two classes of intimacies with regard to which all is honouring. A friendship such as that of Lord Camden adds lustre to a life so brilliant even as Garrick's. The relations he maintained with the Spencers' and others of position and consideration were unclouded. Those, again, he kept up with the leading Frenchmen of the day were equally delightful. The most distinguished men and women of France showed towards him a loyalty and fidelity with which Englishmen are not apt to credit their nation. In all these cases, however, it must be seen that business relations did not interfere, and Garrick's vanity received due homage.

Garrick's nature, indeed, was less complex than uncommon. Vanity, the commonest and most pardonable, though sometimes one of the most cruel of foibles, to use no stronger word, was at the bottom of all Garrick's difficulties. He was, moreover, jealous, more than a little querulous, exigent, peppery, incapable of sustained animosity, endowed with prodigious vitality, and profoundly sweet-natured, using the combined words in their highest significance. This is a combination not often encountered. His traits were not all amiable; he was subservient to success, and timid in the presence of arrogance or assumption, stern only with those whom it was not worth his while to conciliate, and though one of the most generous men that ever lived, he left a not wholly undeserved reputation for stinginess.

Not in the least an ideal hero is a man of this class, yet when his genius is thrown in he remains one of the greatest men and most attractive figures of an interesting epoch. Well known as are the utterances concerning him of Goldsmith and Johnson, it is impossible to omit them from an attempted estimate of Garrick's character. With Goldsmith Garrick had more than one difficulty, and his behaviour with regard to the production of the " Good-Natured Man " was neither very amiable nor very ingenuous. David, indeed, did not believe that this queer, erratic, improvident Irishman was his equal, in some sense, perhaps, his superior, and did not very easily reconcile himself to the idea of conciliating him. He is charged with jealousy of Goldsmith, and the accusation may or may not be just. In refusing to sign the recommendation of Goldsmith as secretary to the Society of Arts he showed more temper than magnanimity, and in the matter of epigrams he was, though in good company, the offender. Goldsmith's vanity was of the nature which could not hear a man praised for any accomplishment whatever without declaring that he (Goldsmith) possessed it in a higher degree. The very childishness of this provokes retort, and a series of epigrams by which Goldsmith was wounded was perpetrated. Garrick's poor contribution to this was—

> " Here lies Nolly Goldsmith, for shortness call'd Noll,
> Who wrote like an angel, but talked like poor Poll."

Then came Goldsmith's reply, "Retaliation," unfinished at his death, in which the character of

Garrick was summed up with marvellous skill and accuracy :—

" Here lies David Garrick, describe me who can,
   An abridgment of all that was pleasant in man ;
   As an actor, confest without rival to shine ;
   As a wit, if not first, in the very first line ;
   Yet, with talents like these, and an excellent heart,
   The man had his failings, a dupe to his art.
   Like an ill-judging beauty his colours he spread,
   And beplaster'd with rouge his own natural red.
   On the stage he was natural, simple, affecting ;
   'Twas only that when he was off he was acting.
   With no reason on earth to go out of his way,
   He turn'd and he varied full ten times a day ;
   Though secure of our hearts, yet confoundedly sick,
   If they were not his own by finessing and trick ;
   He cast off his friends, as a huntsman his pack,
   For he knew when he pleased he could whistle them back.
   Of praise a mere glutton, he swallowed what came,
   And the puff of a dunce, he mistook it for fame,
   Till his relish grown callous, almost to disease,
   Who peppered the highest, was surest to please.
   But let us be candid and speak out our mind,
   If dunces applauded, he paid them in kind.
   Ye Kenricks, ye Kellys, and Woodfalls so grave,
   What a commerce was yours, while you got and you **gave**!
   How did Grub Street re-echo the shouts that you raised,
   While he was be-Rosciused, and you were be-praised !
   But peace to his spirit, wherever it flies,
   To act as an angel and mix with the skies.
   Those poets, who owe their best fame to his skill,
   Shall still be his flatterers, go where he will ;
   Old Shakespeare receive him with praise and with love,
   And Beaumonts and Bens be his Kellys above."

These lines, equally admirable in humour and in

feeling, are of course immortal. Had Goldsmith lived they would have fortified Garrick's recently formed estimate that the writer was worth being conciliated. Very poor beside them seem Garrick's attempts at retort. The following, though weak enough, is perhaps the best :—

JUPITER AND MERCURY.

A FABLE.

" Here, Hermes," says Jove, who with nectar was mellow,
" Go fetch me some clay—I will make an odd fellow :
Right and wrong shall be jumbled—much gold and some
　　　dross ;
Without cause be he pleas'd, without cause be he cross ;
Be sure as I work to throw in contradictions,
A great love of truth ; yet a mind turn'd to fictions ;
Now mix these ingredients, which warm'd in the baking,
Turn to learning and gaming, religion and raking.
With the love of a wench, let his writings be chaste ;
Tip his tongue with strange matter, his pen with fine taste ;
That the rake and the poet o'er all may prevail
Set fire to the head, and set fire to the tail :
For the joy of each sex, on the world I'll bestow it :
This scholar, rake, Christian, dupe, gamester, and poet,
Thro' a mixture so odd he shall merit great fame,
And among brother mortals—be Goldsmith his name !
When on earth this strange meteor no more shall appear
You, Hermes, shall fetch him, to make us sport here ! "

Not less to the point than Goldsmith's lines are Johnson's remarks to Boswell when that worthy spoke to him of Garrick's death. It was in part his own exculpation. Johnson through his entire career resented the success of Garrick, whom he regarded as his inferior, and whose success, if not greater, was at least more rapid than his own. Nevertheless, though often churlish, he liked this companion of his boyhood, and those who thought by attacks on Garrick to please him reckoned without their host. Boswell opened the question at a dinner at Beauclerk's at which were Sir Joshua, Jones (afterwards Sir William), Langton, Steevens, and others, by repeating and proclaiming the justice of an assertion of Wilkes that Garrick had no friends. Johnson was ultimately drawn, and after admitting that there were materials to make friendship in Garrick were he not so diffused, he took up his parable: "Garrick was a very good man, the cheerfullest man of his age; a decent liver in a profession which is supposed to give indulgence to licentiousness, and a man who gave away, freely, money acquired by himself. He began the world with a great hunger for money; the son of a half-pay officer, bred in a family, whose study was to make fourpence do as much as others make fourpence halfpenny do. But when he had got money he was very liberal." Innumerable tributes to Garrick's worth are intercalated among Johnson's growlings. When attending Garrick's funeral Johnson, according to Sir William Jones, said, "Mr. Garrick and his profession have been equally indebted to each other. His profession made him rich, and he made his profession respectable." Again he said in conversation: "Then, sir, Garrick did not *find*, but *made* his way to the tables, the levees, and almost the bed-chambers of the great.

Then, sir, Garrick had under him a numerous body of people, who, from fear of his power, and hopes of his favour, and admiration of his talents, were constantly submissive to him.   And here is a man who has advanced the dignity of his profession.   Garrick has made a player a higher character."   Of the death of Garrick he spoke, as has been said, as that " stroke of death, which had eclipsed the gaiety of nations, and impoverished the publick stock of harmless pleasure."   Johnson, besides proposing to write his epitaph, was willing to have written his life, but was not invited so to do.

What Boswell said about Garrick's having no friends had as much truth as generalizations of the kind often possess.   Garrick's relations at different periods of his life with Hogarth, Burke, Sterne, Fielding, Sir Joshua Reynolds, like those with Lord Camden, were unbrokenly amicable.   With authors as a rule, not wholly through his own fault, he did not " get on."   He did not join the Literary Club until late in life, the year being 1773.   Sir John Hawkins says erroneously that he was never admitted.   In the manner of seeking or consenting to be a member he offended the prejudices or susceptibilities of Johnson, who regarded his manner as cavalier.   When he joined, however, he became a popular member, and on his death—on which occasion, somewhat curiously, the club, which had long existed without any distinguishing appellation but simply as the Club, first took its name—Johnson made expiation for whatever ill-nature he may previously have exhibited, saying, when an election in Garrick's place was proposed, that a successor worthy of such a man could not be found, and insisting upon a grass widowhood before they proceeded to another election.

In most cases of feud or quarrel one is compelled to espouse the side of Garrick. In his dispute with Goldsmith he was wrong. He made, however, all possible amends. A quarrel between him and Johnson almost sprang out of the production of " Irene," and Johnson said with characteristic asperity, " Sir, the fellow wants me to make Mahomet seem mad, that he may have an opportunity of tossing his hands and kicking his heels." Unhappy enough was the death scene which Garrick introduced. Garrick, none the less, in producing the play sought to render a service to an old friend, and Johnson in demurring to his alterations was taking up a line to which managers who are also actors have always objected. Johnson, moreover, not only said things concerning actors with a reference scarcely oblique to Garrick, as when he spoke of a player as " a fellow who claps a lump on his back, and a lump on his leg, and cries, ' I am Richard the Third,' " or declared that a ballad singer stood higher, but wrote what he knew must be wormwood, referring to the stage as a condition which made " almost every other man, for whatever reason, contemptuous, insolent, petulant, selfish, and brutal."

Quarrels with actors constituted a portion of Garrick's daily life. Those over whose head in harlequin

fashion he bounded were little likely to be pleased
by his agility; older men resented in the manager
the dictator; younger men thrust into positions of
untenable rivalry saw or pretended to see in him a
man jealous of their success, and determined to
thwart it. Self-assertion and meanness of this kind
seem all but inseparable from the stage. No man
less than Garrick merits the charge of endeavouring
to impede the progress of younger actors. Now
and then, as in the case of Powell, he became, after a
long absence from the stage, uneasy as to whether
he was, indeed, being forgotten and replaced. As a
rule, however, he challenged fearlessly comparisons
with all, a Barry as soon as a Macklin. Not an
actor of eminence was there in the period over which
his management extended to whom he did not offer
an engagement, ordinarily on advantageous terms,
and those of them who could be trusted, as Sheridan,
Macklin, Barry, Smith, and others, were allowed to
play his own favourite parts. That his measures were
at times unpleasant, that he was angry and a trifle
supercilious with his inferiors, is no serious imputation. A letter is in existence from one of those he
employed saying that but for his dictatorial manner
and shortness of temper he would be an angel. His
actresses were the chief plagues of his life. Before his
marriage the hopes that he might throw the handker-
chief among them kept them in order. In his later
years they were in a state of perpetual mutiny. Not
easily conceivable are the airs and pretensions of
women such as Mrs. Abington, Mrs. Yates, and

Miss Younge. Garrick treated all with judgment and firmness. How successful was his conduct is shown in the fact that so soon as his hand quitted the reins the coach was upset.

In his constant disputes with men such as Colman, whose loyalty and worth are above dispute, as much right must be accorded Garrick as is to be hoped in a case in which men of worth fall out. Colman ceased in later days to be "Coley," angry words passed, and early intimacy was never resumed. The letters of both show, however, respect, and Colman owns that his wounds have never been more than skin deep. When Home's tragedy of "Douglas" was shown to Garrick it was returned with an opinion that it was totally unfit for the stage. There is no reason to believe that Home resented this utterance, which, however, was unpopular in Edinburgh, where Garrick was freely satirized. No cause exists for thinking that Garrick's opinion was wrong. "Douglas" before its production had undergone very serious alteration, and Johnson moreover called it a foolish play, and said there were not ten good lines in it.

Amends were made, anyhow, by Garrick, who took great pains with Home's subsequent pieces, and contracted with their author a close friendship. Of Dr. Armstrong, whose tragedy of "The Forced Marriage" Garrick similarly rejected, the manager made an enemy. Addressing Strahan, David Hume says, 13th March, 1770: "I am sorry to hear that Dr. Armstrong has printed his Tragedy among his

Miscellanies. It is certainly one of the worst pieces
I ever saw, and totally unworthy of his other productions. I should have endeavoured to dissuade
him from printing it had he been a man advisable.
But I knew that he keeps an anger against Garrick
for above twenty years for refusing to bring it on
the stage; and he never since would allow him to
be so much as a tolerable actor. I thought, therefore, it was wiser not to meddle in the affair."
Exactly characteristic is this of the kind of enemies
which Garrick made.

Some men were capable of surmounting such
unworthy feelings. Smollett, whose bitterness
against Garrick, similar in origin, found venomous
utterance, made in his History, as has been seen, ample
amends. Mickle, who thought himself ill-used
because Garrick had refused a tragedy of his, inserted
in his "Lusiad" an angry note against the actor. Soon
afterwards he saw Garrick as Lear act for the first
time. During the first three acts he did not speak;
in a fine passage in the fourth act he sighed, and
turning to the friend who accompanied him, said, "I
wish the note was out of my book."

There were others than Mickle and Smollett with
whom Garrick had to deal. Robert Dodsley, the publisher, familiarly known as Doddy, elected to quarrel
with Garrick for not producing his "Cleone," which
Garrick called " a cruel, bloody, and unnatural play,"
and of which Johnson said, " I am afraid there is
more blood than brains." When the piece was produced at Covent Garden Garrick wrote a letter of

congratulation and an offer of service, to which Dodsley replied coldly and peevishly. Garrick wrote once more accordingly :—

> " MASTER ROBERT DODSLEY,—When I first read your peevish answer to my well-meant proposal to you, I was much disturbed at it; but when I considered that some minds cannot bear the smallest portion of success, I most sincerely pitied you; and when I found in the same letter that you were graciously pleased to dismiss me from your acquaintance, I could not but confess so apparent an obligation, and am with due acknowledgments,
> " Master Robert Dodsley,
> " Your most obliged,
> " DAVID GARRICK."

In regard to Jephson, whose plays Garrick did produce, and to whom before that time he had lent money, Garrick comes out with flying colours. His conduct was gentle, considerate, chivalrous, and the indignation of this gentleman—who was Master of the Horse to the Lord-Lieutenant of Ireland—at an application for some kind of security for sums of money that had been lent him, is more than a little whimsical.

A veritable thorn in the flesh was Richard Cumberland, a voluminous dramatist and a man of some position. For some reason or other Johnson and Goldsmith would not admit him into their set, and Garrick even, when he could trust the company, burst out against him, " Damn his dish-clout face; his plays would never do if it were not for my patching them up and acting in them." No inconsiderable space of the Garrick correspondence is taken up by this man's petulance or abjectness.

Murphy, destined also to be a biographer of Garrick, was not less intractable, and being more intemperate was more to be dreaded. Garrick was the victim at his hands of most forms of attack or insinuation, yet seems to have behaved to him with indulgence if not with cordiality. Alternately arrogant and obsequious, Murphy accepted favours and repaid them with insult. He had the grace to be penitent, however, and it was not without some sort of impetuous and ebullient sentiment that he undertook to write a life of Garrick which is in part an apologia for his own. He described Garrick as a " mean, sneaking little fellow," but when asked concerning his acting he was wont to throw up his hands and eyes, exclaiming, " Oh, my great God ! " The Rev. Professor Hawkins, Mackenzie, the " Man of Feeling," and Shirley, the author of "The Black Prince," are among those who took mortal offence at Garrick's non-recognition of their merits, and Shirley even wrote a pamphlet in which Garrick is attacked. From these men we descend to the Ralphs and the Hiffernans, not even then reaching the depths of infamy, since below them we have Bickerstaffes and Kenricks. Into a cloaca such as this a modern reader is not anxious to be led.

No mention is here made of Foote, who was Garrick's most dreaded enemy, and who, like the others, was nowise slow to accept favours of the man he derided. Foote's attacks upon Garrick were not, however, due to any grievance he had, or fancied he had. They were, indeed, the offspring of pure love of mischief and the delight in inflicting torture which is inherent in some natures. From Foote are derived most of the stories as to Garrick's extreme stinginess. He it was who said that Garrick walked out with the intention to do a generous action; but, turning the corner of a street, he met with the ghost of a halfpenny, which frightened him. He told Rogers that Garrick invited Bishop Hurd to dine with him in the Adelphi, and "after dinner, the evening being very warm, they walked up and down in front of the house. As they passed and repassed the dining-room windows Garrick was in a perfect agony, for he saw that there was a thief in one of the candles that was burning on the table; and yet Hurd was a person of such consequence that he could not turn away from him to prevent the waste of his tallow." When, again, Foote and some others at the Chapter Coffee House were dropping money into the hat of a decayed player, Foote said, "If Garrick hears of this he will certainly send in his hat."

Silly as well as ill-natured are these and a score similar stories which Foote invented, or of which he constituted himself the mouthpiece. Other would-be wags caught the infection, and sneers at Garrick's parsimony were employed by those to whom he had shown himself liberal.   There was, as has been said, a kind of justification of these remarks.   Though princely in some forms of expenditure, Garrick was prudent, careful, and in a sense parsimonious.   After the ridiculously elaborate and long unpaid-for funeral which incurred the grave censure of Johnson, Henderson, the " Bath Roscius," and the successor of Garrick, wrote a significant but ill-natured " impromptu " which does little credit to his heart. He draws a picture of the ghost of Garrick watching the procession, not knowing it was his own, and bursting into approval of its economical arrangements.   The closing lines are :—

> Alas ! poor Garrick, in Elysian meads,
> Where new delight to new delight succeeds,
> Still shall the phantom wealth thy steps pursue,
> And tinge thy pleasures with a *careful* hue.

Garrick's payments to authors were liberal. Murphy himself bears witness that it was with Garrick " a fixed principle that authors were entitled to the emolument of their labours," and opines that by that generous way of thinking he held out an invitation to men of genius.   That Garrick was not a stingy manager must be believed.   In those days as in these, pinching and illiberality in management were not the steps to fortune, and Garrick, besides giving away larger sums of money than any other man of his day, left behind him £100,000, an immense sum for those times.   From the charge of avarice he is best defended by the statement of Johnson : " Yes, sir," said Johnson, " I know that Garrick has given away more than any man in England that I am acquainted with, and that not from ostentatious views. Garrick was very poor when he began life ; so that when he came to have money, he probably was very unskilful in giving away, and saved when he should not. But Garrick began to be liberal as soon as he could ; and I am of opinion the reputation of avarice which he has had has been very lucky for him, and prevented his having many enemies. You despise a man for avarice, but do not hate him. Garrick might have been much better attacked for living with more splendour than is suitable to a player ; if they had had the wit to have assaulted him in that quarter, they might have galled him more. But they have kept clamouring about his avarice, which has rescued him from much obloquy and envy." This vindication is capable. To alter Montaigne, however, To be *careful* or *prudent* a man must be so by temperament, not by interest. Garrick pinched in matters of detail and was splendidly liberal. Many of those who inveighed most strongly against him had tasted, if they had not drunk deep, of his bounty. His faults do not even lie in the direction of parsimony. He did not always give pleasantly, but he gave. His gravest defect was his habit of surrounding himself with flatterers, tools, and toadies, to whose reports he listened. To maintain their places these men invented when they had nothing to report. Garrick, too, always failed to grasp the truth that the man who betrays to him the confidences of others will carry back his own in exchange. Making allowance for want of moral fibre, Garrick is one of the most interesting and delightful personalities that ever rendered illustrious the most popular and most fascinating of professions.

CHAPTER XVII.

OF Garrick as an actor it remains to speak. No
such analysis of his performances as was supplied by
Hazlitt in the case of Kean, or by Leigh Hunt in
that of the Kembles, is accessible. We are worse off,
indeed, than we are with regard to Betterton and the
actors subsequent to the "Restoration," of whom
Pepys has given us silhouettes, and Colley Cibber
portraits. From various sources, however, it is
possible to obtain a fair estimate of Garrick's merits
and qualities, and a German, Lichtenberg, in his
"Ausgewählte Schriften" has left a fairly close
description of his performance in his principal
characters.

That Garrick had the frenzied inspiration of Kean
seems improbable. His passion must, notwithstand-
ing, have been no less remarkable than his versatility.
Slowly and grudgingly he won acceptance as the equal
of Betterton. This he seems to have been. Men are
all praisers of that which they admired in their youth,
and reluctance on the part of a veteran to accept artists
of to-day as the equals of their predecessors has
never been conclusive evidence. Exactly analogous
to the difficulties experienced by the few who,
knowing Garrick at his best, had vivid recollections

of Betterton, are those of the few living admirers of Rachel who have to reconcile themselves to La Bernhardt. To us of later date Garrick presents himself as the equal of Betterton in all respects. In the most famous theatrical picture ever painted Sir Joshua shows us Garrick between tragedy and comedy. In his case alone among actors previous to the present century it is impossible to say whether he was greater in tragedy or comedy, whether Lear, Archer, or Abel Drugger was the most absolute masterpiece. He seems himself to have leant to light comedy, to the Archers and Rangers of previous playwrights. In an unpublished letter (Forster MSS., viii., 78) to the Rev. Charles Jenner, he says in 1770, " The _comédie larmoyante_ is getting too much ground upon us, and if those who can write the better species of the comic drama don't make a stand for the genuine comedy and _vis comica,_ the stage in a few years will be (as Hamlet says), like Niobe, all tears." Frank mirth is aimed at in the few pieces constituting his existing dramatic baggage. The alterations of Shakespeare and other great dramatists impudently classed as his works are serious and lachrymose from whatever point they are regarded. Many of his _pièces d'occasion,_ moreover, he has had the grace to leave unprinted. What are entitled to be called his dramatic works, though principally adaptations such as " Miss in her Teens," " Bon Ton," the "Guardian," and the "Irish Widow," are thoroughly humorous and genuinely diverting.

While admitting that Garrick's great distinction

was his universality, Johnson maintained that his one defect was his inability to play " an easy, fine-bred gentleman." Against this must be put Garrick's declaration, that Johnson once praised an actor in Lichfield who played Sir Harry Wildair, detecting in him " a courtly vivacity," whereas, said Garrick, " he was the most vulgar ruffian that ever went upon boards." Derrick praises especially Garrick's Archer (in which Garrick enacts a gentleman masque-rading as a valet), and says, " He is the footman, the gallant, and the gentleman by turns ; his addresses to Cherry [a waiting maid at an inn] are easy and jocular ; with Mrs. Sullen [a lady of fashion un-happily married] he is polite and unaffected, particu-larly in the gallery scene, where the gentleman's education ought to shine upon the manners of the footman ; and he talks of pictures and mythology. He is perfectly happy in wishing Aimwell joy of his marriage ; his changing to resentment and despon-dency on finding himself disappointed ; and his sudden transition to content and satisfaction on find-ing that his friend is really a lord."

George Christopher Lichtenberg, Professor of Natural Philosophy in Göttingen, visited England in 1770 and 1775, and in the latter year wrote much concerning Garrick's performances. He draws an eminently attractive picture :—

> " In his limbs there is the most exquisite symmetry, and the whole figure of the man is thoroughly neat and elegant. The most experienced eye cannot discover a blemish in any part, or in the combination of parts, nor

yet in his movements. . . . With every appearance of ease and confidence, he hits the mark exactly. His walk, the way in which he shrugs his shoulders, or folds his arms, or puts on his hat, now shading his eyes with it, now cocking it to show his forehead, doing all this with the easiest movements of his limbs, as if each one of them were his right hand—all this, indeed, it is delightful to behold. It gives one pleasure to observe how completely his mind seems to be present in every muscle. . . . Garrick is really strong, and extremely nimble and energetic. In the boxing scene in the ' Alchemist ' he runs and skips, poising himself now on one, now on the other of his well-shaped legs, so that he appears to hover in the air. In the dance in ' Much Ado about Nothing ' he is at once distinguishable by his graceful and agile movements. When I saw him in this dance the people actually had the impudence to cry *encore* to their Roscius! . . . Altogether his expression is the most lively, clear, and speaking I have ever seen. When he is serious, the spectators are serious too ; they furrow their brow or smile just as he does ; and in his private joys and friendly ways, in his asides, when he seems to be taking the audience into his confidence, there is such a sweetness and trustfulness of look that all hearts fly, as it were, to the fascinating man."

An account picturesque enough and full enough of detail to resemble a portrait by Clint, is given by Lichtenberg, of Garrick as Archer, and Weston as Scrub, a country bumpkin servant. Garrick, in his light blue and silver livery, and with a rich laced hat and red feather, comes forward :—

" Bright, brisk, and knowing, his smart hat cocked airily a little on one side, and not in the least overshadowing the brilliant face . . . . full of confidence in his calves and his new dress, with firmness and decision in every movement."

Depicting the scene between the two, Lichtenberg says :—

> "With the easy grace peculiar to him, Garrick throws himself into a chair, rests his right arm upon the back of Weston's (i.e. Scrub's) seat, and leans forward for a little confidential chat. The skirts of his splendid livery hang down gracefully, and in the folds of the coat and the person of the man, one line of beauty succeeds another. Weston sits in the middle of his chair, as becomes him, but somewhat far forward, a hand on either knee. He seems dumbfoundered, and his cunning eyes are fixed on Garrick. If anything is expressed on his face, it is the affectation of dignity struggling with the paralyzing sense of the horrible contrast between him and his companion. . . . Whilst Garrick lolls easily in his chair, Weston, with stiffened back, tries by degrees to out-top him, partly from feelings of respect, but partly, too, that he may now and then steal a comparison, when Garrick is not looking him in the face. When Archer at length, in his easy way, crosses his legs, Scrub attempts to do the same, and at last, but not without some assistance from his hands, he happily accomplishes this feat. All this is done with eyes either fixed or looking stealthily. At last, when Archer begins to stroke his splendid silk-stockinged legs, Weston almost instinctively imitates the actor over his miserable red worsted stockings, but immediately after collapses on his chair, and, with a feeling of humility that calls forth one's pity, quietly gathers his green apron over all."

An animated idea of Garrick's Archer is obtained from this, but it may almost be said that Weston has the lion's share of the commendation. Garrick, who had himself played Scrub, after seeing Weston in it, did not again attempt it. He owned that in the scene described, on watching Scrub's behaviour, he was hard set to keep his countenance. For Weston, indeed, he had a great admiration, and on seeing his Abel Drugger, declared it one of the finest pieces of acting he ever saw, and sent Weston 20*l.* on his benefit.

In a similar style Garrick played the various parts he essayed in light comedy, winning "golden opinions" in those in which lightness and airiness were of more importance than distinction. Davies, in the *Dramatic Miscellanies* (ii. 409), gives a good description of Garrick's Leon in "Rule a Wife and Have a Wife," by Beaumont and Fletcher, a part he assumed, leaving to Woodward that usually preferred of the Copper Captain.

Garrick's person did not suit Leon, and various lines of description had to be excised. So excellent was his acting, however, that the idea of inadequacy of size did not present itself. "He wore the disguise of folly," says Davies, "so exactly and humorously, that he presented the complete picture of a Wittol. When he put on the man of courage and asserted the honest rights of a husband, no one of a more brawny or sinewy figure could have manifested more fire or beautiful animation. The warmth of his spirit was so judiciously tempered, his action so correspondent to his utterance, his whole deportment so significant and important, that I think I never saw him more universally captivate the eyes and ears of an applauding theatre."

Of Sir John Brute, Lichtenberg says :—

"Sir John Brute is not only a dissipated dog, but Garrick makes of him too a conceited old coxcomb. On a wig which suits his years tolerably well, he has put a small fashionable laced hat in such a *nonchalant* way that it does not touch any more of the forehead than is already covered by the wig. In his hand he has one of those oak sticks with a kind of chopper to it, which the young bloods carry with them on their morning promenades in the park (the time for which, here, is from ten to three) and with which they give themselves the air of regular Drawcansirs, a kind of bludgeon as rough and unpolished as the clodhoppers from whom its use is borrowed. This bludgeon Sir John uses to emphasize his words with a thump, especially when none but women are present, or occasionally, in his rage, to deal a blow, where no one is at hand to resent it. Almost every theatre has its passable sot, for the obvious reason that opportunities of studying the part are abundant. And besides, it is in the nature of such tipsy parts to have no strictly defined limits. Nevertheless, Garrick acts the sottish Sir John in such a way that I should certainly have recognized his extraordinary talent had I previously heard nothing of him, and if I had seen him only in one scene of this play. In the beginning he wears his wig straight, and one sees the full, round face. Afterwards, when he comes home quite drunk, his face looks like the moon a few days before the last quarter, nearly half of it being obscured by the wig. The part which one does see is flushed and greasy, yet it is extremely friendly, and thus makes up for the loss of the other half. The waistcoat is open from top to bottom ; the stockings hang in wrinkles ; the garters are loose and—very mysterious—are not a pair. It is a wonder Sir John has not picked up shoes of both sexes too ! In this pickle he enters his wife's room, and to her anxious inquiry what is the matter with him (and she had good reason for putting this question), he replies, ' As sound as a roach, wife.' Yet he does not stir from the doorpost, against which he leans as heavily as if he wanted to rub his back on it. He then becomes in turn brutal, tipsily wise, and again friendly, all to the loud applause of the audience. In the scene where he falls asleep he amazed me. The way in which, with closed eyes, swimming head, and pallid face, he quarrels with his wife, and melting his r's and l's into one—into a sort of dialect of medials,—now abuses, now falters out scraps of morality (on which he is the most sickening commentary) ; then the way in which he moves his lips, so that one cannot tell whether he is chewing, or tasting something, or speaking—all this as much exceeded my expectation as anything else I have seen this remarkable man do. I wish you could hear him say ' pre-ro-ga-tive ' in this part. It is only after two or three efforts that he is able to get as far as the third syllable."

In Lord Foppington he had to compete with re-collections of Cibber, by whom, in fact, though the n ame was given it by another, the character was in-vented. Cibber's exquisite insolence, affectation, and sangfroid are crystallized in a delightful picture by Grisoni, and some sympathy may still be felt with those who held that Garrick never reached the ineff-able impertinence of his predecessor. In his own Lord Chalkstone, a part in which he was always wel-comed, he retained some recollections of Lord Fop-pington. Lord Townly was not held one of his most successful parts. His Ranger, Mrs. Siddons, who most probably saw it only on his farewell performance of the character, declared delightful, and his Benedick was held a comic masterpiece, his raillery in especial being full of vivacity and charm.

As Bayes, in "The Rehearsal," Garrick had three more or less formidable rivals, Colley Cibber, his son Theophilus, and Foote—the part was, indeed, also played by Mrs. Mountfort, and even by Mrs. Clive. Of three of the representatives, Davies gives a tolerably good description. Colley Cibber dressed Bayes "like a smart coxcomb. In the delineation of the character, he made him sufficiently ridiculous ; but I thought he rather exhibited the laughter at Bayes's extravagances than the man that was en-amoured of them. His son, Theophilus, displayed more vivacity in Bayes than his father ; by the in-vention of new-raised troops, or hobby-horses, and other novelties, with some fresh jokes upon the actors, he drew the public to it for three weeks successively. —But Theophilus mixed too much grimace and false spirit in his best acted parts."

" Mr. Garrick, when he first exhibited Bayes, could not be distinguished from any other gay well-dressed man ; but he soon altered it to a dress he thought more suited to the conceit and solemnity of the dramatic coxcomb. He wore a shabby old-fashioned coat, that had formerly been very fine ; a little hat, a large flowing brown wig, high-topt shoes with red heels, a mourning sword, scarlet stockings, and cut-fingered gloves. The difference between Garrick and his immediate predecessors was very conspicu-ous. They, by their action, told the spectators that they felt all the ridicule of the part ; he appeared quite ignorant of the joke that made against him. They seemed to sneer at the folly of Bayes *with* the audience; the audience laughed loudly *at* him. By seeming to understand the satire, they caught at the approbation of the pit; he gained their loudest plaudits, without letting them know he deserved it. They were in jest; he was in earnest."

Somewhat nebulous in expression and more concerned with accidents than essentials is this, but it serves to show a phase of Garrick's acting.

In a more pronounced style of comedy was his Abel Drugger in "The Alchemist," in which his most realistic effects appear to have been produced. The story is familiar of a Lichfield grocer who took with him to London an introduction from Peter Garrick to David, which was not delivered. Questioned upon his return as to the reason of his non-delivery of the letter, he vowed to Peter that he had gone first to the theatre and seen David, who was playing in Abel Drugger. From this entertainment he came away with the conviction that the actor's acquaintance was not to be desired, "for," said he, "though he be your brother, he is one of the shabbiest, meanest, most pitiful hounds I ever saw." Similar anecdotes are narrated concerning many actors. The present story, which is told by Macklin, is conceivable, but has probably been coloured. That the part was one of Garrick's masterpieces is, however, certain. Wilkes (Derrick) says, "Abel Drugger is certainly the standard of low comedy; and Mr.

Garrick's playing it the standard of acting in this species of comedy."

Sir John Brute, in "The Provoked Wife," to which previous reference has been made, was another character in which Garrick overleaped all rivalry. Quin, one of whose favourite parts it was, might say that Garrick would only be "Master Jacky Brute," and might find one here and there to accept the opinion. Lichtenberg was, however, as has been seen, enchanted with Garrick, and the general opinion awarded the younger actor the supremacy, especially so far as regards the revelation of some signs of breeding behind his debauched behaviour. His drunkenness, as may be supposed, was unsurpassable. Don Felix, Kitely, and Lord Chalkstone were all of them triumphs. Lord Townly alone among his comic characters seems to have come short of greatness.

Concerning the Hamlet of Garrick more is known than of any other tragic representation of the last century. We have the testimony of Partridge in "Tom Jones," so curiously concordant with that of the grocer who saw Garrick in Abel Drugger. There is first the sentiment of terror conveyed sympathetically to Partridge when Hamlet sees the Ghost. "Nay," says he to Jones, "you may call me coward if you will; but if that little man there upon the stage is not frightened, I never saw any man frightened in my life." Then comes the subsequent resentment of Partridge upon being told that the exponent of Hamlet is the best player. "He the best player ! Why, I could act as well as he myself. I am sure if I had seen a ghost, I should have looked in the very same manner, and done just as he did. And then, to be sure, in that scene, as you called it, between him and his mother, when you told me he acted so fine, why, Lord help me, any man—that is any good man that had such a mother—would have done exactly the same. I know you are only joking with me; but indeed, madam, though I was never at a play in London, yet I have seen acting before in the country ; and the king for my money ! he speaks all his words distinctly, half as loud again as the others. Anybody may see he is an actor."

The evidence of Partridge as to Garrick's trepidation is borne out by Lichtenberg, who gives a full description of the scene. Cutting out what he says of the dress, scenery, and opening business, I take up Lichtenberg's account after the utterance by Horatio of the words, " Look, my lord, it comes."

> " At these words Garrick turns suddenly round, and at the same moment staggers back two or three paces with trembling knees, his hat falls to the ground, both arms—especially the left—are nearly extended to the full, the hand as high as the head, the right arm more bent and the hand lower, the fingers spread out and the mouth open. There he remains standing, with legs far apart, but still in a graceful attitude, as if electrified (*sic*), supported by his friends. His features express such horror that I felt a repeated shudder pass over me before he began to speak. The almost appalling silence of the assembly, which preceded the scene and made one feel scarcely safe in one's seat, probably contributed not a little to the

effect. At last he speaks, not with the beginning but with the end of a breath, and says in a trembling voice, 'Angels and ministers of grace defend us,' words which complete whatever may yet be wanting in this scene to make it one of the sublimest and most terrifying of which, perhaps, the stage is capable. The Ghost beckons him ; then you should see him, with his eyes still fixed upon the Ghost, while yet speaking to his friends, break loose from them, although they warn him not to follow, and hold him fast. But at last, his patience exhausted, he faces them, and with great violence tears himself away, and, with a swiftness which makes one shudder, draws his sword on them, saying, ' By heavens, I'll make a ghost of him that lets me.' Then, turning to the Ghost, he holds his sword out: 'Go on ; I'll follow thee ;' and the Ghost moves off. Hamlet remains standing still, his sword extended before him, to gain more distance ; and when the audience have lost sight of the Ghost, he begins to follow him slowly, at times stopping, and then going on again, but always with his sword extended, his eyes fixed on the Ghost, with dishevelled hair and breathless, until he, too, is lost behind the scenes. You may easily imagine what loud applause accompanies this exit. It begins as soon as the Ghost moves off, and lasts until Hamlet likewise disappears."

Not less animated is the description in a second letter of a subsequent scene. Lichtenberg continues :—

"In the fine soliloquy, ' O that this too too solid flesh would melt,' &c., Garrick is completely overpowered by the tears of just grief for a virtuous father, for whom a frivolous mother no longer wears mourning, nor even feels grief, at a time when every parasite of the court should still be wearing black—the most unrestrained of all tears, perhaps because they are the only alleviation which in such a struggle between one duty and another

duty an honest heart can procure. Of the words, 'so
excellent a king,' the last word is quite inaudible : you
only perceive it by the motion of the mouth, which closes
immediately afterwards firmly, and trembling with agita-
tion, as if to repress with his lips the only too clear indi-
cation of the grief which might unman him. This way
of shedding tears, which shows the whole burden of
inward grief, as well as the manly soul suffering under it,
carries one irresistibly away. At the end of the soliloquy
he mixes just anger with his grief ; and once, when he
strikes out violently with his arm to give emphasis to a
word in his indignation, the word (to the surprise of the
audience) remains unuttered, choked by emotion, and
only follows after a few seconds, when tears begin to
flow. My neighbour and I, who had not yet exchanged
a word, looked at each other and spoke. It was irresistible."

This conveys an idea of power truly tragic, and
such as few succeeding actors have rivalled.

Davies even, under the influence of this magical
presentation, becomes almost eloquent, or at any rate,
rises above the dead level of his ordinary criticism.
Comparing Garrick, after the custom, with Wilks
and Spranger Barry, he says that in his speech at the
end of the second act—

> " The play's the thing,
> Wherein I'll catch the conscience of the king,"

he rose superior to all competition. " His self-
expostulations and upbraidings of cowardice and
pusillanimity were strongly pointed and blended
with marks of contemptuous indignation. The
description of his uncle held up at once a portrait of
horror and derision. When he closed his strong

paintings with the epithet *kindless villain*, a tear of anguish gave a most pathetic softness to the whole passionate ebullition." Still further light upon the Hamlet is cast by an anonymous correspondent of Garrick, who inundated the actor with criticism, much of it not likely to be wholly to Garrick's taste, but whose letters were judged worthy of preservation.

In tragedy Lear appears to have been Garrick's greatest part. This character, seldom seen of late until its recent revival by Mr. Irving, was held by Sheridan to be Garrick's masterpiece. O'Keefe also says concerning Garrick, " I liked him best in Lear. His saying, in the bitterness of his anger, ' I will do such things—what they are, I know not,' and his sudden recollection of his own want of power, were so pitiable as to touch the heart of every spectator. The simplicity of his saying, ' Be these tears wet?—yes, faith,' putting his finger to the cheek of Cordelia, and then looking at his finger, was exquisite." (" Recollections," i., p. 81.)

In the delivery of the curse, Garrick was taxed with being too deliberate, and not yielding to the impetuosity which the occasion required. So complete was the mastery over his public which he obtained, that it is difficult to see the justice of these complaints. Davies declares that he " rendered the curse so terribly affecting to the audience, that, during the utterance of it, they seemed to shrink from it as from a blast of lightning," and adds, " His preparation for it was extremely affecting; his throwing away his crutch, kneeling on one knee, clasping his hands together, and lifting his eyes towards heaven, presented a picture worthy the pencil of a Raphael."

Wilkes (Derrick) leaves also a fair description of portions of the Lear, or, at any rate, of the points at which the highest effects were created. It must be remembered that it was Tate's mangled version, with a happy termination, in which Garrick was seen.

" With what emphatic rage does he pronounce,

> Darkness and devils—saddle my horses ;
> Call my train together.

" What heart of sensibility is there that does not swell with horror at the awful solemnity with which he utters the curse of

> Blasts upon thee.
> Th' untented woundings of a father's curse
> Pierce every sense.

" How beautifully expressive appears the bitterness of his anger, subsiding into a reflection upon his own folly !   How artfully does he endeavour to suppress the justly provoked tear, when he says,

> Old fond eyes,
> Lament this cause again, I'll pluck ye out,
> And cast ye with the water that ye lose
> To temper clay.

" His manner of conveying his feeling here, makes every other eye overflow ; the alteration of his countenance from sensibility to madness, the foolish laugh, and indeed his whole performance of the mad part, must impress everybody capable of the smallest tenderness. I never see him coming down from one corner of the stage, with his old grey hair standing, as it were, erect upon his head, his face filled with horror and attention, his hands expanded, and his whole frame actuated by a dreadful solemnity, but I am astounded, and share in all his distresses; nay, as Shakespeare in some different place, with elegance, observes upon another subject, 'one might interpret from the dumbness of his gesture.'"

Bannister told Rogers that the manner in which Garrick in "Lear" said, "O fool, I shall go mad," absolutely thrilled him. Of the magical power of Garrick's eye we hear constantly, and in the portraits, indeed, that are preserved, an idea of its power of expression is conveyed. A description of it is given in a scarce little publication, the *Theatrical Review*, for the year 1757, and beginning of 1758. The anonymous author of this, though he censures Garrick's management, says, "Mr. Garrick may have faults, as an actor, but to me, I must own, they are as much lost as the spots in the sun, only visible to long-sighted astronomers." Of Garrick's eyes he writes: "His eyes have been ever and universally admired; their cut is what a painter would call bold and perfect; their size big, the pupil large, strong, lively, active and variable, its colour dark, surrounded and set off with a due proportion of white, that gives to its every motion a brilliancy, a distinctness, a life, that speaks in every glance."

Concerning other celebrated performances, any amount of raptures may be gathered. His Richard was said by Richard Brinsley Sheridan to have been firm, but not terrible enough. This wrung from Mrs. Siddons the protest, " God bless me, what could be more terrible?" followed by an explanation how at rehearsal he bade her, " as he drew Lady Anne from the sofa, follow him step by step, so that he should keep his face to the audience ; as he acted much with his eyes. During the performance she was so overcome by the fearful expression of his face, that she forgot his instructions, but was recalled to herself by a look of reproof, which, she said, she could never think of without terror."

His greatest effect seems to have been obtained in what is known as the tent scene, in which he awoke to the necessity of action, after his ghostly visitation. Derrick says of this, " I do not recollect any situation in tragedy, in which he appears to more advantage than that in which he rises and grasps his sword before quite awake ; nor could anything afford a finer subject to a masterly painter, than his manner of receiving Catesby." Concerning Hogarth's print of this scene, it does not, in Derrick's opinion, do all the honour he could wish to the great painter. The terror with which Garrick received Catesby yielded by degrees to his sense of the urgency of action, and before long his former spirit and intrepidity were restored. Among other scenes selected for praise, are those in which Buckingham retires in disgust at Richard's refusal of the crown, and the subsequent jubilation of Richard when his schemes are successful. " What fire lights up his eye, what satisfaction glows in his countenance, when he thus expresses himself" in words which Cibber had the audacity to interpolate in Shakespeare :—

> " Why now my golden dream is out ;
> Ambition, like an early friend, throws back
> My curtains with an eager hand, o'erjoy'd
> To tell me what I dreamt is true . . . . a crown, etc."

In speaking of his imperfections, and drawing a parallel between himself and the remainder of humanity, he was always " galled and uneasy," and even " cross-grained " and splenetic. In the scene of wooing of Lady Anne he was held to be eclipsed by Barry, the tone of voice of " this darling of nature " being " happily insinuating," and his manner " perfectly engaging." Somewhat conventional are the adjectives Derrick employs, and he is more than a little tedious in repetition, but he conveys a fair idea of the subject.

In Macbeth also, Garrick is held to have made a success, a somewhat surprising statement to those who are familiar with the picture by Zoffany, showing Garrick like a little man disguised as a footman, and Mrs. Pritchard in a costume even more horrifying. The more judicious of Garrick's critics practically avoid all mention of this character and of Othello, in both of which parts he was at a disadvantage compared with Quin. George Selwyn, indeed,

openly awards the preference in Othello to Quin,
saying, after witnessing Garrick in the part, "I
saw Garrick act Othello that same night, in which
I think he was very unmeaningly dressed, and
succeeded in no degree of comparison with Quin,
except in the scene where Iago gives him the first
suspicion of Desdemona. He endeavoured throughout to play and speak everything directly different
from Quin, and failed, I think, in most of his alterations." Murphy's criticism on Macbeth, conveyed
in his correspondence with Garrick, is favourable—it
could not well be other—but leaves also room to
suppose that the conception and execution were not
wholly to his mind. Davies, however, gives to the
dagger scene, and the banquet scene, as presented by
Mrs. Pritchard and Garrick, unstinted praise. He
declines to separate the two players, whose merits, he
says, were equal and transcendent.

The beginning of the scene after the murder "was
conducted in terrifying whispers. Their looks and
actions supplied the place of words." After dwelling
on the fragmentary speeches, "I have done the deed,"
etc., which, he holds, supply "only an outline to the
consummate actor," Davies continues with some criticism too naïve and too characteristic of the age not
to be quoted. The italics are mine. "The dark
colouring, given by the actor to these abrupt
speeches, makes the scene awful and tremendous to
the auditors! The wonderful expression of heartfelt
horror, which Garrick felt (? conveyed) when he
showed his bloody hands, can only be conceived and

described by those who saw him! *The expression of* 'sorry sight,' *is certainly not happy now.* Words which were highly expressive and energetic above one hundred and fifty years ago, have, by length of time, lost their importance. Davenant, fifty years afterwards, altered 'sorry' to 'dismal;' *but perhaps a better word than that might still be substituted.*"

From the scene which followed Lady Macbeth had long since been removed by the players. The surprise, the hypocrisy, and the fainting of Lady Macbeth, when she hears the news with which she is familiar, used to move audiences to ridicule! "Mr. Garrick," says Davies, "thought that even so favourite an actress as Mrs. Pritchard would not, in that situation, escape derision from the gentlemen in the upper regions."

To the scene with the ghost of Banquo, Garrick is said first to have lent its full terror. Those who had seen Garrick's predecessors, with their drowsy and ineffectual manner, held that the pith of Macbeth was drawn in the first two acts. On being told this, Garrick smiled ironically, observing that he should be "very unhappy if he were not able to keep alive the attention of the audience to the last syllable of so animated a character."

Mrs. Pritchard in this scene showed "admirable art, in endeavouring to hide from those present the frenzy of her husband. She smiled on one, whispered to another, and distantly saluted a third; in short, she practised every possible artifice to hide the transaction that passed between her husband and the vision his disturbed imagination had raised." She tried vainly, meanwhile, "by reproving and angry looks," to conceal her own uneasiness, and stimulate him to a sense of manhood.

Julius Cæsar Garrick did not play, although he contemplated so doing. He gave Hotspur in "a laced frock and a Ramillies wig," a costume which even in those days was found "insignificant," and the part did not count among his successes. His Faulconbridge was also a failure, and the delivery by so insignificant-looking a man, of the heroic speeches assigned the character, rendered them "unimportant and inefficient." In the dying scene in "King John" he rose to the height, stirring deeply with terror the spectators. "Every word of the melancholy news uttered by Faulconbridge, seemed to touch the tender strings of life, till they were quite broken, and he expired before the unwelcome tale was finished." As the King in the second part of "King Henry IV.," Garrick was held to triumph over disadvantage of figure, and his delivery of the more pathetic passages is extolled. He is charged with denying, through jealousy, the merit of Powell in this character.

Of serious characters outside Shakespeare, Jaffier in Otway's "Venice Preserved" stands foremost. Like other tragedians, Garrick originally chose Pierre in the same play, which is regarded as the more remunerative part. In the more tender portions of both characters, he was, it was held, eclipsed by Barry, and in Pierre had even to regard Mossop as a rival. In Jaffier he maintained his position to the end, the scene in which in a frenzy he saw his friend on the rack being presented with such extraordinary force, that men trembled at the picture. Derrick judged this performance worthy of a criticism almost as elaborate as he bestows upon Lear and Richard. Unlike Davies, he finds the tender aspects those in which Garrick stood highest, holding that nowhere else is a picture so exquisite presented of conjugal love and friendship. The audience, we are told, was convulsed with tears.

Osmyn in Congreve's "Mourning Bride," and Lusignan in Aaron Hill's "Zara," an adaptation from Voltaire, wind up the list of characters with which it is necessary to deal. In Osmyn we learn that Garrick acted with inexhaustible fire. His Lusignan was distinguished by elocutionary ability and by charm and distinction of manner.

Singularly few were the parts in which Garrick did not win acceptance. In those even which he gave up to others he appears to have scored. It was natural to avoid a combat when, as was occasionally the case with Macklin, Quin and Barry, the guns were all on the other side. Now and then he was scolded by his friends for taking a part altogether beneath him, such as Costar Pearmain in the " Recruiting Officer"; another time he showed his marvellous command by playing Master Johnny in " The Schoolboy." Much valuable praise is bestowed upon Garrick by his French friends and admirers, and much rapturous eulogy by enthusiasts such as Hannah More.

From the "Correspondance" of Grimm and Diderot we get the best idea of Garrick's abilities, and even of his appearance :—

> "Garrick est d'une figure médiocre, plutôt petite que grande. Il a la physionomie agréable et spirituelle, et un jeu prodigieux dans les yeux. Sa vivacité est extrême. Il a beaucoup d'esprit, une grande finesse, et une grande justesse ; il est naturellement singe et il contrefait tout ce qu'il veut" (vol. iv. p. 502).

The strongest evidence to his variety is given a couple of pages earlier, where his manner and method are shown :—

> " Le grand art de David Garrick consiste dans la facilité de s'aliéner l'esprit, et de se mettre dans la situation du personnage qu'il doit représenter ; et lorsqu'il s'en est une fois pénétré, il cesse d'être Garrick, et il devient le personnage dont il est chargé. Aussi, à mesure qu'il change de rôle il devient si différent de lui-même, qu'on dirait qu'il change de traits et de figure, et qu'on a toute la peine du monde à se persuader que ce soit le même homme. On peut aisément défigurer son visage : cela se conçoit ; mais Garrick ne connaît ni la grimace, ni la charge ; tous les changements qui s'opèrent dans ses traits proviennent de la manière dont il s'affecte intérieurement ; il n'outre jamais la vérité, et il sait cet autre secret inconcevable de s'embellir, sans autre secours que celui de la passion. Nous lui avons vu jouer la scène du poignard dans la tragédie de *Macbeth*, en chambre, dans son habit ordinaire, sans aucun secours de l'illusion théâtrale, et à mesure qu'il suivait des yeux ce poignard suspendu et marchant dans l'air, il devenait si beau qu'il arrachait un cri général d'admiration à toute l'assemblée. Qui croirait que ce même homme, l'instant après, contrefait avec autant de perfection un garçon pâtissier qui, portant des petits pâtés sur sa tête, et bayant aux corneilles dans la rue, laisse

tomber son plat dans le ruisseau, et stupéfait d'abord de son accident, finit par fondre en larmes."

From portraits of Garrick, numerous as these fortunately are, we obtain no such vivacious idea of his acting. A fair idea of his appearance is presented. No picture, however, of Garrick in action —and the Garrick Club can boast the possession of a dozen—conveys so living an idea as Grisoni's picture of Colley Cibber as Lord Foppington, or Clint's picture of Kean as Sir Giles Overreach, both in the same collection.

According to surviving records Garrick acted between 1741 and 1776, 2251 times. In his opening season he played 138 times. The smallest number of times he was seen in a season was in 1765-66, when he played 10 times. From the autumn of 1763 to that of 1765 he was, however, unseen, being abroad. He played practically about one hundred different characters.

It is as an actor that Garrick appeals to us, and not as a dramatist. A list of the plays, which were assigned him, or the authorship of which he claimed, may be seen in the "Biographia Dramatica" of Baker, Reed and Jones, to which list of 39 pieces must be added an alteration of "Mahomet" and some similar experiments. A few of Garrick's plays have, as has been said, ingenuity of construction and vivacity. On the whole, like that of Christian in the "Pilgrim's Progress," his march towards immortality will be the speedier and the more comfortable when the burden of his general dramas falls from him. His occasional verses are sometimes happy. What Johnson said of his talk is almost true of his verses—" Garrick's conversation is gay and grotesque. It is a dish of all sorts, but all good things. There is no solid meat in it: there is a want of sentiment in it."

A curiously complex, interesting, and diversified character is that of Garrick. Fully to bring it before the world might have taxed his own powers of exposition.

THE END.

INDEX.